THE GIFTS OF GOD
and the
AUTHENTICATION OF A CHRISTIAN

An Exegetical Study of 1 Corinthians 8-11:1

PAUL DOUGLAS GARDNER

WIPF & STOCK · Eugene, Oregon

Wipf and Stock Publishers
199 W 8th Ave, Suite 3
Eugene, OR 97401

The Gifts of God and the Authentication of a Christian
An Exegetical Study of 1 Corinthians 8–11:1
By Gardner, Paul Douglas
Copyright©1994 by Gardner, Paul Douglas
ISBN 13: 978-1-5326-0218-4
Publication date 4/20/2017
Previously published by University Press of America, 1994

Contents

Acknowledgements

I am deeply grateful to many people who have helped me along the way to achieve my ambition of writing a detailed study on this part of 1 Corinthians. I am specially thankful to those who gave me great encouragement to pursue doctoral studies when I was often tempted to give up. My supervisor for this work was Professor Morna D Hooker, the Lady Margaret Professor of Divinity at Cambridge University. She patiently offered wise advice throughout my studies. Her encouragement, that I should work closely with the text, has led me to a deeper appreciation of the apostle Paul as both writer and theologian. Dr Douglas de Lacey offered valuable encouragement at a time when I thought the work might never be finished. Mrs Ruth Ferguson and Revd Moira Hansen devoted many hours to reading discussing and commenting on aspects of the work.

This work could never have been written without financial and other forms of support. I therefore wish to thank the following:
the Department of Education and Science (UK) for a major studentship; the Hockerill Educational Foundation; the Tyndale Fellowship; Oak Hill College for financial support and a sabbatical in which to complete my work; Mr and Mrs M F Gardner; the Revd D L Gardner and Dr J M Gardner, my parents, for financial support and for first introducing me to the Bible.

I would also like to thank my children, Jonathan, David and Hannah, for their prayers and for living so long with a father who has seen to little of them. But, above all, I am deeply grateful to my wife, Sharon, who has supported and encouraged me in so many ways.

πάντα εἰς δόξαν θεοῦ

Abbreviations

Biblical references to a chapter and verse(s), without specifying a book, indicate that the book being referred to is *1 Corinthians*. Occasionally, the immediate context clearly refers to another book. Should there be any ambiguity then '1Corinthians' is spelled out.

All commentaries on 1 Corinthians are cited by author only and appear separately in the commentary list at the end.

Other works are cited by author and short title. Where this may be ambiguous, the short title is also given in the bibliography.

ABR	=	*Australian Biblical Review*
AnBib	=	*Analecta Biblica*
ANF	=	*The Ante-Nicene Fathers* (Anne Arbor: 1979, eds Roberts and Donaldson)
AV	=	*Authorised (King James) Version*
BA	=	*The Biblical Archaeologist*
BAGD	=	*A Greek-English Lexicon of the New Testament and Other Early Christian Literature,* (Chicago: 1979, ET by W F Arndt and F W Gingrich revised and augmented by F W Gingrich and F W Danker)
BDB	=	*A Hebrew and English Lexicon of the Old Testament* (Oxford: 1976, F Brown, S R Driver, C A Briggs)
BDF	=	*A Greek Grammar of the New Testament and Other Early Christian Literature,* (London: 1961, F Blass, A Debrunner and trans by R W Funk)
Bib	=	*Biblica*
BibS	=	*Biblische Studien*
BiTr	=	*Bible Translator*
BJRL	=	*Bulletin of the John Ryland University Library of Manchester*
BTB	=	*Biblical Theology Bulletin*
BZ	=	*Biblische Zeitschrift*

BZAW	=	*Beihefte zur Zeitschrift für die alttestamentliche Wissenschaft*
CBQ	=	*Catholic Biblical Quarterly*
ch(s)	=	*chapter(s)*
CJT	=	*Canadian Journal of Theology*
CTJ	=	*Calvin Theological Journal*
CTM	=	*Currents in Theology and Mission*
DSS	=	The Dead Sea Scrolls
EpRev	=	*Epworth Review*
EQ	=	*Evangelical Quarterly*
Esp	=	*especially*
ET	=	English Translation
EvTh	=	*Evangelische Theologie*
ExT	=	*Expository Times*
FRLANT	=	*Forschungen zur Religion und Literatur des Alten und Neuen Testaments*
Heb	=	Hebrew
HibJ	=	*Hibbert Journal*
HistRel	=	*History of Religion*
HTR	=	*Harvard Theological Review*
ICC	=	*International Critical Commentary*
IEJ	=	*Israel Exploration Journal*
Interp	=	*Interpretation*
ISBE	=	*International Standard Bible Encyclopaedia*, (Grand Rapids: 1979-88, ed Bromiley 4 Vols)
ITQ	=	*Irish Theological Quarterly*
JAC	=	*Jahrbuch Für Antike und Christentum*
JBL	=	*Journal of Biblical Literature*
JETS	=	*Journal of the Evangelical Theological Society*
JSJ	=	*Journal for the Study of Judaism in the Persian, Hellenistic and Roman Period*
JSNT	=	*Journal for the Study of the New Testament*
JSOT	=	*Journal for the Study of the Old Testament*
JSS	=	*Journal of Semitic Studies*
JTS	=	*Journal of Theological Studies*
LS	=	*A Greek-English Lexicon* (Oxford: 1901, eds H G Liddell and R Scott, 8th edition)
LXX	=	The Septuagint
Neot	=	*Neotestamentica*
NeotestSem	=	*Neotestamentica et Semitica*. Studies in Honour of Matthew Black (Edinburgh: 1969, eds Ellis and Wilcox)

New Docs	=	*New Documents Illustrating Early Christianity* (ed Horsley)
NICNT	=	*New International Commentary on the New Testament*
NICOT	=	*New International Commentary on the Old Testament*
NIDNTT	=	*The New International Dictionary of New Testament Theology*, (Exeter: 1975-78, ed Brown 3 Vols)
NIV	=	*The New International Version*
NKZ	=	*Neue kirchliche Zeitschrift*
NT	=	New Testament
NovT	=	*Novum Testamentum*
NTS	=	*New Testament Studies*
OED	=	*Oxford English Dictionary*
OT	=	Old Testament
PPJ	=	*Paul and Palestinian Judaism* (E P Sanders, London: 1977)
RB	=	*Revue Biblique*
RdQ	=	*Revue de Qumran*
ref	=	reference
RExp	=	*Revue and Expositor*
RelSRev	=	*Religious Studies Review*
RestQ	=	*Restoration Quarterly*
RHPhR	=	*Revue d'Histoire et de philosophie religieuses*
RS	=	*Religious Studies*
RSR	=	*Recherches de Sciences Religieuses*
RSV	=	*Revised Standard Version*
RThPh	=	*Revue de théologie et de philosophie*
RThR	=	*Reformed Theological Review*
RV	=	*Revised Version*
S-B	=	*Kommentar zum Neuen Testament aus Talmud und Midrasch* (München: 1922-28, eds H L Strack and P Billerbeck, 4 Vols)
SBLDS	=	*Society for Biblical Literature Dissertation Series*
SBT	=	*Studies in Biblical Theology*
StBTh	=	*Studia Biblica et Theologica*
SJ	=	*Studies in Judaism*
SJT	=	*Scottish Journal of Theology*
SNTSMS	=	*Society for New Testament Studies Monograph Series*
SNT	=	*Supplements to Novum Testamentum*
StEv	=	*Studia Evangelica*
TDNT	=	*Theological Dictionary of the New Testament*, (Grand Rapids: 1964-1976, ed Kittel, ET Bromiley 10 Vols)
ThLZ	=	*Theologische Literaturzeitung*
ThPh	=	*Theologie und Philosophie*

TLG	=	*Thesaurus Linguae Graecae. Canon of Greek Authors and Works* (New York: 1986, eds L Berkowitz and K A Squitier 2nd edition)
TS	=	*Theological Studies*
TZ	=	*Theologische Zeitschrift*
TNTC	=	*Tyndale New Testament Commentaries*
TOTC	=	*Tyndale Old Testament Commentaries*
TynB	=	*Tyndale Bulletin*
TToday	=	*Theology Today*
UBS	=	United Bible Societies
VT	=	*Vetus Testamentum*
WT	=	wilderness traditions
WThJ	=	*Westminster Theological Journal*
ZPE	=	*Zeitschrift für Papyrologie und Epigraphik*
ZThK	=	*Zeitschrift für Theologie und Kirche*
ZNW	=	*Zeitschrift für neutestamentliche Wissenschaft*

Unless otherwise stated, abreviations for primary sources are those cited in JBL 95 (1976), 335-338.

Abbreviations of Qumran documents not mentioned in JBL 95:
4QDib Ham = Words of the Heavenly Lights (also 4Q504)

Other Abbreviations:
P Coll Youtie — Colectaneae Papyrologica. Texts published in Honor of H C Youtie, ed A E Hanson (Berlin, 1976, 2 Vols).
P Köln — Kölner Papyri 1, (Cologne, 1976 eds B Bramer and R Hubner).
P Oxy — *The Oxyrhynchus Papyri* (London, eds Bowman, Haslam, Shelton, Thomas).
Thorikos Test. — *Thorikos and the Laurion in Archaic and Classical Times* (Ghent, 1975 eds Mussche *et al*) 33-42.

Abbreviations for Philo are in Vol 10, xxxv-xxxvi of *Philo,* in *Loeb Classical Library* (London: 1962 trans F Colson in 10 vols)

Refs to *Midrash Rabba* are from the Soncino Press edition in 10 Vols (London: 1961 eds H Freedman and M Simon).
Refs to *The Talmud* are from the Soncino Press edition in 18 Vols (London: 1961 ed I Epstein).
Refs to the *Mekilta* are from the Jewish Publication Society of America edition in 3 Vols (Philadelphia: reprinted 1976 trans Lauterbach).

Preface to the 2017 Reprint Edition

It is just over twenty years since this work was first published. In that time several great commentaries and many articles and monographs have been published on 1 Corinthians and on the chapters examined in this book. Since many have interacted with the work, often very graciously, I would have been happiest to rewrite the whole, taking into account many very valuable comments. At this stage that is not possible, but this work does offer a detailed exegetical background for ideas that I have developed and applied to the whole epistle in the Zondervan Exegetical Commentary on 1 Corinthians (Grand Rapids: Zondervan, 2018). Since I refer to this work in that commentary, I hope this reprinting will be useful.

There were various errors in this work, including a few spelling mistakes and some wrong accenting, to which reviewers and others have drawn attention. It has not been possible to correct these. However, one misspelled statement can be corrected here, and it remains the goal of the work:

πάντα εἰς δόξαν θεοῦ

Revd. Dr. Paul D. Gardner

1. Introduction

The legitimacy of eating meat which had been offered to idols was but one of the questions posed to Paul by the Corinthians ... His response is so subtly argued that a correct interpretation of every verse is essential if we are to understand not only his position but that of the Corinthians.[1]

Too often commentators on 1 Corinthians 8-10 have spent so much time examining the broader issues that they have failed to engage satisfactorily with the detail of Paul's arguments. It is the purpose of this thesis to attempt that detailed exegesis and, in doing so, to present possible solutions to the larger problems.

1.1 Chapters 8-10: The Issues

The broad problems with which the interpreter is confronted when examining these chapters are several.

First, some scholars[2] have noted that there is an apparent contradiction between chs 8 and 10 in the way Paul handles the issue of 'idol meat'. Differences in Paul's argument are also noted between 10:1-22 and 10:23-11:1. It is said that 10:1-22 reflects a harsh approach that forbids the eating of idol meat, while 10:23-11:1 and ch 8 reflect a more reasoned ethical response. Any work on these chapters must decide how this apparent contradiction is best to be handled.

Second, how does ch 9 relate to the (apparently) single theme of idol meat in chs 8 and 10? Is Paul offering himself by way of example, or has he temporarily changed subjects in order to defend his apostleship?

Third, what does the word ἐξουσία mean in ch 9 and why was this so important to Paul?

Fourth, the examples in ch 10 drawn from the wilderness traditions[3] are said by many to indicate that Paul was moving into a discussion of the sacraments. Whether these verses are, in fact, dealing with the

---

1   Murphy-O'Connor, "Food" 292.
2   For an outline of the different positions held by a number of scholars see section 1.2 below, and the exegesis of the text.
3   Hereafter WT.

sacraments and thus what the links are between chs 9 and 10 are important questions that must be addressed.

Fifth, the relationship between the issue of 'idol meat' (8:1), 'knowledge' (8:1, 2, 7 etc.) and 'love' (8:1, 3), both in these chapters and in the letter as a whole, has caused much discussion and requires detailed consideration.

Sixth, is there a common factor which links the several different issues Paul confronts in the whole epistle? For example, is the subject of gifts (chs 12 and 14) related to meat offered to idols, or is the subject of meat related to the sexual problems discussed in 5:1ff?

For most scholars the answer to these and other problems of the epistle has lain in the construction of hypotheses concerning the background of the Corinthian church and relationship between Paul and the church. Our own work seeks not to prejudge these issues. In fact the hypothesis presented at the end of this dissertation is amenable to a number of hypotheses concerning the historical and social background of the Corinthians. However, although some of these reconstructions would not substantially affect our own hypothesis, several have been influential in guiding the interpretation of much of the text of the epistle so we shall now outline the more important of them, while postponing most interaction with them until those places in our own exegesis where this is appropriate.

1.2   The Background: hypotheses

Until recently, apart from the various commentaries available on the whole letter, there had only been one close examination of chs 8-10.[4] In this work, W. T. Sawyer posited a clear hypothesis for the Corinthian situation. He examined the issue of meat offered to idols and its possible background, before going on to argue that Paul's opponents were Jewish and nomistic. He emphasised the connection between the opponents in 1 Corinthians and those in 2 Corinthians and concluded: 'in both epistles the opponents belonged basically to the same group'.[5]

From this connection he deduced that Paul was 'strong' and was defending his apostleship against the weak who were over-scrupulous Jewish Christians.[6] Chs 8-10 provided a theological 'basis by which Paul dared to allow the "strong" at Corinth to eat things sacrificed to idols'.[7] The three points the 'strong' were obliged to consider before

---

[4]   In 1968 Sawyer, *Problem* 4, was able to say that chs 8-10 'have escaped much scholarly interest'. Such is not the position today. Many articles have been written on aspects of these chapters since the mid sixties. Scholars such as E. E. Ellis, G. D. Fee, R. A. Horsley, and J. Murphy-O'Connor stand out for their contribution to studies on 1 Corinthians.

[5]   Sawyer, *Problem* 150; esp *contra* Georgi, *Gegner*.

[6]   Ibid 258.

[7]   Ibid 212.

eating meat offered to idols were: 1) Was a person's 'Conscience' hurt? 2) Was 'Fellowship' disrupted? 3) Was the goodness of the created order affirmed?[8] Sawyer's examination of the background to these chapters centred almost entirely on Jewish customs and debates about eating meat. Not much attention was paid to hellenistic background material and the final conclusion is somewhat predictable: 'This seemingly important controversy at Corinth was understood by Paul to be related to a larger issue, the growing rift between Jewish and Christian wings in the Church'[9]

In 1981, W. L. Willis redressed this imbalance and examined the hellenistic background to chs 8-10.[10] An important further aspect of this work is that Willis sought to identify 'fundamental norms and themes which are operative here [in 1 Corinthians 8 and 10] as a part of Paul's ethical thought'.[11] Two notable strengths of his dissertation are i) the recurring discussion through the exegetical sections of the importance of 'love' in these chapters as a 'hallmark' of the church,[12] and ii) the detail of the examination of hellenistic meals. However, the work suffers from virtually ignoring the possibility of a Jewish background and from its failure to address ch 9.

Looking back to earlier work on the epistle, we find that pre-nineteenth century scholars usually viewed the epistle as a response to a series of different issues connected by two factors: i) the desire of Satan to split a church and ii) leaders who had been corrupted by a desire for prominence.[13] In the last century, however, commentators sought to reconstruct the historical situation in Corinth in the attempt to find a common factor behind these individual problems.

In 1831 F. C. Baur attempted to define the characteristics of the 'parties' mentioned in 1:12. Two groups existed in the church: the one being Paul/Apollos and the other Christ/Peter. He believed that Paul faced Judaizers in Corinth as he had done in Galatia. The attacks on Paul were seen, then, as a new step in the Judaism/Paulinism controversy.[14]

---

8   Ibid 201-213.
9   Ibid 260. See further on Sawyer's thesis in 2.1.1 below.
10   Willis 7-64.
11   Ibid 4.
12   Cf Furnish, *Love* 112-114, 116.
13   Chrysostom 2ff; Calvin 9; inter al. Chrysostom regards the given names of the apostles in 1:12 as 'masks' behind which pompous leaders hide. There is no separate 'Christ' group, for Paul 'added this of himself, wishing to make the accusation the more grievous, and to point out that by this rule Christ must be considered as belonging to one party only' (24-25). Calvin 27 also takes this position on the Christ group.
14   Baur, "Christuspartei"; Cf Baur, *History* I 61ff. Cf Baur, *Paul* I 269ff. This reflects his dialectical understanding of history: 'Principle stood opposed to principle; and only the future development of Christianity could decide which of

While there are places that conceivably indicate that Paul's opponents were Jewish (e.g., chs 7, 8 and 10), the fact that Jewish problems did arise does not necessitate the presence of a 'Judaizing' group.[15] Further, it must be conceded that there is little evidence of an on-going battle of such proportions between a Pauline and Petrine Christianity as Baur's reconstruction requires.[16]

Many at the end of the nineteenth century expressed dissatisfaction with Baur's thesis. In connection with 1 Corinthians, Godet claimed that some hellenistic influence was present among Paul's opponents.[17] He still viewed the Christ-party as Judaizers but argued that 'nothing authorizes us to ascribe to Peter a conception of the Gospel opposed to that of Paul'.[18] The Peter party was distinct and conceded more liberty than the legalists in the Christ party, but even the rigorists were people involved in 'unsound speculations' rather than pharisaical Jews. Godet also suggested a likely parallel among Gnostic writers.[19]

In 1908 Lütgert argued, contra Bauer, that Paul was being attacked by antinomian hyper-pneumatics, even Gnostics. They were the Christ party.[20] Lütgert saw only this one camp opposing Paul: a pneumatic, hyper-Paulinist and Gnostic group.[21] He also attempted to connect this pneumatic group with Paul's own preaching of liberty by suggesting that Paul's original Gospel had been radically affected by hellenistic thought in the Corinthian situation and had moved from its original content.

Lütgert argued that the Corinthian correspondence gave no indication of Judaizing problems.[22] The Corinthians despised rather than feared Paul because he was not imposing, and because the evidence of power and Spirit seemed to be missing.[23]

---

the two principles would acquire the predominance over the other'. (Baur, History I 63.)

[15]   Cf Conzelmann 14 n 108. Luther 9. Luther laid the groundwork for seeing some of the problems arising from a Judaizing Christianity.

[16]   Schoeps, Paul 78ff also suggests the controversy centres on Judaizing elements.

[17]   Godet 33-34; in 63ff. he allows for the existence of four separate groups at 1:12.

[18]   Ibid 72.

[19]   Ibid 77.

[20]   Lütgert, Freiheitspredigt.

[21]   Ibid esp cf 49ff for criticisms of Baur, also cf Schmithals, Gnosticism 118ff.

[22]   Ibid 51. Lütgert states sarcastically: 'Judische Gegner des Paulus können nur Nomisten gewesen sein. Eine Streitschrift gegen Luther kann doch nur von einen Papisten ausgegangen sein! Von wenn denn sonst?'

[23]   Ibid 68-69: '... sie hassen und fürchten ihn nicht, sondern sie verachten ihn, sein äusseres Auftreten, seine Rede hat nichts Imponierendes, sondern ist schwächlich [2 Kor 10,10: er ist ein ἰδιώτης τῷ λόγῳ.. Ihnen ist er kein Apostel. Warum nicht? Der Beweis des Geistes und der Kraft fehlt ihm, das ist aber für sie das entscheidende Kennzeichen des Apostels'. This approach is also reflected in Savage, Power.

However, there are problems with Lütgert's thesis. Firstly he remained too tied to the attempts to ascribe the opposing views to one 'party' and to equating that with the Christ party. The Christ party is only mentioned in 1:12 (unless 2 Corinthians 10:7 is also a reference to such a party).[24] Secondly, the whole hypothesis rests upon an examination of 2 Corinthians 10-13. Such a procedure is deficient in a number of respects: i) it is not necessarily certain that 1 Corinthians 1 and 2 Corinthians 10-13 are written to the same situation.[25] ii) The 'parties' are not mentioned (with the possible exception given above) in 2 Corinthians 10-13. iii) This hypothesis fails to demonstrate why 'Christ crucified' is not enough for the Gnostics. What was the content of their belief that made them differ from Paul at such a fundamental level and yet apparently not be so harshly dealt with by him as the Galatians had been? iv) While this hypothesis deals adequately with 1 Corinthians 1-4, and with 2 Corinthians 10-13 (if its premises are accepted), it fails to give an adequate account of 1 Corinthians 8-10.

Schlatter built on Lütgert's hypothesis of Jewish-Gnostic opponents (influenced by their hellenistic environment), but believed that their theology had been derived from a speculative Palestinian Judaism.[26] This hypothesis is more systematically worked through than Lütgert's. New leaders from Jerusalem arrived in the church and claimed they belonged to Peter. However, they were not Judaizers in the accepted sense.[27] As the influence of these new leaders increased, so their criticism of Paul became sharper. When the Corinthians appealed to Paul or even Peter the new leaders responded with an appeal to Christ. This was their expression of spiritual independence.[28]

Schlatter saw the difference between Paul and the opponents as a 'different conception of the Gospel'. The Corinthians substituted wisdom for faith.[29] This wisdom was not specifically Greek in conception, but rather reflected Jewish 'wisdom' ideas that came to prominence under syncretistic hellenistic pressures. Paul's letter therefore spoke against the self-centred theology of the 'wise' men. The wise expressed their wisdom through freedom. Paul did not discourage freedom but showed how in specific situations freedom should be balanced by love, thus avoiding an 'autonomous ethic'.[30]

For example, 1 Corinthians 8 is seen as dealing with a specific instance of the exercise of 'freedom', while in 10:1ff., Paul returns to the

---

24   Kümmel 208 rejects this possibility.
25   Barrett, *Essays* 14ff. concludes that the links should not be made too closely between these passages.
26   Schlatter, *Church* 174ff; also *Bote* 28ff, 41ff.
27   Schlatter, *Bote* 29: 'Eine Neigung, das mosaische Gesetz in die Gemeinden zu bringen, hatten dieser Männer nicht'.
28   Schlatter, *Church* 174.
29   Ibid 175ff.
30   Schlatter, *Bote* 154.

question of what precisely makes a Christian, that is, the nature of the Gospel.

Schlatter's emphasis on 4:6 and 4:8 and their specific association with a pneumatic group laid the basis for the later talk of 'over-realized eschatology'.[31] The desire to see one main common theological problem arising from one set of opponents who were Gnostic was more carefully discussed than before and, while criticised in its detail, laid the basis for the work of scholars such as Schmithals,[32] Marxsen,[33] and Wilckens.[34]

However, Schlatter still relied on a particular interpretation of 2 Corinthians 10-13 and there was confusion to be seen in the way he described a development from the Petrine 'party' and others, into the main thrust of one overwhelming 'Christ party'.[35] With the passage of time two foundations of the hypothesis have been questioned. Firstly, it is now broadly argued that a developed libertine Gnosticism did not exist in the sixth decade A.D.[36] and secondly, some have maintained that there is insufficient evidence that the opposition was Jewish.[37]

A detailed study of the supposed hellenistic origins of Pauline thought was made by R. Reitzenstein. He viewed Paul himself as a Gnostic and deliberately set himself against further examination of a Jewish component in this Gnosticism which, he said, had been one-sidedly stressed.[38] In an examination of the words πνευματικός, γνῶσις and πνεῦμα, he sought to show close links with the mystery religions. Paul was a πνευματικός and had a 'mystical connection with Christ'. This is what Χριστοῦ εἶναι means in 2 Corinthians 10:7. It does not refer to a 'Christ party' — an idea which was added in 1:12 'under the demands of rhetoric'.[39] For Paul the centrality of the message lay in the cross. The spiritual man balanced his γνῶσις with love. This balance with love is the key to the difference between Paul and his opponents, for both sides are enthusiasts, but the one with love is the mature Christian who keeps the cross before him.[40]

His interpretation of chs 8-10 is immediately influenced by his hellenism/Gnosticism hypothesis. Of the irony in 8:1 concerning people

---

[31]   See below.
[32]   Schmithals, *Gnosticism* 122, says, 'Schlatter's characterization of the Corinthian heresy is correct on the essential points'.
[33]   Marxsen, *Intro* 74ff.
[34]   Wilckens, *Weisheit*.
[35]   Schlatter, *Bote* 28ff; 67ff; *Church* 174ff.
[36]   Wilckens, *Weisheit*.
[37]   Cf Reitzenstein, *HMR* 73; 426ff.; Schmithals, *Gnosticism* 123; Munck, *Paul* 148ff. (see 149 n 1 for specific criticism of Schlatter on this point.) A combination of these two points gives Munck a forceful argument against Windisch who built on both Lütgert and Schlatter (cf Munck, *Paul* 174, and Windisch 23ff.)
[38]   Reitzenstein, *HMR* 73.
[39]   Ibid 427.
[40]   Ibid 494ff.

who think they 'know', he says: 'the idea of the graduated vision in the mysteries shows through here'.[41] 10:3-4 is regarded as 'an obvious transfer of OT ideas into the perspective of the mysteries'.[42] Few would now regard this as 'obvious', and most commentators now believe it is ill-conceived to impose technical mystery-religion vocabulary onto Paul's own use of certain words, such as πνευματικός and γνῶσις.[43] For example, Bultmann also insisted on a Gnostic setting for the Corinthian church but, while agreeing that Gnosticism arose in hellenism, he believed it entered the church 'mostly through the medium of hellenistic Judaism that was itself in the grip of syncretism'.[44]

W. Schmithals argued that Gnosticism provided the context for 1 Corinthians but refused to accept that it arose in Palestinian Judaism. Γνῶσις, he believed, was a *terminus technicus* of all religious language of Paul's day.[45] He found the root of the idea in the *Corpus Hermeticum* where the issue was not mysticism but myth: 'To possess Gnosis means nothing other than to know just this myth in its existential import'.[46]

Although others have presented hypotheses based on Gnostic ideas,[47] none has achieved the detail presented by Schmithals.

In brief response, it must be said that hypotheses centred upon the presence of Gnostic ideas at Corinth do, in themselves, provide a reasonable understanding of the epistle: that is, provided they are acceptable in their premises. However, debate has raged as to whether these are *probable* or acceptable hypotheses. Certainly Schmithal's view does take seriously the existence of a religious vocabulary which appears only rarely elsewhere in Paul's letters, but many have argued that pre-Christian Gnosticism did not exist. It is not our purpose here to repeat the work of others on this question, though it is our opinion that the arguments for a fully developed Gnosticism in Corinth at the time of Paul's writing have been found wanting.[48]

41   Ibid 381.
42   Ibid 416.
43   See 2.1 below.
44   Bultmann, *Theology* I 171: 'The Gnostic Spirit enthusiasts whom Paul opposes at Corinth are of Jewish origin'. Also cf "Γινώσκω" 708ff, where he suggests that Paul opposed Gnostics, while himself being influenced by such mythological ideas.
45   Schmithals, *Gnosticism* 146.
46   Ibid 147.
47   Cf Wilckens, *Weisheit;* Kümmel, *Intro* 200ff; Drane, *Libertine* 100; Marxsen, *Intro* 72ff; Winter, *Pneumatiker passim.*
48   See Arai, "Gegner"; Conzelmann 15; Ellis, "Wisdom" 84; Nock, *Background;* Manson, *Studies* 193ff; Wilson, "Gnostic?" 67ff; Pearson, *Pneumatikos;* Hurley *Man* 6ff (who argues that even Gnostic terminology found in the NT implies no more than that the same words were used as *later* became technical terms in Gnosticism. To prove that individual words imply Gnosticism, Gnostic content and thought complexes must be demonstrated to be present in the context); Wedderburn, *Gnosticism* 189ff; esp Yamauchi, *Gnosticism.* In a final chapter of the second edition of this book, Yamauchi interacts with many other scholars but is still convinced of his own conclusions. Also Fee 11.

In the light of this debate, some have preferred to talk of 'enthusiasts'
or 'spirituals', thereby partly leaving open the questions of the
provenance of these ideas, whether from mystery cults or from
Gnosticism.[49] Others have talked of 'proto-gnosticism'.[50]
Of course the problem here, as with many other hypotheses, lies in
how much it is possible to distinguish between the background that was
Paul's, and that he drew upon, and the background that was the
Corinthiaṅs'. It is all too easy to forget that, while Paul himself may
have had Jewish ideas in mind when he spoke of γνῶσις and σοφία, he
may have been deliberately *re-defining* Greek pagan concepts in a
manner obvious to the Corinthians, but not so obvious to those studying
the text 2000 years later.

An interesting contribution to the discussion about the cultural and
religious background to the problems Paul faced in Corinth is provided
in the work of J. Dupont. In a detailed examination of specific words and
concepts, he suggested a biblical-Jewish setting was shared by Paul and
the Corinthians. For example, he concluded that the antithetical formulae
'to know God' or 'be known by him' had no comparison in hellenistic
mysticism. The formulae were derived directly from the OT and the
Jewish view of God's knowledge of his people and their love for God.[51]
He explored the difference between πνευματικός and ψυχικός,
between 'enthusiasm' and νοῦς, and in a careful analysis could find no
satisfactory hellenistic background. His judgment merits quotation:

> Tout nous permet d'affirmer qu'en parlant de 'psychiques' et de
> 'pneumatiques' saint Paul est tributaire d'une terminologie biblique, et que,
> si les Corinthiens employaient les mêmes expressions, celles-ci, même sur
> leurs lèvres, ne se expliquent bien qu'à partir d'un milieu littéraire juif.[52]

Against all those advocating a 'Gnostic' religious *milieu,* he
maintained that even the term γνῶσις itself came from Jewish thought.
He did allow that some other allied words such as 'liberté', 'en
conscience' and 'πλήρωμα' may have been derived from popular Greek

---

[49]   Bornkamm, *Paul* 71ff; Lake 222ff. (who finds his main evidence in 2
Corinthians 10-13); Knox, *Enthusiasm* 9ff; Käsemann, *NTQT* 125ff; Hemphill,
Charisma 50ff; Thiselton, "Realized" 512ff.
[50]   The problems of defining such a concept were indicated in the Messina
Conference of 1966 (See Bianchi *Gnosticismo*). Yamauchi *Gnosticism* allows
for the idea of proto-gnosticism. (Cf Conzelmann 15; Barrett, *Essays* 12; and esp
Hurley, *Man* 5ff.) Proto-gnosticism is merely descriptive of possible thought
forms and words that were later used in Gnosticism. Thus hypotheses accepting
this background vary considerably, e.g. in emphasising the Jewish or Greek
background, or taking different stances on the 'groups' etc. Conzelmann, Barrett,
and Hurley, all talk of factors present in Corinth from which Gnosticism
emerged, but their reconstructions of the Corinthian situation vary considerably.
[51]   Dupont, *Gnosis* 87.
[52]   Ibid 180.

philosophy, although only 'd'une manière très indirecte', being mediated through hellenistic Judaism.[53]

However, Dupont's hypothesis does not adequately address the unusual frequency with which certain words such as γνῶσις, σόφος, and πνευματικός appear in this epistle. If these words are explicable against a Jewish background, then some explanation is needed as to their notable absence from an epistle like Galatians. Dupont in fact suggests that the position of the 'strong' is founded in a charismatic gnosis derived from Judaism, while the weak are Jews worried by legal impurities.[54]

From time to time the integrity of the Corinthian correspondence and especially chs 8-10 has been challenged. Although few commentators have doubted Pauline authorship, a number of different literary reconstructions have been proposed.[55]

The problem with such hypotheses is that they are very subjective. A hypothesis that seeks to answer the textual issues without resort to literary and source-criticism is to be preferred because it deals with the evidence already in hand. Conzelmann perhaps best summarises the conclusions of a number of scholars on this issue,

> There is no conclusive proof of different situations within ⋅l Corinthians. The existing breaks can be explained from the circumstances of its composition. Even the complex that gives the strongest offense, chs 8-10, can be understood as a unity.[56]

Another hypothesis that has been influential in the last decade is that presented by A. C. Thiselton.[57] He proposed that the Corinthian situation could best be explained as a problem with 'over-realized eschatology'. While others such as Bruce,[58] Munck,[59] Käsemann,[60] and Barrett[61] had pointed the way to this position, Thiselton develops it with the whole epistle in view.

'Realized eschatology' indicates a belief and behaviour centred upon the presence already of the fullness of promised eschatological blessings. As Barrett says, 'for them there is no "not yet" to qualify the

---

53   Ibid 529, 538. For the impact of Dupont's thesis on his reading of 8:7, see our exegesis below.

54   Ibid 532-534. The Jewishness of parts of 1 Corinthians has been examined by many. Cf Wilckens, *Weisheit;* Davies, *PRJ;* Hurley, *Man* 23-26; Ellis, "Wisdom".

55   The most notable are Weiss xxxix ff; Schmithals, *Gnosticism* 87ff; Héring xiii ff. but see also the interesting hypothesis of Hurd 290ff. His Table 7 provides a summary of his own position. We refer to these different reconstructions as they affect the interpretation of the text.

56   Conzelmann 4.

57   Thiselton, "Realized".

58   Bruce 49ff.

59   Munck, *Paul* 165.

60   Käsemann, *ENTT* 171.

61   Barrett 109.

"already" of realized eschatology'.[62] Käsemann links such ideas closely
to Gnosticism: the 'Enthusiasts at Corinth had already felt themselves
lifted above temptation ... '.[63]

Thiselton carefully seeks to demonstrate[64] that 'realized eschatology'
is in fact a 'sufficient cause' though not a 'necessary cause'[65] for each of
the diverse problems encountered in the epistle. He argues that the error
of eschatology causes misconceptions of the gifts and the Spirit, and also
accounts for the discussion in chs 1-4 of attitudes to ministry.[66] He
suggests that in every section of the epistle there is evidence of 'both a
realized eschatology and an enthusiastic theology of the Spirit on the
part of the Corinthians'.[67]

Thiselton's hypothesis does demonstrate the pervasive discussion of
eschatology in the letter and emphasises that eschatology and an
'enthusiastic theology of the Spirit' are closely linked throughout the
epistle. However, it is not at all clear how Paul's great emphasis on the
theology of a crucified Christ fits into the anti-enthusiastic stance that he
is supposed to be taking. Have the enthusiasts moved beyond the need to
'actualize the "crucifixion with Christ"'?[68] Is not Paul's own
'enthusiasm' bound to the cross (1:23-24, 30-31)?

We have mentioned a number of ways in which hypothetical
reconstructions of the social, cultural or literary background to this
epistle have sought to address some of the 'issues' to which we referred
above. We have not sought exhaustively to criticise any of them. In
some cases this has already been done by others, but our purpose has
been simply to set the scene for the work which follows. In different
ways, this dissertation is indebted to many of the scholars mentioned.
However, it is also our intention to show that it is possible to approach
chs 8-10 without a prior commitment to a particular 'background' and to
make coherent sense of the argument Paul presents.

1.3   Method

We have indicated earlier that the interpretation of parts of 1
Corinthians is often affected by the hypothesis proposed for the setting
of the whole. Sometimes this has meant that the text itself has been
virtually ignored. In a devastating criticism of the extravagancies of
certain hypothetical reconstructions, R. P. C. Hanson has warned of the

62   Loc cit.
63   Käsemann, ENTT 171.
64   In spite of Ellis' criticisms of the 'over-realized eschatology' hypothesis.
Ellis, "Crucified" 73ff.
65   Thiselton, "Realized" 512.
66   These chs turn 'not in the first instance on questions about wisdom'
(513).
67   Ibid 523.
68   Ellis, "Crucified" 74.

need for careful controls.[69] The criterion of authenticity of a reconstruction must rest on some part of the documentary evidence:

> as every hypothesis removes the reader one step further from the documentary evidence, so it renders the reconstruction progressively more unlikely. Ingenuity is no substitute for probability.[70]

The ensuing work, therefore, has deliberately sought to examine the text in considerable detail. As the work progresses, it is our belief that a possible reconstruction of the particular religious problem faced by Paul is in fact suggested by his reasoning. The argument for this hypothesis is cumulative and it is laid out in the final chapter. The final decision for the reader as to whether the hypothesis merits further consideration must rest on the results of exegetical work.

There are possible dangers in relying on *Paul's* reasoning to provide details concerning the beliefs of those to whom he was writing. The problem has been highlighted recently with regard to interpretations of Galatians. Lyons argues that most interpretations of Galatians are built on 'mirror reading'. This involves taking statements made by Paul, and supposing that, through these, it is possible accurately to describe the position of Paul's 'opponents'. Lyons notes that, while Paul's responses might be to 'charges' from opponents, he might also be responding 'to misinformation, misunderstanding, or mistaken conclusions of hypothetical arguments which he himself has constructed in order to refute them'.[71]

Barclay also warns about these dangers which, he observes, are more acute if the text concerned is strongly polemical. The polemical nature of an argument may itself distort our understanding of the 'opponents'. However, Barclay's article attempts to demonstrate that 'mirror reading' can be subjected to a number of controls. While the method is never likely to produce certainty regarding the opponent's position, when these controls are employed it can produce more or less satisfactory hypotheses. He suggests that categories such as 'virtually certain', 'highly probable', 'probable', 'possible' etc., are useful ways of defining the value of hypotheses arrived at through mirror reading.

The problem of mirror reading is not as acute when examining 1 Corinthians as it is when looking at Galatians. First, much 'mirror reading' in Galatians attempts to reconstruct the position of a *third* party: those who were trying to lead astray the people to whom Paul was

69   Hanson, "Clement" 517ff. This is a review article of a work by Morton Smith and contains a serious questioning of the whole basis upon which Morton Smith's idiosyncratic hypotheses are founded. Hanson is dealing, of course, with reconstructions surrounding the Gospels material, but his general statements are aimed broadly at biblical scholarship and his warnings need to be heeded.
70   Ibid 519.
71   Lyons, *Autobiography* 96-97.

writing. In our examination of 1 Corinthians we have sought partially to reconstruct the views of those to whom Paul was *directly* writing. Secondly, we shall argue below that, while Paul disagreed with some of those to whom he wrote, chs 8-10 are not polemical in nature and thus at least one of the dangers in mirror reading is less problematic here than in Galatians.

However, mirror reading is used in some places in this dissertation as a means to providing a working hypothesis through which, it is hoped, we can better understand *Paul's* argument. We have sought to control this method in a number of ways. Firstly, the hypothesis presented at the end of this dissertation rests, we believe, on considerable *cumulative* exegetical evidence rather than on the mirror reading of one particular statement. Secondly, we have sought to emphasise the consistency in *Paul's* argument through these three chapters, thereby seeking to discover the issues of most concern to *him*, rather than building too much on those sections, such as 8:3 and 8:10, where we have cautiously 'mirror read' the position of the Corinthians. We believe that we have not over interpreted these chapters, although we recognise that we might be tempted to call 'highly probable' what others would call only 'possible'![72]

Method in exegesis also requires a mention. We have taken seriously the many scholarly debates which concern these chapters and, where these are significant, we have sought to draw attention to the different perspectives represented among scholars. It has been impossible exhaustively to describe the history of exegesis of each verse within the limitations of this dissertation, but we have always aspired to indicate what we believe to be the strengths and weaknesses of other positions.

Exegesis inevitably requires considerable discussion of the meaning of words, phrases etc. For too long the diachronic method and etymological word study has formed a substantial part of exegesis. Although this linguistic approach has been challenged through the years, notably by Saussure,[73] it had not been seriously questioned among the majority of biblical scholars until the publication of Barr's work on semantics in 1961.[74] Even though most scholars now admit the validity of Barr's criticisms of the diachronic approach, all too few apply his recommendations within their work. Some still seem not to have heard of him at all![75]

The principle established by Saussure was that a 'synchronic' understanding of a language unit should take precedence over the

---

[72]   See Barclay's list. "Mirror Reading" 85. We hope that none will class it as 'Incredible'!
[73]   Saussure inaugurated this discussion in *Linguistics* (1915).
[74]   Barr, *Semantics*.
[75]   Note the *misuse* of biblical words (from 1 Corinthians) to be found in Detzler's, *Living Words*.

diachronic. The synchronic understanding deals with 'logical and psychological relations that bind together coexisting terms and form a system in the collective mind of speakers'.[76] Silva summarises Saussure's understanding of diachronic linguistics as 'studies of those relations, *unperceived* by the collective mind' that 'bind together successive terms'.[77]

The usefulness of etymology in exegesis must be subject, therefore, to careful controls. It is not and cannot be a guide for the present semantic range of a particular word.[78] In this dissertation we have sought to take such strictures seriously and it is believed that this has borne useful results. The work demands an examination of specific problematic linguistic units (words, phrases or sentences), but the method employed has given priority to examining the semantic value of these units within their own context. However, we shall also see that Paul's use of language, at least on occasions, was stimulated probably by a conscious awareness of the historical root of the word or phrase being used. Of course demonstrating this is not an easy task and, on occasion, the most that can be said is that Paul *may* have had a root meaning in mind.[79]

The dissertation proceeds by means of the verse by verse exegesis for which Murphy-O'Connor appealed in the opening quotation of this chapter.

1.4   The Aims

We have introduced some of the basic issues and problems with which we are confronted when approaching chs 8-10 and we have presented some of the principle hypotheses constructed to deal with those issues. Through a detailed study of the text of chs 8-10, our aim is to show that a satisfactory resolution of those issues does present itself and that a hypothesis can be formulated to explain the nature of the religious problem Paul believed he was facing in Corinth.

Specifically, this means that we intend:

i)   clearly to portray the *logical progression* of Paul's argument, without resort to source critical reconstructions;

ii)   to show how γνῶσις and ἀγάπη are linked to this discussion of meat;

iii) to contend that ch 9 is an integral part of Paul's argument in chs 8 and 10;

---

[76]   Saussure, *Linguistics* 99-100.
[77]   Silva , *Meaning* 37 — paraphrasing and quoting Saussure, *Linguistics* (our emphasis).
[78]   Barr, *Semantics* 107.
[79]   For further discussion of the possibility of this demonstration cf Porteous, "Present", and Barr, "Isaiah". Also cf the brief discussion of this issue in Silva, *Meaning* 47ff.

iv) to suggest that the 'sacraments' are not the main issue addressed in ch 10;

v) to demonstrate the substantial links between chs 8-10 and other parts of this epistle;

vi) to advance our understanding of the nature of the underlying *religious* problem Paul faced at Corinth.

2. The Person Who Is Loved By God.

Exegesis of 1 Corinthians 8

2.1   Idol meat, knowledge, and love (Verses 1 - 3)

The subject of εἰδωλόθυτα is introduced by the phrase Περὶ δέ, a formula found on six occasions in this epistle.[1] It is generally agreed, in the light of 7:1, that Paul was referring to subjects raised in a letter he had received from the Corinthians.[2] However, there is less agreement on several matters in these opening verses: i) What was the nature of the εἰδωλόθυτα mentioned? ii) Was Paul quoting from the Corinthian letter with the formula οἴδαμεν ὅτι ...? iii) How was γνῶσις functioning in the Corinthian community? iv) How did Paul expect ἀγάπη to function and what did οἰκοδομέω mean?

2.1.1   Εἰδωλόθυτα

The subject raised by the Corinthians concerned εἰδωλόθυτα. It is said that this pejorative word was drawn from the debate between Jews and Hellenists. The normal Greek word for meat sacrificed to idols was ἱερόθυτον (cf 10:28). In that Jews despised meat that had been in contact with pagan ceremony they coined the word εἰδωλόθυτον to describe it.[3] However, caution is necessary here, for it is not clear that eating meat offered to idols would have been a matter of debate among Jews. It is possible, we suggest, that the word was actually coined around the time of the Jerusalem Council and was of *Christian* origin. If this was the case, then the word may have been used to describe the sort

---

1   7:1, 25; 8:1; 12:1; 16:1, 12. Cf 8:4.
2   Calvin 134, Weiss 169 and most modern commentators.
3   Κρέα (8:13) indicates that meat was the issue.

of idol meat which Christians generally, for all their new-found freedom, felt unable to eat.[4]

The only possible pre-christian uses of the word that we have encountered[5] are in 4 Maccabees 5:2 and Sibylline Oracles 2:95. The latter book shows regular signs of a Christian redactor and is likely to be dated well into the first century AD.[6] The similarity of context and vocabulary to Acts 15 also suggests that, at this point, the Christian redactor has been at work.

Compare Acts 15:29:

ἀπέχεσθαι εἰδωλοθύτων καὶ αἵματος καὶ πνικτῶν καὶ πορνείας.

with Sib Or 2:95:

αἷμα δὲ μὴ φαγέειν, εἰδωλοθύτων δ'ἀπέχεσθαι.

4 Maccabees probably emanates from the same period.[7] Charlesworth suggests the period between AD 19 and 54. Towards the end of this period a word, coined in a Christianity subject to Judaizers, might easily have been taken back into Judaism.

Apart from these two uses of the word, and those in the NT, the earliest use of the word appears to be in Clement of Rome. It is only after that the one other *Jewish* source cited in *BAGD* 221 (*Pseudo Phocylides* 31) is to be noted. The word is then used in the Church Fathers.

If we are right in this suggestion, then it means that the use of the word in 8:1 is extremely early and typically expresses Christian abhorrence of pagan sacrifices, within the context of the early church debate about the nature of the liberties Christians were allowed.

We have already established the point that hypotheses concerning the Corinthian situation have dictated the interpretation of the text. This is evident in what people have said about the meaning of εἰδωλόθυτα in chs 8 and 10, for we have no corroborative evidence in the use of this word for a specifically *Jewish* problem.[8] However, it is important now to review the major hypotheses which seek to explain the problem Paul faced here.

Those such as Reitzenstein, who belonged to the *religions- geschichtliche Schule*, believed that the mystery religions provided the

---

4   See 'Additional Note' (ch 4 below). The term 'idol meat' is widely used in discussions on these chapters (cf Willis, *Idol Meat!*). By this we mean meat that, at some stage, was sacrificed to idols.

5   *TLG* and normal reference sources have been used.

6   Charlesworth, *Pseudepigrapha* I 331-332.

7   Ibid II 533. Dupont-Summer, *Machabées* 78-85 suggests AD 117-118.

8   It should be noted that in Rev 2:14, 20, where Εἰδωλόθυτα is used, the situation is one of syncretism, not Jewish sensibilities; cf Sweet, *Revelation* 87-93.

necessary background to the word.[9] Heitmüller's work had led the way in suggesting that an understanding of theophagy in mystery religion sacrifices gave Paul his basis for a sacramentalism designed to achieve mystical union with Christ.[10]

For those who adopted a 'sacramentalist' view of the eating, problems arose with chs 8-10. On the one hand it appeared Paul built his argument from a direct comparison with hellenistic sacramentalism (10:1-22) and came to a rigorist position, while on the other hand it seemed Paul denied sacramentalism and discussed the issue from an ethical perspective (8:1-13; 10:23-11:1).[11] Most assumed that the problem Paul faced was that all meat, wherever it was sold, would have been offered at such hellenistic ('sacramental') sacrificial feasts.

This school of thought has since been so profoundly criticised that, in 1955, G.B. Caird said 'Attempts ... to show that the Christian sacraments were derived from the hellenistic mystery religions ... [are] wrong-headed'[12] Among others, Nock argued that 'in pagan initiatory rites ... meals were meals, with no known special significance save in Mithraism — and Mithraism was not ... a notable force in the world around nascent Christianity'.[13] Yet for scholars such as Bornkamm[14] its influence remains in their interpretation of these chapters. Even Conzelmann, who is so cautious in the Introduction to his commentary,[15] draws on the work of this school uncritically when addressing 10:21.[16]

Willis[17] set out to demonstrate that the 'alleged conflict' between the 'sacramentalist' view of idol meat and the 'ethical' arguments of chs 8 and 10:23-11:1 'misunderstands both the character of pagan cult meals and Paul's arguments'.[18] There is no need to repeat his work here, but some of his findings may be usefully summarised. They certainly give a

9   See 1.2 above. Cf Loisy, *Mystères* esp 356-360.

10   Heitmüller, *Taufe*. On supposed theophagy in the NT era see Smith, *Theophagy*. For the impact of these views on chs 8-10: Lietzmann 45, 50-51.

11   So Weiss xl-xliii who probably influenced Loisy, *Mystères*. Both assign 10:1-22 to an earlier letter. Ch 8 and 10:23ff are assigned to a second letter.

12   Caird, *Apostolic* 96. The criticisms of the 'sacramentalist' position of the *religionsgeschichtliche Schule* have spanned the decades. Cf the early work of Kennedy, *Mystery Religions* esp 220-223; Wagner, *Pagan Mysteries* esp 268-294. More recently a cautious revival of some of the ideas is seen in Klauck, *Herrenmahl*.

13   Nock, *Background* 133.

14   Bornkamm, *Paul* 191-193, and "Herrenmahl".

15   Conzelmann 15.

16   Ibid 174 esp nn 44-47.

17   See above p 3.

18   Willis 11.

possible understanding of the background that caused the Corinthian question concerning idol meat.

Willis describes three traditional interpretations of these meals: i) sacramental, ii) communal, and iii) social. The sacramental position emphasizes theophagy while the communal concerns the 'sharing' of the meal with the deity who is assumed to be present. The third view is that the meals were eaten before the deity. In other words, while the communal meal was an occasion for 'conscious worship', in the social meal 'the focus is on the social relationship among the worshippers' even though 'due regard was given to the deity and a portion allotted to him'.[19]

In the light of these positions, Willis' work offers an examination of papyri and inscriptions relating to four important pagan cults: Eleusis, Dionysus, Mithras, and Sarapis and Isis.[20] His conclusions[21] are that there is 'no evidence at all' that meals had sacramental significance, but considerable evidence that the 'social interpretation' is correct. Many meals were not 'religiously significant' even if they took place in a temple. According to Willis, the problem Paul faced was one of Christians eating sacrificed meat at social occasions which were sometimes 'in a temple' (8:10). The motivation of these Christians was 'social'. An additional motivation may have been provided by possession of 'knowledge''and 'privileges' (ἐξουσία).[22]

The problem with this study is that not all the evidence Willis uses *has* to be read in the way he suggests. He points to several invitations to eat at a banquet of a god. Most of these come from the Oxyrhynchos Papyri and so were not necessarily such prominent social occasions in Paul's day. But even if they were, they are open to different interpretations. Horsley suggests a 'communal' understanding of what was going on, supporting this from a rather different invitation to the *kline* of Sarapis from the usual.[23] Normally, in the small number of such invitations available, a named individual invites someone to a 'banquet of the Lord Sarapis'. Sometimes this seems to be in a temple, or in a room off a temple, and sometimes elsewhere.[24] But in *P Köln 57* it is a god who invites:

καλεῖ σε ὁ θεὸς
εἰς κλείνην γεινο(μένην)

---

19   Ibid 20.
20   Ibid 22-47.
21   Following Kane, "Meal" 343-349.
22   Willis 62-64.
23   *New Docs* 1 5-9.
24   *P Oxy 1484*: ἐν τῷ θ(ο)ηρίῳ; *P Coll Youtie*, 51-55 cited in *New Docs* 1 5: ἐρωτᾷ σε Νικεφόρος δειπνῆσαι εἰς κλείνην τοῦ κυρίου Σαράπιδος ἐν τῷ λοχίῳ τῇ κγ ἀφ' ὥρας θ.

ἐν τῷ θοηρείῳ
αὔριον ἀπὸ ὥρας θ´

Horsley cites this as 'the most clear-cut evidence that 'these banquets had a fundamentally religious character: Sarapis was considered as being present for the dinner'.[25] The editor of *P Yale 85* goes further and argues that *'kline* in Egypt was a technical term for religious observance ... We may thus conclude that an invitation to dine εἰς κλείνην Σαράπιδος is an invitation to a specific kind of religious observance'.[26] Even where meals were essentially private and at home it is possible that they were under the direction of a priest of Sarapis.[27]

While Willis is probably correct in denying that these meals had 'sacramental' significance and is also right to stress their social aspect, he overstates his case in largely denying the so-called 'communal' understanding. Apart from the implication drawn by Horsley from *P Köln 57*, Willis does not allow sufficiently for the fact that papyri invitations do exist which are for obviously *non*-religious gatherings. For example, *P Oxy 926*:

καλεῖ σε Ἡραθέων
δειπνῆσαι εἰς τὴν ἐπί–
κρισιν αὐτοῦ ἐν τῇ οἰ–
κίᾳ αὐτ[ο]ῦ ἥτις
ἐστὶν ε ἀπὸ ὥρ(ας) [θ]

Given the existence of invitations like this to non-religious meals,[28] it is at least possible that all banquet invitations mentioning a god were to gatherings where the participants were in fact *conscious* of the religious nature of the event and where, perhaps, the presence of the god was assumed. Willis' argument is not fully convincing here.

Sawyer examined the issue from a different perspective looking in some detail at Jewish dietary regulations. His conclusion, following Barrett,[29] Manson,[30] and others, was that probably some had come under the influence of the 'Peter group' and so εἰδωλόθυτα referred to all meat offered to idols wherever it was eaten. Sawyer argues that Jews were forbidden to eat this meat for a number of reasons including improper slaughtering, or because an animal was 'unclean'. However, the main reason was simply that the food was contaminated by having

25   *New Docs* I 6.
26   *P Yale 85* p 263.
27   *P Yale 85* p 264.
28   See also various wedding invitations in the Oxy. Papyri; cf *P Oxy 1214*: an invitation to a birthday meal.
29   Barrett 44, also *Essays* 54.
30   Manson, *Studies* 200.

been in the hands of an idolater.[31] Thus these people were not making distinctions about *where* the food was eaten. For them the problem was as acute in the situation of 10:25 and 27 as it was when the food was eaten ἐν εἰδωλείῳ (8:10). It was *Paul* who introduced a distinction of *place*.[32]

Sawyer's emphasis on the Jewish background does not adequately confront the problem of 8:7 which seems to refer to Gentile converts. Much of his discussion[33] is also based on rather tortuous and sometimes very weak logic that begins by seeking to demonstrate a similarity between 2 Corinthians 11:4 and Galatians 1:6-9, and subsequently between 2 Corinthians 11 and 1 Corinthians 8-10. His logic seems to be this: the problem at Galatia was caused by nomistic Jews. Links between Galatians 1:6-9 and 2 Corinthians 11:4 suggest Paul faced a similar problem at Corinth. Links between the latter chapter (especially v 29 and its reference to ἀσθενής and σκανδαλίζω and 1 Corinthians 8-10 again suggest a Jewish nomism was the issue. After examining further parallels between 1 Corinthians 9 and 2 Corinthians 12 he concludes that:

> The only logical explanation for this [the parallels] is that on both occasions he was defending his apostleship and in both epistles the opponents belonged basically to the same group [34]

The problems with this approach are considerable. For example, Paul does not say that the confrontation in 1 Corinthians is with Jewish people. If some of the ways in which Paul responds are with so-called 'Jewish' ideas like σκανδαλίζω, then it need prove no more than that *Paul* was a Jew and used terms like this regularly! Certainly, whatever the source of the problem at Corinth, Paul used Jewish concepts in his response, seeing the OT as written to provide 'warnings' for all the people of God.[35]

Fee has argued that in the context of ch 8 εἰδωλόθυτα appears to refer specifically to the meat offered as sacrifice *in a temple*. However, most commentators suggest that it was a more general term given to sacrificed meat offered for sale in the market place. Assuming a Jewish issue, it is said that the reference cannot be to meat eaten 'in a temple' because

---

31   Cf *M Abod Zar* 2:3, 5 etc. Also cf Kohler "Dietary Laws" in *The Jewish Encyclopaedia* IV 597, quoted by Sawyer. Strangely, Sawyer does not discuss *why* idolaters might have profaned food.
32   Sawyer, *Problem* 166.
33   Ibid 142-150.
34   Ibid 150.
35   See below on 10:1-14.

Jews would never have gone to a temple.[36] Fee is unconvinced by this and other arguments for the 'Jewish' perspective. Building his discussion on 8:7 he states: 'The offended person, whose conscience is weak, is not a Jewish Christian, but a gentile convert'.[37] Against those who would propose an outside influence upon these Christians in the form of a Petrine/Judaizing polemic, he insists: 'There is not a hint in the text that his [the convert's] anxiety over idolatry has an outside source.'[38] For Fee, the meat in 8:1 is specifically that offered and eaten ἐν εἰδωλείῳ .

Fee supports his case from 10:1-22 where εἰδωλολατρία is the issue (10:7). He argues that the real problem was the mixture in hellenistic temples of πορνεία and eating at sacrificial meals. As in the OT,[39] so in Corinth, sexual sin and eating meals in the presence of a deity were subject to the judgment of God. This, he suggests, may also explain the problem of πορνεία dealt with in ch 6.[40]

The emphasis on eating 'in a temple' and on the subject of 'idolatry' is important but the adamant conclusion that Jewish sensibilities were not an issue overstates the case. Dupont and others have demonstrated at least the *possibility* of the 'strong' being Jewish gnostics or proto-gnostics.

It is our view that not enough information is given to be certain whether converted Jews or converted Gentiles were causing Paul most problems here. Verse 7, as we shall see, clearly refers to former pagans but we cannot deduce definitively the origin of the so-called 'strong'. Of much greater significance, we believe, is the study of how Paul *deals* with the issues confronting him, for it is this that reveals insights into Paul's teaching and it is this which is most accessible in the text before us. Paul had to face people who were eating this meat and the seriousness of that problem is amply illustrated by his use of words like μολύνω (8:7), πρόσκομμα (8:9), ἀπόλλυμι (8:11), and σκανδαλίζω (8:13). However, his initial response appears to digress from the subject for he talks now of γνῶσις.

---

36   Cf Fee's summary of this perspective: "Εἰδωλόθυτα" 182. Robertson on 8:10 adopts the common position on ἐν εἰδωλείῳ: 'In order to show how the *offendiculum* (Vulg.) arises, he takes an extreme case', 171.

37   Fee, "Εἰδωλόθυτα" 183.

38   Loc cit.

39   Num 25:1-2; cf 1 Cor 10:6-8.

40   Ibid 187.

2.1.2   A Corinthian saying

There is widespread agreement among scholars that v 1b contains a quotation from a Corinthian letter to Paul: "all of us possess knowledge".[41]

Paul's use of οἴδαμεν, it is said, is a deliberate attempt to disarm the Corinthians by saying that he has what they have,[42] before immediately qualifying the statement in v 1b. However, if it is accepted that Paul agreed with the statement then there is at least an apparent contradiction with v 7. Conzelmann addresses the problem by commenting on v 7: 'Paul still grants even now that his opponents have objective knowledge, but not that they have understanding in the proper sense'.[43] Even this, however, leaves a tension in v 1 itself between Paul's *theory* and his *practice*.

The clause οἴδαμεν ὅτι cannot confidently be said to *introduce* a quotation. Willis has pointed out that this clause occurs only in 8:1 and 8:4.[44] The unusual nature of this phrase may indicate that the whole sentence is part of a *Corinthian* quotation. Thus, says Willis, 8:1 contains the *Corinthian* statement, 'We know that we all possess knowledge, and 8:4 contains their statement, 'We know that an idol is nothing in the world'. Willis further argues that, if the Corinthians were saying οἴδαμεν frequently about various subjects, Paul's repeated οὐκ οἴδατε; ... is probably a deliberate contrast with them. Taking οἴδαμεν ὅτι as part of a quotation avoids the possible contradiction between 8:1a and 8:7[45] but also avoids the tension most see in v 1, where Paul otherwise seems to be agreeing (in theory) that 'we know' and then moving directly to qualifying this (in practice). Willis argues, therefore, that Paul is holding together theory and practice more clearly than most scholars suggest.[46]

However, there are two possible problems with doing this. The first is that it gives rise to an apparent tautology in 8:1. In effect it seems as if the Corinthians were saying 'We know that we know ...! Secondly, if Paul is arguing that *not* all possess knowledge (8:7), to what was he referring in passages like 2 Corinthians 4:6 or Romans 15:14 where he seems to attribute knowledge to all Christians?

---

41   Hurd 68 lists 24 commentators adopting this position. Hurd himself proposes that the slogan came from Paul's first preaching at Corinth (p 279).
42   So Chrysostom 261-262. Cf Weiss 214; Héring 67.
43   Conzelmann 146.
44   For οἴδαμεν δὲ ὅτι or ... γαρ ὅτι see Rom 2:2; 3:19: 2 Cor 5:1 etc.
45   Cf Lock, "Suggestion" 65-67. He suggests that the first person plural verbs came from the Corinthians and second plural from Paul, thus effectively requiring that the whole of vv 4-6 be a quotation from the Corinthians.
46   Willis 70.

The tautology is more apparent than real. The Corinthian 'strong' are clearly one of the several groups to be found in the church. We shall demonstrate below that they regarded 'knowledge' as a possession that marked them out in some way. Hence, it is quite understandable that they should say, 'We know that we all possess knowledge. In other words, i) not all people did grant them this fact, and ii) the knowledge being referred to was a *particular* γνῶσις.[47] Their tone was probably defensive: 'this is what we know we have (whatever anyone else may say)'. Certainly the sentence need not be regarded as tautologous.

The issue of the *meaning* of 'knowledge' is dealt with in the next section. Suffice it to say that we believe both Paul and the Corinthians use the word to describe a particular gift of the Spirit. Paul calls these gifts χαρίσματα and believes that they are given to people in a *discriminating* way by the Spirit. It is *this* sort of 'knowledge' that we believe the Corinthians were claiming to possess. It was *this* knowledge that Paul later said (8:7) that *not* all possessed. We shall expand on this below.

Following Willis, then, we suggest that Paul's qualification, which starts in v 1b and continues in v 7, addresses a slogan of the Corinthians in which they emphasize *themselves* to be possessors of knowledge. It is stated in a way that is somewhat typical of their arrogance.[48]

2.1.3 Γνῶσις

The link between knowledge and idol meat has been much debated. Below, we suggest that the text itself shows the nature of the link.

It is to be noted[49] that the word γνῶσις occurs more frequently in 1 Corinthians than elsewhere in the NT.[50] This fact combined with the appearance of other words like πνευματικός[51] and σοφία gives rise to the suggestions[52] that Paul faced Gnosticism in Corinth.

Schmithals held that 8:1-9:23 and 10:23-11:1 came from epistle 'B', in which the Corinthian response to the admonitions of Paul in epistle 'A' is heard. Paul had spoken against the worship of idols in 10:14-22 (epistle A), but then a new problem of meat offered for sale *outside* the temple was raised. To this, Paul responded in agreement with the Gnostic position that 'we all have knowledge, but placed the practice of

47   See 2.1.3 below.
48   Cf other refs to arrogance e g 1:26-31; 3:3-4, 18-23; 4:6-8, and below on 'boasting'.
49   Cum Reitzenstein, *HMR*; Dupont, *Gnosis*; *inter al.*
50   Γνῶσις appears ten times in 1 Corinthians. The many occurrences of the verb γινώσκω in this epistle are also relevant.
51   See 4.4.1 below.
52   Above 1.2.

eating in the context of love.[53] The problem lay in the 'typically Gnostic' belief that 'to participate in pagan cultic meals from a deliberately "Christian" stance' would demonstrate that the 'demons have indeed been conquered'.[54]

We have already suggested that Gnosticism was unlikely to have provided the background. Scholars who have proposed a Jewish background to 'knowledge''and 'wisdom' were also mentioned above. But in our opinion neither case has been finally proven. Perhaps the most that can be said is that γνῶσις was part of the religious vocabulary of the hellenistic age and was, for some reason, especially prominent in Corinth.

However, it is important to return to the text if we are to move beyond these more or less reasonable hypotheses and discover more about 'knowledge' and the problem faced by Paul in Corinth. We believe it is possible to establish how this knowledge (whatever its roots) was *functioning* in the community — at both a theoretical and practical level. Schmithals correctly indicates that the relationship between γνῶσις and εἰδωλόθυτα centred on the need to *demonstrate* something.[55] This is apparent in the text:

i)   Verse 10 makes it clear that trouble for a 'weaker' person is caused in *seeing* τὸν ἔχοντα γνῶσιν. Possession of γνῶσις seems possibly to have involved the *deliberate* policy of being seen eating idol meat. This is supported by Paul's use there of the word οἰκοδομέω. While he intended criticism by using this word,[56] it does seem that the 'knowledgeable eating' in some way was designed to set an example or even cause jealousy. That this 'building up' in knowledge was a deliberate policy is probably further supported by Paul's contrast in v 1c, in which he said that it was 'love' which 'built up'. Unless there was a deliberate policy of the 'strong' to 'build up' the weak to eat idol meat, it is difficult to explain why the weak were tempted to copy the one with γνῶσις. We return to this later.

ii)   Paul says that ἡ γνῶσις φυσιοῖ The word φυσιόω connotes a flaunting of something or of oneself over *against* another.[57] This becomes evident in 4:6 where one person is not to be 'puffed up' against another. In 4:18 and 19, the flaunting of the Corinthian ways is against the ways of Paul 'in Christ' (v 17). This word indicates a *deliberate* effort to contrast oneself with another. Interestingly, in 13:4 Paul says 'love does not flaunt itself' — a similar contrast to that found in 8:1.[58]

53   Schmithals, *Gnosticism* 224-229.
54   Ibid 226.
55   Loc cit.
56   See below 2.1.5. .
57   Φυσιόω appears six times in 1 Cor, otherwise only in Col 2:18.
58   To a considerable extent ch 13 is a commentary on ch 8.

From *Paul's* perspective, then, it is already to be seen that the *function* of γνῶσις in the community was divisive. But what was this γνῶσις?

We have mentioned above that all Christians had a certain 'knowledge'. However, the sort of knowledge addressed in ch 8 was not possessed by all (8:7). In fact, Paul possibly emphasized this distinction between types of knowledge by his use of the article (ἡ γνῶσις) in v 1c and v 7.[59] There are other indications that a distinctive form of γνῶσις is the subject of discussion in this epistle.

Chapter 13 demonstrates this by contrasting certain possessions or 'faculties' with love. 'Tongues', 'prophecy', 'faith to remove mountains' are listed with 'knowledge', and all are contrasted with love. In the light of ch 12, it is reasonable to assume that these are to be classed as χαρίσματα which are evidently *not* possessed by every Christian (12:4-11). Exactly how this χάρισμα of γνῶσις is to be differentiated from the γνῶσις that all Christians have is not easy to discern. 'Faith' perhaps offers an analogy. All Christians are required to have faith in Christ but presumably not all have this distinctive 'faith to remove mountains' (13:2). These gifts from the Spirit seem to be more intense and given for a specific purpose to 'build up the church'. Perhaps they were felt to be the product of a more immediate personal, or even visionary,[60] experience of the presence of the Holy Spirit in the individual.

Attention is first drawn to γνῶσις in Paul's own description of the church in ch 1. It is something with which God has 'enriched' them (1:5). Γνῶσις and λόγος are among the charismata of which they lack none.[61] Since Paul mentions other charismata in 12:4-10 and that different individuals receive different gifts, it may reasonably be suggested that two things are presupposed in chapter 1: firstly, that λόγος and γνῶσις were prominent gifts, therefore receiving particular mention, and secondly, that although all had gifts not all actually had γνῶσις.

It seems likely, therefore, that the γνῶσις mentioned in 8:1 was in fact the charisma from ch 1.[62] Γνῶσις was one of several gifts of God for his church, designed to benefit the community (cf 12:4, 28-31; 14:1).[63] This

---

59   Oslhausen 135 says of ἡ γνῶσις in v 7: 'a certain defined knowledge is there spoken of'.

60   Dupont, *Gnosis* 145.

61   See discussion of these 'spiritual gifts' in Fee 39.

62   Ellis, *Prophecy* 61.

63   Surprisingly, this link between chs 1 and 8 is rarely developed. Among those who develop only the most general link, cf Conzelmann 27, 140; Barrett 37-38; Weiss 7, 215; Wolff II 4. Most commentators do not even suggest γνῶσις in 8:1 might be the gift of the Spirit, e. g. Héring, Goudge, Thrall, Prior, Lenski, Senft, Schlatter, Willis. However, cf Fee 366 n 34: 'Their γνῶσις is a gift of the Spirit, which enlightens them to act in a certain way'.

argument is supported by Paul's contrast in ch 13, which is essentially between love and gifts of the Spirit (13:1-3).

It is difficult to deduce from the text exactly what this gift of the Spirit really was, because Paul's concern, as we shall see, was with the *function* of γνῶσις. They may have been abusing it, but Paul was still thankful that they had received it (1:5). In fact Paul gave very little information about the gift at all, perhaps because it was a subject raised by the Corinthians rather than the apostle himself. However, it is possible to deduce three things about this gift apart from the fact that it came from the Lord, by grace, and was given for these 'last days' (1:4-9).

Firstly, it was not simply speculative and theoretical knowledge. It will be seen later that some commentators have tried to resolve the apparent contradiction between vv 1 and 7 by suggesting that Paul agreed with the theory but not with the practice. But this is to misunderstand how knowledge functioned for the Corinthians. It may have begun with theoretical statements such as 'an idol does not exist', but part of their understanding of this gift was that it had to be *practised*.[64] Knowledge was practical:[65] they ate in idol temples and wanted others to do so (8:10). Those with knowledge worked it out in the community and did not separate theory from knowledge.

Secondly, from 2:12 it is possible to deduce that knowledge for Paul involved correctly discerning the things given by God. Dunn has persuasively argued this point.[66] He begins with the reference to the gift mentioned in 12:8: 'word of knowledge'. This, he says, may express 'more of Paul's reaction against Corinthian *gnosis* than his agreement with it', because of the contrast in 8:2 between knowing and not fully knowing. He goes on to suggest that 2:12 sheds light on what Paul meant: 'Now we have received ... the Spirit which is from God, that we might understand the gifts bestowed on us by God'. 'Word of knowledge' may, therefore, denote

> Some charismatic insight into 'the things given us by God' ... some understanding of the relationship of God to the believer(s), some recognition of the charismatic dimension (τὰ χαρισθέντα) to the believer's life individually or as a community. Since 'knowledge' in this more O T sense includes the overtones of 'acknowledgement' we may

---

64   Pearson, *Pneumatikos* 42; Parry 131. While caution must be exercised here with regard to 'mirror-reading' (see p 13 above), the evidence for our view that knowledge was a gift to be practised is cumulative. Further, we argue below that this was how *Paul* viewed knowledge and we see no exegetical reason to suggest that the Corinthians understood the gift differently.

65   Barrett, *Essays* 54, who deduces this from both ch 10 and 6:13.

66   Dunn, *Spirit* 218-219.

assume that some practical application of the *gnosis* was explicit or implicit in the 'word of knowledge'.[67]

Thirdly, we may perhaps deduce from the use of the perfect ἐγνωκέναι in 8:2 that such knowledge was received on a particular occasion. Perhaps such occasions were often repeated (12:8), but experiences were being used as the basis for arguing that certain people now 'had knowledge'. Paul did not allow this deduction (cf 8:2b where an ingressive aorist is used).[68]

In summary, it seems that this γνῶσις was possibly a revelation from God given to particular individuals at a particular time or times. It was given to build up the community, that is, it was to be *practical*. It was given so that the church might 'understand the gifts bestowed on us by God'.

2.1.4   Ἀγάπη

The dominance of the concept of love in these chapters is noted by Furnish.[69] Its focus is the church, which is the understood object of the verb οἰκοδομέω. This becomes clear on examination of the meaning of οἰκοδομέω (see below). However, our understanding of ἀγάπη must also account for its use in v 3 where God is the object.

Paul rarely talked of love for God. Stauffer mentions only Romans 8:28 and this verse.[70] Barrett says that 'it is more characteristic of Paul to describe man's response to God as faith rather than love'.[71] But Paul has already talked of love *for* God in 2:9, where he quoted from a composite of Jewish texts.[72] 8:3 appears deliberately to build on the teaching of chs 1-3. There the emphasis was on the electing call of God (1:26-29) who had saved his people (1:18) by his power (2:5). Love for God was seen to rest, as was faith, in God's prior work through his Spirit.

Two important aspects of Paul's view of love are to be found in i) its relationship to the death of Christ, and ii) its link to the work of the Spirit. In ch 1 the death of Christ was at the centre of Paul's understanding of God's wisdom (his plan) to save his people. It was the 'word of the cross' that was the power of God to those 'being saved' (1:18). Paul said 'Christ [is] the power of God and the wisdom of God' (1:24). It was the death of Christ that brought 'new life' (Romans 6:4-

---

67   Ibid 219.
68   Héring 67.
69   Furnish, *Love* 112-115.
70   Stauffer, "Ἀγάπη" 50 n 140. Cf 2 Thess 3:5.
71   Barrett 190.
72   Nestle[26] mentions Sir 1:10: τοῖς ἀγαπῶσιν αὐτόν. On possible sources for 2:9 see Weiss 58-59.

11) but, supremely, in Christ's death was the *love* of God shown. As God's new creatures, people were to be controlled by Christ's love, 'For the love of Christ controls us ... he died for all, that those who live might live no longer for themselves but for him who for their sake died and was raised' (2 Corinthians 5:14-15). Love for God and love for neighbour, therefore, arose out of a proper response to the prior love of God for man.

It is for this reason that Paul made the link in 8:11, 12 between sinning against a brother 'for whom Christ died' and 'sin against Christ'.[73] For Paul, 'brother' was a synonym for Christian, but his addition of 'for whom Christ died' emphasized the centrality of the death of Christ as a motivation to love the brother.

The work of the Holy Spirit was what enabled the life of love to be lived. Because of this close relationship between love and the work of the Spirit, love became the *demonstration* that a person possessed the Spirit and was therefore a Christian. It is important to understand this in Paul's theology because it ultimately helps explain the difference between faith and love in Paul. For Paul, possession by the Spirit of God indicated that a person belonged to Christ (Romans 8:9-11) and was one of the elect. Paul's understanding of the process involved here is perhaps most clearly expressed in Romans 5:5: 'The love of God has been poured into our hearts through the Holy Spirit who has been given to us'.[74] Thus, it was love for God rather than wisdom or knowledge (2:7-9), which was the evidence of having 'received not the spirit of the world, but the Spirit which is from God' (2:12).

Although Barrett believes Paul would more normally have used the word 'faith', we may now suggest why he did not in 8:3. Galatians 5:6 helps clarify the distinction: 'For in Christ Jesus neither circumcision nor uncircumcision is of any avail, but faith working through love'. It is wrong simply to say here that faith is theory and love is practice.[75] Rather, love is a description of *faith* in practice. As Ridderbos says: 'faith expresses itself, so to speak, in love'.[76] The chief sign of faith, in Paul's view, was love. As has been noted, the person of faith was the one who had believed in Christ crucified and had the Spirit of God. If this was the case, and love was the evidence in the community that a person had faith, then it is not surprising that Paul saw it as pre-eminent among the fruit of the Spirit (Galatians 5:22).

---

[73]   See 2.4.3 below.
[74]   We understand τοῦ θεοῦ as an objective genitive. Cf Cranfield, *Romans* I 262. For additional arguments in favour of this see Wright *MPG* 138-139.
[75]   Rightly Betz, *Galatians* 264.
[76]   Ridderbos, *Galatians* 191; cf Smedes, *Love* 96.

It is perhaps because early Christians saw in Christ's death God's covenant love for his people that, in their desire to be Christ-like, *love* came to figure so prominently.[77] No doubt love was also regarded as of fundamental importance as Christians sought to follow Christ's reaffirmation of the OT law: to love God and one's neighbour.[78] The words of Christ, enshrined in the Johannine tradition, also indicate love to be the mark of a true Christian: 'By this all men will know that you are my disciples, if you have love for one another' (John 13:35). While the Christ-centredness of Paul's statement that love 'builds up' is not immediately to be seen in 8:1-3, we have seen that it is evident in 8:11-12 and it does become evident in Paul's summary of this section in 11:1, 'Be imitators of me, as I am of Christ'. Finally, it is more especially evident in his use through the next few chapters of the word οἰκοδομέω. In practice, love marked out those who belonged to God, for it showed that they had faith in Christ crucified and that the Spirit was at work in their lives.

The concept, also found in 8:3, of being 'known by God'[79] built on the OT tradition in which God 'knew' his people in an electing way.[80] But it is in 13:12 that Paul's particular contrast is made more explicit between man's knowledge (now ἐκ μέρους and awaiting completion) and God's knowledge of man which is already full: καθὼς καὶ ἐπεγνώσθην. This partial nature of man's knowledge is precisely the point of 8:2. Love for God rested on God's election and showed itself in the community through love for the brother (8:1b). Héring is surely correct in saying: 'Love for God is therefore the true sign of election' (cf Romans 8:28-30).[81]

2.1.5   Οἰκοδομέω

Paul could talk of his own apostolic authority as one who 'built up' the community (2 Corinthians 10:8; 12:19; 13:10) and, more generally, of the need for the Christian church or community to be built up.[82] In 1 Corinthians this distinction becomes obscured as Paul's own 'building up' was used as an example for others in the church to follow (cf 4:6, 16; 11:1). In 3:9, Paul called the church at Corinth θεοῦ οἰκοδομή. He had laid the foundation, and commanded that anyone who built on it (ἐποικοδομεῖ) should use proper materials (vv 12-15). In 3:16 he called the Corinthians the ναὸς θεοῦ. Paul's thoughts were driven by the

77 Note the repetition of Rom 13:8, 9c, 10. See Willis 74.
78 Mark 12:30-32; cf Gal 5:14.
79 Cf also Gal 4:9; Mat 7:23; 25:12.
80 Cf (LXX) Num 16:5; Jer 1:5; etc. Cf Murphy-O'Connor, "Ghetto" 559.
81 Héring 68.
82 Michel, "Οἰκοδομέω" 141.

knowledge that they were in the messianic age, an age in which the Spirit had come (3:16), and an age moving towards 'the Day' of Judgment (3:13). The foundation Paul laid was Christ (v 11).

This 'building' metaphor was probably drawn from the OT,[83] where rebuilding or 'building up' the temple and the cities was regarded as part of God's future covenantal blessings on Israel. The goal of the building was the completion of the promises of God.[84] Paul seemed to regard the church as the renewed temple, built on its messianic foundations and within which the Spirit of God dwelt.[85]

The 'building up' was designed to help the church, and individuals who comprised the whole, to become what they were. They were the holy temple of God (3:16-17). Any building had, therefore, to follow God's wisdom and plans, and not man's (2:16). The attitude in which this was to be done had to be one of service to Christ (4:1). 2 Corinthians 5:1-5 is a reminder that Paul regarded the Spirit (cf 3:16) as a guarantee of an eternal building.

The use of οἰκοδομέω in 1 Corinthians 8:1b is not a specific allusion to the OT themes prominent in ch 3. However, the word probably did come to mind in light of his earlier comparison of his own work and the building work of the Corinthian leaders. Parallels between the two chapters make this likely: in ch 3 Paul had mentioned wrong building leading to 'destruction'.[86] In 8:10-11 'building' on the basis of knowledge wrongly applied to eating idol meat could also lead to destruction.[87] People who built incorrectly perhaps thought they were wise (3:18) or that they had 'knowledge' (8:2), but they had yet to become wise (3:18) and did not yet know as they ought to know (8:2).[88]

Οἰκοδομέω in ch 8, we suggest, came to mind in the light of Paul's earlier discussion of the subject. At the heart of the word was Paul's concern for the *church* — a church that was Christ's and should be united in service of Christ rather than divided as one group flaunted something over another. Thus, the outworking of theory into practice

---

[83]   This is demonstrated in various studies. Cf Vielhauer, *Oikodome* 9-15; 85-86; Bonnard, "L'église"; Ridderbos, *Paul* 429-432.

[84]   In Acts 15:16 James' speech drew upon this picture using Amos 9:11 and Jer 12:15.

[85]   Ridderbos, *Paul* 430. Cf Is 28:16; 65:21-22; 66:1; Ezek 36:10, 36; 37:24-28: Jubilees 1:17. Among those agreeing that Paul draws on such ideas in 1 Cor 3 are: Barrett 90; Héring 24; Conzelmann 77-78. Also see Gärtner, *Temple* 56-60, who demonstrates parallels between this section in Paul and ideas in the Qumran texts.

[86]   Φθείρω: *BAGD* 857: in the sense of 'punish with eternal destruction'. Cf 2 Pet 2:12; Jude 10, 11 (with ἀπώλετο).

[87]   On the ironic use of οἰκοδομέω: Vielhauer, *Oikodome* 94.

[88]   Note the use of εἴ τις δοκεῖ in 3:18; 8:2.

was to be tested by examining the type of building that was being done. Love, in practice, builds up the church. Knowledge, in practice, puffs up the individual.

2.1.6   The function of γνῶσις

Verses 1-3 introduce both the main topic for chs 8-10 (εἰδωλόθυτα) and the main theological problem that concerned Paul.

It is likely that Paul was quoting from a Corinthian letter. Either he included himself in agreement with their statement or, as we feel is more likely, οἴδαμεν ὅτι is also part of the quotation. The double use of a first person plural verb (οἴδαμεν and ἔχομεν) draws attention to those who have raised the issue: 'We, [the ones who are 'strong'] know that we all possess knowledge ...' In either case, v 1b qualifies v 1a, but with the latter interpretation v 7 offers no problem at all because Paul never formally agrees that 'all' have knowledge. In fact, he denies it.

There is some evidence in these three verses to suggest that Paul's problem with γνῶσις at Corinth lay not in the fact that the Corinthians possessed the gift but in the way they allowed it to *function* in the community.

We have suggested that Paul viewed γνῶσις as a gift of the Spirit with which this church had been particularly 'enriched' (1:4-7). There is no indication that Paul decried this gift *per se*. In ch 1 he had thanked God for it and he regarded it as useful in 'building up' the church (14:6). However, Paul's qualification of γνῶσις was stern and abrupt. Even though spiritual gifts were given to 'build up' the church (14:1-5, 12), Paul said their γνῶσις puffed them up. Being 'puffed up' involves a flaunting of something for one's own benefit, but the nature of a charisma like γνῶσις is that it is given for this age, is partial (13:10), and will cease (1:7; 13:8). There is little about it that warrants a person being puffed up. What then was Paul's problem with γνῶσις in this context?

We noted that the use of the word φυσιόω lent weight to Schmithal's assertion that the issue centred on the need to *demonstrate* something. *We propose that it was precisely this demonstrative function that Paul opposed.* What the Corinthians believed becomes clearer in v 3 and through the rest of ch 8.

Paul contrasted love with knowledge. What makes love different in *this* context is not simply its permanence (ch 13), but its *function*. Negatively, it is 'not puffed up' (13:4). Positively, it 'builds up' (8:1d). It was centred in 'love for God', the possession of which *demonstrated* that 'one is known by God' (8:3). We have seen that from earliest times in the church the practice of love demonstrated that a person was a Christian, and in Paul's theology was integrally related to belief in Christ crucified and the work of the Spirit in a person's life.

The issue Paul confronted was 'what is it that demonstrates that a person is "known by God"?' Paul's response was: '... if a person loves God, *this* person (οὗτος is emphatic[89]) is known by God'. It seems possible, then, that the clause οὗτος ἔγνωσται ὑπ' αὐτοῦ was not a clever twisting of the subject, nor a play on words in which Paul showed that it was God's knowledge that is really important.[90] The point of comparison was between γνῶσις and ἀγάπη, not between γνῶσις of man and γνῶσις of God.

Paul was not comparing God's knowledge with 'the characteristically gnostic idea of the spiritual ascent of the soul to God'.[91] Nor was Paul saying 'the appropriate stance for Christians is not *knowing* God, but *being known*, which is seen in loving God ...'.[92] Paul certainly believed that to be true, but to make that point of 8:3 is to read it in the light of Galatians 4:9. Neither was Paul saying 'Christian behaviour is not predicated on the way of knowledge ... but on the way of love, which is in fact the true way of knowledge'.[93]

Given Paul's response describing the function of ἀγάπη, it seems likely that the Corinthians were using this gift of the Spirit (γνῶσις) as a demonstration that 'this one is known by God', i.e., one of God's elect. Paul turns the Corinthians back to the command of the Law and of Christ, that God's people are to *love* him and love their neighbour. 8:3 makes the first point and 8:1d (οἰκοδομέω) makes the second.[94]

2.1.7   Summary

Paul regarded love for God as evidence that a person was known by God (8:3). For the Corinthians, 'knowledge' seems to have usurped this function of love. This is evidenced in the fact that it 'puffs up', suggesting that the Corinthians were flaunting it in demonstration of something. A contrast, with Paul's emphasis on 'this man' (v 3) being the one who is 'known by God', suggests that γνῶσις may have been

89   Moule, *Idiom* 122. *BAGD* 596. The emphatic nature of this apodosis becomes more apparent when contrasted with the more general apodosis of another εἴ τις... clause in v 2. Cf also Rom 8:9.

90   So several scholars: Conzelmann 141; Allo 198; Lietzmann 37 (who adds that this phrase puts us in the 'Bereich hellenistischer Mystik'); Weiss 217-218 *inter al.*

91   Barrett 190.

92   Willis 81.

93   Fee 368.

94   See comments on 'mirror reading' (above p 13). Here the emphatic οὗτος adds weight to our suggestion, but a working hypothesis like this must be supported in other ways. Below we seek to show that this reconstruction is suggested in a variety of different ways and that it makes sense of some of the more intractable problems faced in chs 8-10.

flaunted by certain Corinthians as that which demonstrated that they were known by God. This is the main contrast in these verses. It is not primarily a contrast between knowledge of man and knowledge of God (although Paul's emphasis on the incompleteness of wisdom in ch 3 and knowledge in ch 13 is vital to his argument). It is a contrast between knowledge which leads to boasting, and love which is for the benefit of the church and is Christ-centred.

In this instance the Corinthians flaunted their knowledge by eating idol meat. This is the quite direct link between εἰδωλόθυτα and γνῶσις. Paul not only showed that love was the true marker of the one known by God but, in v 2, he began to show the real problem with knowledge. Knowledge was not appropriate as a 'marker'. It was incomplete and imperfect. This was a point he would develop later in ch 13. Gifts of the Spirit were limited in function (13:1-3) and, with special reference to knowledge (13:8-12), their function had to be seen in the light of 'the perfect' which would come. Chs 12 and 14 address the positive use of the gifts of the Spirit and describe their proper *function* in the church. But neither γνῶσις, nor any of the spiritual gifts, was intended to function as evidence of election or community membership. In fact, they could not possibly do so, for the Spirit apportions them as he wills, to different people different gifts (12:4-11), and 'knowledge' is not in everyone' (8:7).

2.2   There is one God (Verses 4 - 6)

Schlatter comments on v 4, 'Das ist die Erkenntnis, auf der die Freiheit der Gemeinde in dieser Sache beruht'.[95] However, there is a difference of opinion again concerning the extent of possible quotations from a Corinthian letter.

Willis has argued that, 'Omitting the Pauline qualification of 5b, the Corinthians' defense is cogently set forth in 8:4-6'.[96] The structure of the three verses, he suggests, supports his view. From the 'fundamental confession of monotheism' in 8:4, the Corinthians have concluded that idols do not exist. 'This confession is elaborated in v 5 to take notice of the apparent being of many gods and lords', then in v 6 the whole is summed up in a 'creedal confession'.[97] Certainly, it has long been assumed that v 6 is pre-Pauline,[98] although Willis' view that it is a quotation from the Corinthians has not been put forward by many.[99]

---

[95]   Schlatter 96.

[96]   Willis 86.

[97]   Ibid 84.

[98]   Kramer, *Christ* 95; Murphy-O'Connor, "Cosmology".

[99]   Although see Grosheide 192. For trenchant criticisms of Willis on this see Fee 371 n 10.

The use of περὶ indicates a return to the issue of εἰδωλόθυτα raised in the Corinthian letter.[100] As in v 1, so in v 4 οἴδαμεν ὅτι may introduce a quotation (the ὅτι therefore being recitative in vv 4a and 4b). This is the position the *RSV* takes. However, following similar arguments to those put forward for v 1, οἴδαμεν ὅτι could also be regarded as part of the Corinthian statement.[101]

Most commentators view vv 5-6 as Paul's qualification of the position taken by the Corinthians who have written to him. Willis takes issue with this, saying that the affirmation of monotheism does *not* suit Paul's purpose here. In other words, these two verses represent the argument or 'knowledge' of the *Corinthians*. Into the middle of this, Paul introduced the point he wished to stress: (v 5b) 'as indeed there are many "gods" and many "lords"'. In this, says Willis, Paul was leaving the way open for his argument in 10:18-22. On this view, the 'Corinthians' defense is cogently set forth in 8:4-6' *less* v 5b!

This is an attractive reading because it assigns to the Corinthians, who were insisting that idols meant nothing, the apparently more hypothetical clause beginning καὶ γὰρ εἴπερ, while attributing the definite statement (ὥσπερ εἰσιν ... v 5b) to Paul.[102] Though this is plausible, we shall see that v 6 can make sense as a *continuation* of v 5b, that is as a continuing *qualification* of the Corinthians' statements of v 4. Thus, accepting v 4 as a quotation from the Corinthians, we shall seek to show that vv 5b-6 are Paul's careful qualification of that position.

However, the problem faced by nearly all commentators remains: how is it best to understand v 5a? Is this the beginning of Paul's opinion[103] or does it reflect the position of the Corinthians that at a hypothetical level they might allow for the existence of λεγόμενοι θεοί?[104] Or is it that Barrett is right in saying that, at this stage, Paul expresses 'no definite opinion'?[105]

---

[100] Faw ("Thessalonians" 221) suggests that between 7:1 and ch 16 περὶ δέ introduces points of reply to the Corinthians and that, in some places, reference back to their letter was made simply by using δέ or περί as here 8:4 (περί). Further papyri evidence confirms this use of περὶ δέ, and possibly a similar use of περί. In a private letter from a freedman to his patron (c first century BC — BGU Vol IV, no 1141) we read:

εὐλαβῶς ἔχων προεγνωκ[ῶς/έναι με] περὶ των δακτυλιδίων [γεγονέναι] ὧν ἐπόησε ὁ Ερως.... Περὶ δὲ τῆς σκιᾶς φανερόν μοι ἐγενήθη ἐκξητήσαντι ἠλλάχθαι μεν τὴν πορφυρᾶν ὑπὸ τοῦ Διοδώρου καὶ μὴ δεδωκέναι σοὶ ...

[101] Willis 88. So also Osborn "ΣΥΝΕΙΔΗΣΙΣ" 178.
[102] So also Parry 130; Grosheide 192; Hurd 120-122. Cf Fee 371 n 10.
[103] Conzelmann 142; Fee 372.
[104] Parry 130.
[105] Barrett 192.

The phrase καὶ γὰρ εἴπερ is rare in Greek literature. Those examples that we do have confirm the conclusion of *LS* that the phrase is used 'mostly to imply that the supposition agrees with the fact'.[106] If this is so, then it seems reasonable that it functions as the introduction to 'Paul's cautious argument'[107] against the statement of the Corinthians in v 4. This argument becomes less cautious in v 5b and v 7, reaching its climax in 10:18-22.[108]

Grammatically, it is worth noting that εἰσιν is placed forward in both vv 5a and 5b which suggests an emphasis on the word.[109] Also there is considerable weight given to the first person plural pronoun in v 6, beginning Ἀλλ' ἡμῖν. Bearing these points in mind, these verses may be paraphrased:

> (v 4) You say, in support of your action in eating food offered to idols: 'We know that an idol does not exist in the world and that there is no God but one'. (5) For even if[110] (in the face of your denial) there are what might be called gods either in heaven or on earth — in fact there are indeed many gods and many lords — (6) yet rather (ἀλλα) it is among *us* that there is one God the Father ...

It seems to us that Paul's main qualification of what the 'strong' were claiming was that it was only partly true. In what Hurd rightly calls a 'henotheistic-sounding statement',[111] Paul conceded the real existence of gods but claimed that in the *Christian* context only the one God was recognised.[112] We return to the implications of this shortly, for it will be helpful now briefly to examine the possible background to Paul's apparent ambivalence on the subject.

Horsley has suggested that in Judaism there were two traditions of polemic against false gods.[113] The first, 'in Deutero-Isaiah, derided the heathen gods as nothings and their worship as foolishness.' This tradition, he argues, was largely followed by Hellenistic Jewish literature and Wisdom literature. The second tradition, later followed in apocalyptic Jewish literature (such as 1 Enoch and Jubilees), is exemplified in Deuteronomy, Jeremiah, and Malachi. Here the criticism

106 *LS* 420. We have found less than a dozen occurrences. A search for καὶ γὰρ εἴπερ with ὥσπερ produced one ref in Aristotle (*De generatione animalium* 723b 27). Searches used *TLG*.

107 Hurd 122.

108 'So-called gods' need only imply that Paul would rather call them 'demons'. Cf Fee 372.

109 Lenski 338; Weiss 220.

110 *BAGD* 220.

111 Hurd 122.

112 Paul was not a henotheist but he did accept the reality of demonic powers at work in the world.

113 Horsley, "Gnosis" 38, following Bousset, *Religion*.

of idolatry centres on seeing it 'as the service of demons'. Horsley contends that the Corinthians followed the hellenistic-wisdom tradition which Paul modified in line with the apocalyptic tradition.

The evidence for this distinction of positions is not entirely satisfying. In Horsley's 'Deutero-Isaiah' tradition, it is not as clear as he suggests that heathen gods do not *exist*. Certainly they are regarded as 'nothings', but this is in *contrast* with the power and knowledge of Yahweh. In Isaiah 44:9 idol *makers* are, like the things they make, 'nothings' (תֹהוּ). In Isaiah 41:29 the works of the gods are 'nothing'. Indeed anything may be regarded as 'nothing' if set against God, even nations (40:17) and princes and rulers (40:23). The Israelite *perspective* is to be that false gods are 'nothing'. Only Yahweh can do anything for them. Interestingly Isaiah 65:11 refers to a table being set to the god of Fortune גַּד which becomes, in the LXX, τῷ δαιμονίῳ τράπεζαν.

Further, it is possible that the Corinthians themselves had parts of Deuteronomy 32 in mind — a chapter which Horsley regards as representing the position that later appears in the 'apocalyptic' tradition. This chapter establishes the concepts of 'no god' and 'foolish worship' but also refers to demon worship:

Ἔθυσαν δαιμονίοις, καὶ οὐ θεῷ. θεοῖς, οἷς οὐκ ᾔδεισαν (32:17)
Αὐτοὶ παρεζήλωσάν με ἐπ’ οὐ θεῷ παρώργισάν με ἐν τοῖς εἰδώλοις αὐτῶν (32:21)
or again:
οὐκ ἔστι θεὸς πλὴν ἐμοῦ (32:39)

An emphasis on this latter text and others in the chapter to the exclusion of the former two could lead to the same position Horsley lays at the feet of Hellenism. We will suggest later that Paul set the 'balance' right from Deuteronomy 32.

Even if Horsley is correct in his analysis, the most interesting point that arises from the text is that Paul's handling of the problem demonstrated the Corinthian knowledge to be inadequate. Paul had pointed to the wrong manner in which γνῶσις was being allowed to function in the community and had shown how incomplete it was (v 2). He then introduced his qualification of their knowledge: gods and lords *do* exist. Establishing this additional aspect of the truth opened the door for his second attack on the way knowledge was being used in Corinth.

Thus, in v 3 we see that Paul attacked knowledge at a fundamental religious level: it did *not* indicate those who were 'known by God', — only love could do that. Verses 5-6, we suggest, carry his argument forward on a second level: their 'knowledge' was inadequate anyway.

We must now return to the discussion of v 6. The precise nature of Paul's teaching here has been discussed at length[114] and further detailed analysis is not needed here. Some commentators believe parts of this verse, in particular the phrase τά πάντα, are drawn from Stoicism.[115] Murphy-O'Connor has challenged both the suggested parallels and the method used by these scholars. Instead he suggests that the text has an essential unity found in its single movement: from (ἐξ), to the point of arrival (εἰς), and the entrance way (δία).[116] He persuasively argues that the nature of this movement is not cosmic but salvific. 'If the structure of the verse suggests a single movement, it must be one or the other. It cannot be both'.[117] Even τά πάντα, he demonstrates, is used regularly in a salvific sense, especially in the Corinthian correspondence.[118] The most interesting aspect of this article is his insistence that Paul is *not* arguing that everything comes from God, therefore 'food offered to idols comes from God, and so may be eaten by Christians'.[119] As he rightly points out, Paul is addressing the 'strong' in this passage, and they already believe that! Rather, Paul's purpose is to help the Corinthians progress in their knowledge.

The 'us' of v 6a is Paul and the church, but this was much more than a simple agreement with the Corinthian affirmation of monotheism. Paul reminded these Christians that this one God is the 'Father'.[120] He was drawing attention to the familial, or brotherhood, aspect of the Christian faith. 'The calculated repetition of *adelphos* in vv 11-13' is to be seen as part of the necessary context within which v 6 must be read.[121] But, tentatively, we wish to suggest more than this.

Earlier we commented that the Corinthians themselves might have had Deuteronomy 32 in mind when they claimed οὐδὲν εἴδωλον ἐν κόσμῳ. When Paul returns to the discussion about idols and the reality of

---

114   Cf Murphy-O'Connor, "Cosmology"; Dunn, *Christology* 179-183; Kramer, *Christ* 95-99; Horsley, "Gnosis"; Kerst, "Taufbekenntnis" *inter al.*

115   Cf Conzelmann 144; Lietzmann 38; Dupont, *Gnosis* 344-345.

116   Murphy-O'Connor, "Cosmology" 264, following Sagnard, "1 Corinthiens". Bengel 634, 'εἰς αὐτὸν, in eum ... Finis fidelium.' Cf Horsley, "Background" 132-135.

117   Loc cit.

118   He cites 2:10-13; 9:22-23; 12:4-6; 2 Cor 4:14-15; 5:18; 12:19; Rom 8:28, 31-32. Dunn, *Christology*, 329 n 69 argues that Stoic parallels are closer than the Pauline parallels cited. However, even he admits that Paul has adopted those Stoic formulae and this accounts for the obvious differences with the Stoic phrases!

119   Op cit 265 (*contra* Godet).

120   This need not be a 'baptismal acclamation', *contra* Murphy-O'Connor "Cosmology" 266.

121   Loc cit.

demons in ch 10, he directly quotes from Deuteronomy 32 twice (in 10:20 from 32:17, and 10:22 from 32:21). It is clear from a study of that chapter in Deuteronomy that it would suit both sides of the Corinthian debate in different ways. It refers to an idol as a 'no god' (v 21), and yet mentions sacrifices to demons (v 17), and making God jealous with 'strange gods' (v 16). We have seen how it might have been applied by the Corinthians, and the direct application of the passage by Paul in 10:20, 22 will be examined later. However, it is also possible that there is an allusion to it here in 8:6. In the light of the use of Deuteronomy 32 in 10:20-22, possibly Paul saw it as an 'obvious' passage to use in this controversy and may already have had it in mind in ch 8. If he actually recognized a *Corinthian* allusion to the chapter, then his desire to teach his own understanding of that passage would be obvious.[122] In the nature of the case this cannot be proven but the possibility must be considered.

In Deuteronomy 32:6 the Israelites are challenged:

ταῦτα κυρίῳ ἀνταποδίδοτε οὕτω, λαὸς μωρὸς καὶ οὐχὶ σοφός; οὐκ αὐτὸς οὗτός σου πατὴρ ἐκτήσατό σε καὶ ἐποίησέν σε καὶ ἔκτισέν σε;

The use of 'Father' for God is rare in the OT, and yet the influence of Deuteronomy 32:6 on later Jewish use of the concept is to be noted.[123] If Paul does have this in mind, then this is additional evidence that he is not thinking in terms of cosmology, but of the chosen people who have been created and redeemed by God.[124] The fact that God is their particular creator and father becomes the basis for an appeal to a proper understanding of idols.[125] Seen in this light, the whole of v 6 is directly related to the Corinthians. Possibly it draws on earlier forms of a creed, but it seems to be put together by Paul for this situation.[126] The careful structure of this verse, and its close relationship with v 5b should be noted, for this also indicates that we have here a Pauline compilation.

v 5b   *There are many gods*
                 and many lords
But for *us*

A *Corinthian* allusion to Deut 32 might well have been based on Paul's own teaching about idols on his first visit.

[123]   Schrenk, "Πατήρ" 978.

[124]   See also 1:28.

[125]   On the use of 'Father' for God cf *Tg Onk* and *Jon* on Deut 32:6 and 32:18. Jub 1:22-28; 2:20; 3 Macc 7:6; Jos *Ant* 5:93; Tob 13:3-5.

[126]   Thus we agree with Dunn: 'The formulation in 1 Cor. 8.6 is directed wholly to the situation of the Corinthians ... *it is hard to recognize an earlier formulation behind it*'. (*Christology* 181, his emphasis.)

There is one God
> the Father, from whom are all things[127]
> and to whom we go

and one Lord
> Jesus Christ, through whom are all things
> and through whom we [come to God]

Given that in the OT the existence of many gods and many lords is granted,[128] as it is in v 5, and that 'we' refers to the people of God, we must ask what the precise nature is of Paul's qualification of the Corinthian position of v 4.

Some suggest that Paul argues that, 'gods *become* gods by being believed in, and faith in the *one* God and the *one* Lord creates freedom no longer to recognize these powers'.[129] But we have seen that Paul emphasizes in v 5b that these gods and lords *do* exist. It is wrong to suggest that because v 6 begins 'for us' therefore v 5 was actually stating something that was only true 'for them' (the 'weak' or pagans generally) *subjectively*.[130] This distinction between an 'objective' Christian view that gods do not exist and a 'subjective' pagan view that they do[131] seems far from Paul's mind. In v 7 we shall see that Paul's concern is with *real* defilement with idols and idol meat. If it were not, then there would be no need for the strong statements of 8:9ff.

The distinction Paul points to here is explicit in 10:14-22. Idols are nothing, but demons do indeed exist and can truly, not just subjectively in the mind of the worshipper, be worshipped. The 'demons' of ch 10 are the gods and lords of 8:5. The contrast with the Christian is, therefore, the traditional Jewish one: for *us* there is only one God who is true and who is Father of those who are his because, when God's people compare him and his works with anything else at all, the rest is 'nothing'. If people forget this context, they are vulnerable to demons (10:14-22). He is 'God of gods and Lord of lords' — noticing again Paul's balanced structure in these verses.

2.2.1 Summary

Paul returned in v 4 to the practical issue arising from the abuse of the gift of knowledge. The Corinthians had argued that idols did not exist and, therefore, that εἰδωλόθυτα might be eaten. Paul did not allow the adequacy of this position, adding that 'gods' and 'lords' really did exist. In ch 10 he amplified this in terms of worshipping demons.

---

127 With Murphy-O'Connor, "Cosmology" 264.
128 Cf also Deut 10:17.
129 Conzelmann 145.
130 *Contra* Fee 373.
131 Loc cit.

In v 6 Paul emphasized the sovereignty of the one God's unique work for his people whom he brought into being. He is known, therefore, as Father. From him (ἐξ οὗ) come all things (for his people) and 'to him (εἰς αὐτόν) 'our own being leads'.[132] The mediator of this work is the one Lord, through whom (δι᾽ οὗ) are all things and through whom (δι᾽ αὐτοῦ) *we*, as Christians, continue our existence before God.

In verses 1-3 Paul showed that knowledge was functioning as love was supposed to function. Paul then began to modify Corinthian 'knowledge'. Knowledge that acted on a belief in monotheism was inadequate unless filled out by an understanding that 'gods' and 'lords' did exist as real demonic powers. As Paul would go on to show, this meant that 'falling' was a *real* danger, one from which the Corinthians, for all their affirmation of monotheism, were not immune.

2.3   A radical challenge to the Corinthians (Verses 7 - 8)

A number of questions face the reader in these verses. What is their relationship to vv 4-6? Who is referred to in v 7b as 'weak in conscience'? What does 'Conscience' mean, and how can it be defiled? Who proposes the view of food presented in v 8?

2.3.1   The relationship between vv 1, 4-6 and 7a

Fee[133] insists that the relationship between vv 1 and 7 is best to be explained by differentiating between knowledge at a theoretical level (which all have — v 1), and knowledge at 'the experiential, emotional level' (that not all have — v 7). This seeks to avoid a contradiction between vv 1 and 7. But, as has been noted, there is little evidence that either Paul, *or the Corinthians*, would have separated theory and practice in this way. The gift of knowledge seems to have involved the *practice* of their understanding of God's will. If the 'knowledge' was inadequate or wrong then their practice and experience of it would be wrong. Theory and experience were not divided in this way. Further, the text does not *say* what Fee suggests. The defiling of conscience (v 7), or the possibility of being 'destroyed' (v 11), was not linked by Paul to immature or incomplete experiential knowledge. The use of the article ἡ in 8:7 suggests a certain demonstrative force, perhaps: 'this knowledge we have been talking about'. Paul did not suggest that these 'weak' people should be more knowledgeable. He said that they did not have *this* knowledge and so should be treated appropriately. Finally, it will be seen that also in v 8 Paul was not concerned with distinctions of theory and experience. Wrong knowledge involved wrong actions.

---

132   Barrett 192.
133   Fee 379; also Conzelmann 146.

A different possibility is put forward by Jeremias,[134] who suggests that there were two Corinthian sayings which Paul sought to correct. The first is in v 1a (corrected in vv 1b-3), and the second is in v 4, which Paul corrected here in v 7. 'This knowledge therefore refers in v 7 to the particular statement that 'an idol has no real existence'. This view shows the link between v 7 and vv 4-6 but does not do justice to the links with v 1. There the subject is εἰδωλόθυτα, which is examined in terms of a problem with 'knowledge'. In v 7, Paul began with knowledge and moved directly to eating food ὡς εἰδωλόθυτον. It is not, therefore, easy to divide the first saying from the second.[135]

Thus far, we have argued that the Corinthians have said three things:

i)   'We know that we all have knowledge';

ii)   'We know that an idol does not exist';

iii) 'There is no God but one'.

If γνῶσις was a gift of the Spirit, as defined earlier, then these were not bare statements of theory. As a χάρισμα it was supposed to build up the church in Christ. The Corinthians believed that they were doing this, as Paul ironically pointed out in 8:10. Thus, it is not as simple as some suggest, to say, 'Paul agreed, but wanted them to do it all in love'. There is little indication that Paul did agree, even with iii) above, *in the Corinthian context* of their exercise of a spiritual gift. He qualified ii) and iii) by saying that there *are* other 'lords' and 'gods' ('so-called', because his preference was to call them 'demons'). He qualified i) by saying that their knowledge was incomplete. He denied their religious understanding of the gift: that those who possessed it were 'known by God'. Through his stress on love, building up, and the creation of *God's* people through Christ, Paul turned the emphasis away from boasting to a concern for those who belong to Christ.

In v 7 Paul began to clarify the implications of what he was saying. The verse begins with the strong adversative ἀλλα and emphasis on the negative οὐκ: 'But this knowledge is *not* in everyone'. It may be that Paul meant simply that the gift of the Spirit called 'knowledge' was not possessed by all the Christians. This would make sense in the light of his use of the body metaphor in ch 12, and be a direct contradiction of their statement i) above. However, it is more likely that v 7 refers here to the particular claimed manifestations of knowledge in all *three* of their statements — not as theory, but as statements upon which they based their practice. This practice was, as we have seen, integral to the understanding of the gift. *That* is why the initial question in v 1 was about eating meat offered to idols and the initial answer was in terms of 'knowledge'. The two could not be separated.

---

134 Jeremias, *Abba* 27-274.

135 Héring 72 suggests two different kinds of γνῶσις in vv 1 and 7.

Thus we suggest that Paul was criticizing all three statements of the 'strong' Corinthians.

i)   *Not* all have knowledge.

ii)   *Not* everyone possesses the knowledge that an idol is nothing *with the result that* they can eat εἰδωλόθυτα.

iii) *Not* everyone possesses knowledge that there is 'no God but one' *with the result that* they can go to idol temples and eat.

To begin with, *Paul* does not possess this knowledge! Neither v 4c nor v 6a can be regarded as theoretical statements of monotheism. They are, in effect, contrary 'words of knowledge'. Paul's, in v 6, centres on what God has done in Christ and on understanding better the place of Christ as founder and sustainer of his people. It clearly does not 'puff up' Paul, but builds up the Christian church.

It seems, therefore, that the knowledge of v 7 was the particular knowledge that the 'strong' claimed to have: a spiritual gift which was being abused. Not all possessed the gift and therefore not all possessed 'knowledge', either of Paul's sort (v 6) or the Corinthians' sort summarized in their three statements.

2.3.2   Weak consciences

Much has been written on the use of the word 'conscience' as it is used in these chapters.[136] The modern meaning of an inward moral knowledge or consciousness does not seem to be an entirely satisfactory interpretation in ch 8. The original idea of συνείδησις is said to be '"to have knowledge of something with" another person on the basis of eye-witness'.[137] This knowledge was also sometimes reflexive, as a person reflected on his own actions or thoughts.[138] Pierce has argued that the word later came to indicate a knowledge of the *moral* quality of these actions.[139] As these actions were judged, and a person discovered that he had done wrong, so the negative nature of conscience developed.[140] 'Conscience' came to have a restraining influence on proposed actions considered to be morally wrong. It helped to discern what should or should not be done.[141] The definition of right or wrong was to be found

[136] Cf Gooch, "Conscience"; Eckstein, *Syneidesis*; Horsley, "Consciousness"; Thrall, "Meaning" and "ΣΥΝΕΙΔΗΣΙΣ"; Jewett, *Terms*; Harris, "ΣΥΝΕΙΔΗΣΙΣ"; Sevenster, *Seneca*; Pierce, *Conscience*; Spicq, "Conscience"; *inter al.*

[137] Maurer, "Συνείδησις" 899.

[138] Ibid 900.

[139] Pierce, *Conscience* 21.

[140] Gooch 245.

[141] Thrall "ΣΥΝΕΙΔΗΣΙΣ" argues (*Contra* Pierce, *Conscience*) that, for Paul, 'Conscience' began to function as 'law' had in Judaism — a moral guide to proposed actions.

in some objective set of principles 'beyond the subjective, established instead by reason or the moral community or God'.[142]

After examining ancient uses of σύνεσις, συνειδός, and συνείδησις, Maurer concludes that, until the first century, συνειδός and συνείδησις were 'more often used for self-consciousness in a non-moral sense' indicating that the connection with moral decision making was only secondary.[143]

Spicq and Bultmann both agree that συνείδησις originally meant 'knowledge'. This word, argues Spicq, has been taken from popular speech and evolved by Paul in a direction that 'est plus dépendante des conceptions morales d'Israël que des doctrines des Philosophes'.[144] Bultmann says that this 'knowledge' is centred in a person's judgment of his actions, in the light 'of the demand that is incumbent upon man'. This is a transcendent demand of which all are aware:[145] 'Hence, "conscience" is at one and the same time a knowledge of good and evil and of the corresponding conduct'.[146]

One thing is clear, Paul wrote at a time when the connotation of the words related to 'conscience' was changing. This development mentioned above, that was noticed by Pierce, means that it is specifically in the local context of chs 8-10 that we must first seek the meaning of the word.[147]

This word so dominates this section of this epistle that it may have originated with the Corinthians themselves.[148] In ch 8 the word appears in:

8:7 Καὶ ἡ Συνείδησις αὐτῶν ἀσθενὴς οὖσα μολύνεται

8:10 ἡ συνείδησις αὐτοῦ ἀσθενοῦς ὄντος οἰκοδομηθήσεται ...;

8:12 τύπτοντες αὐτῶν τὴν συνείδησιν ἀσθενοῦσαν εἰς Χριστὸν ἁμαρτάνετε

The masculine participle in 8:10 indicates that here it is the person who is weak and that therefore the conscience might be 'built up'. Verse 11 continues with the discussion of the destruction, not of a conscience, but of a brother. In verse 12 Paul returns to calling the conscience 'weak'. Clearly he is not separating the conscience from the person.[149] That this

142 Gooch, "Conscience" 246.
143 Op cit 904.
144 Spicq, "Conscience" 55.
145 Bultmann, *Theology* I 220.
146 Ibid 217.
147 Συνείδησις appears in the Pauline corpus twenty times; eight times in chs 8-10; eleven other times in the NT.
148 Cf Weiss 228; Maurer, "Συνείδησις" 914; Pierce, *Conscience* 64-65; *inter al.*
149 Jewett's argument is unnecessarily ingenious (*Terms* 422-423). He suggests that the distinction is made in v 10 so that the Corinthians do not

is the case is further seen in 10:28-29 where a person is not allowed to eat on account of τὸν μηνύσαντα καὶ τὴν συνείδησιν. Paul goes on to explain in v 29 that the conscience here is the one that belongs to the informant. Therefore the καί is 'explicative rather than conjunctive'.[150] This is important in providing an understanding of the 'defiling' of the conscience in 8:7. Μολύνεται must be seen as referring to the result on the *person* and not just to a change for the worse in his 'Conscience'. Willis is no doubt correct in saying 'μολύνεται in 8:7 is explained by σκανδαλίζω in 8:13'.[151]

It is far from clear that in ch 8 the word 'Conscience' refers to the person's moral[152] ability to pronounce judgment on what he is about to do or has done. If this is what the word means, then the 'weak' actually have too *strong* a conscience. They are *too* conscientious about what they eat. This is an important point because in v 10 the question to be faced is how a 'weak person' can have his (moral) conscience 'built-up' to the point where he does something that he apparently knows he should not do (i.e., about which he has a 'Conscience'!). Paul shows clearly in vv 9, and 11-12 that, if the conscience is built-up in this way, destruction will follow. Of course, his use of the word οἰκοδομέω is ironic, but the question remains as to how the conscience could be built up to sin.

In order to define 'Conscience' we must look more closely at what was going on in ch 8. Men 'having knowledge (v 10) were arrogantly ('puffed up') eating in idol temples. They seemed to desire specifically to be *seen* (ἐὰν γάρ τις ἴδῃ) doing this because, we suggest, they wanted to flaunt their gift of γνῶσις. The weak person *seeing* them do this, might be built up to being 'defiled' (v 7), or 'destroyed' (v 11). The means by which this destruction would take place was ἐν τῇ σῇ γνώσει — a vigorous condemnation of the 'strong' Corinthian position. It is ironical that the gift which these Christians believed marked them out as elect was leading to the destruction of people 'for whom Christ died'.

---

readily give an affirmative answer to a question which would then read: οὐχὶ ἡ συνείδησις αὐτοῦ ἀσθενής οἰκοδομηθήσεται. He continues: 'The distinction between the weak man and his supposedly edified conscience serves to express the inner disunity — the schizophrenia — which results when the weak man is induced to act against his conscience'. This view takes v 1 in terms of theoretical knowledge that all possess and v 7 as referring to those who were unable to 'assimilate' it. Such a distinction is unlikely. Also Paul's concern is not simply hurt or pain caused to a brother, but the possibility of his 'destruction'.

150   Gooch, "Conscience" 247.
151   Willis 95.
152   Cf Stacey, *Man* 206-221; Fee 387.

There are at least three reasons, then, why συνείδησις cannot easily be interpreted as a guilt-causing 'moral conscience'. Firstly, these 'weak' people seem to have had too *strong* a conscience, one which made them feel guilty for attending idol temples. Secondly, if 'moral conscience' were the issue, then it was the 'strong' whose 'Conscience' was actually weak for it was they whom Paul was addressing and having to educate. It was they who should have had a moral conscience about their behaviour, sensitive enough to recognize that their action might lead to the destruction of a brother. *They* were the ones who had to be made aware (morally) of their sin (v 12). Thirdly, Paul never criticized the weak in this passage, or attempted to have them become more 'knowledgeable'. He accepted them as they were and condemned those who would have changed them. This approach was in line with how Paul reminded the arrogant that they were 'not powerful' (1:26) and that the 'weak' were chosen by God (1:27). Paul had even argued that he was 'weak' in comparison with those who believed themselves to be 'strong' (4:10). However, Paul never condoned lax or inadequate *moral* consciousness. This is evident in 9:19-23 where Paul was prepared to be 'weak' to those who were 'weak' but, in doing so, would not break the 'law of Christ' (9:21-22).

Given the above and the fact that the weak desired to be *seen* to be like the 'strong' even to the point where they were led into real idolatry (vv 7b and 10c), it is quite likely that a 'weak conscience' simply means a 'lack of knowledge of oneself in relation to others'. This is a perfectly possible meaning for the word in Greek,[153] and fits the context well.[154] Firstly, Paul has already shown that the main issue surrounding the problem with 'knowledge' was one of belonging (8:3). Being 'weak' in this sort of self-perception would provide ample motivation to do something known to be wrong. Much-desired group recognition could easily lead to doing many unwise things. If the weak were persuaded that *practised* knowledge — in this case eating idol meat — would demonstrate that they were 'known by God' then their motivation to do that, even if it led to sin, would be obvious. Secondly, this would also explain why the 'strong' were keen to see the weak follow them. They wanted to see the weak 'built up' to a greater sense of security in the community of God — to a certainty of being elect.

Thus we suggest that 'conscience' in verse 7 is being used, not in terms of a moral conscience (one that cannot cope with the decision to

153 Maurer, "Συνείδησις" 899-900.
154 There may be pain attached to such feelings but that is different from a guilty moral conscience. A feeling of inadequacy vis-à-vis the others in the community need not involve a sense of guilt. Gooch, "Conscience" 245, notes that most scholars recognize that a notion of 'bad feeling' is one strand of the word's meaning.

eat such food), but in its earlier use of 'self-awareness'.[155] Maurer pointed to two strands in the use of the word συνείδησις. The one was the moral conscience, but the other, which applies better in 1 Corinthians 8:7, was self-reflection. This he says 'is about being, so that the problem of conscience is especially one of knowledge'.[156] The problem for the weak was, in their view, precisely that they lacked knowledge and self-awareness. They were insecure and felt badly about their position in the church so sought security through the practice of the gift of knowledge. They were unable to assess or discern properly the implications of God's works of grace.[157]

This understanding of συνείδησις makes good sense of v 10. There, having a weak knowledge or consciousness of himself in relation to the group, the weak person might indeed believe that someone who appeared secure before God was worth emulating. Verse 12 makes sense in this light, too. The knowledgeable have 'wounded' the conscience of the weak in encouraging them to believe that without knowledge they lacked something. In other words, the arrogant behaviour of the knowledgeable left the weak feeling even worse and less secure than they did before, because they were being led into sin.

The exegesis of the next few verses, especially 8:8, confirms this view that both sides were seeking *demonstrable* evidence of status before God, and thus further supports the idea that conscience has to do with self-consciousness rather than moral, guilt-causing conscience. Also, the examination later of 10:25-29 will indicate that a similar understanding of συνείδησις makes ready sense of that passage.

We began by saying that the usual understanding of 'moral conscience' raised more difficulties than it seemed to solve. Our conclusion is in line (as mentioned above) with at least one strand of the meaning of συνείδησις in other Greek literature. This meaning does not contain the element of 'moral' decision making.[158] Maurer is close to our position when he says: 'The weak should take the Gospel promise of their acknowledgement by God more seriously than their own knowledge'.[159]

It is interesting that the idea of a *weak* conscience does not appear, as far as we are aware, outside 1 Corinthians or comments on 1 Corinthians in the church fathers. However, there are a couple of occurrences of the

---

[155] Osborn, "ΣΥΝΕΙΔΗΣΙΣ" 175 admits that in Paul 'the original meaning "self-knowledge" is always largely present'.

[156] Maurer, "Συνείδησις" 905.

[157] See below on the recurring theme of judgment and discernment in this epistle.

[158] A view broadly shared in this context with Maurer, Bultmann, and Gooch.

[159] Op cit 915.

idea of knowledge or understanding being 'weak', or of a person being 'weak' in knowledge. One of the clearest is in Wisdom 9:5:

Ὅτι ἐγὼ δοῦλος σὸς καὶ υἱὸς τῆς παιδίσκης σου, ἄνθρωπος ἀσθενὴς καὶ ὀλιγοχρόνιος καὶ ἐλάσσων ἐν συνέσει κρίσεως καὶ νόμων.

The three adjectives describe the man in his relationship to σύνεσις. While seeking wisdom, the writer describes himself as one who is weak, young, and inferior in understanding of judgment and laws. 'Weakness' is his perception of himself as immature in this knowledge. This is perhaps not far removed from Paul's use of the word 'weak' in ch 8.

In Diodorus Siculus 34/35:30b-c Ἡσσόμαι, is used probably for stylistic reasons because ἀσθένεια appeared in the previous sentence, but the meaning is the same: Ὅτι ἡ φρόνησις ... ὑπὸ μόνης τῆς τύχης ἡττᾶται· καὶ γὰρ ἃ διὰ σύνεσιν καὶ ἀγχίνοιαν ... — Understanding is only 'weaker' than Fortune and [ruins] the things [mapped out (Loeb)] through knowledge and shrewdness. Weakness here is primarily contrasted with the strength of Fortune, but again part of the meaning is that people's understanding is not adequate to cope with their planned actions, so Fortune steps in.

To conclude this section, we suggest that those 'weak in their conscience' were people who, reflecting on their own actions and feelings, felt insecure as God's people. Their weakness was not in moral decision-making. As those 'until now accustomed to idols',[160] their weakness in self-awareness is easily understood and it would simply be compounded if they were told that the gift of knowledge (which some did not have) indicated election. They would then be persuaded to eat

160 It would seem obvious that ἕως ἄρτι indicated the weak were converted from pagan (Gentile) backgrounds. However, some have suggested that the weak are those who have *Jewish* sensibilities to eating idol meat. Thus, the 'until now' may be paraphrased, 'until now accustomed to believing idols to be real because they were Jewish', and *therefore* having pangs of conscience about eating something they used to think was wrong. In slightly different ways Dupont (*Gnosis* 532-533) and Schlatter (97-98) take this position. Dupont sees the problem in Corinth as lying between 'un débat où s'affrontent deux tendances de judéo-christianisme' (533). Thus far, we have avoided becoming embroiled in the controversies about the origins of the problems faced by Paul. Our purpose is to examine the nature of the religious problem itself and Paul's way of dealing with it. Here, it would not alter what has been said if the problem of the weak arose among the converted Jews or pagans. Exegetically it should be pointed out, however, that the reference to ἐν εἰδωλείῳ may support a view that the weak were converted Jews — obviously horrified at being told that they could enter temples. But the singular τοῦ εἰδώλου in v 7 may suggest that Paul was not referring *generally* to being accustomed to idolatry but, more specifically, to being accustomed to 'the idol' — in whose temple they now find themselves again (cf Fee 379 n 18). In this case the weak would be converted Gentiles.

idol meat (practising 'knowledge') while knowing that such action was a sin.

Paul did not address this weakness in v 7. He denied that everyone had such 'knowledge', and he showed how the weak really *were* defiled.

The word μολύνω is not so very different in meaning from τύπτω (v 12),[161] but does require some explanation. It is only used once by Paul and seems to refer to a 'staining' with sin[162] — a point that is clearer in vv 11-13 where the weak person is led into sin and judgment. The 'defilement' of their 'self-consciousness' lay in the fact that they thought they were doing something to improve their position when in fact they were being drawn into sin. The 'strong' were causing them to think of themselves as 'weak', thereby 'wounding' them and 'sinning against Christ' (v 12).

If this is the case, it is quite reasonable to assume that οἰκοδομέω originated in the Corinthian camp and had to do with building up self-confidence in a person's own status in the community and before God. Paul's ironic use of οἰκοδομέω in v 10 may demonstrate this: far from confirming the security of election this knowledge denied it, for a 'brother' 'for whom Christ died' might be 'destroyed' (v 11). Also explained by this understanding of the text is the emphasis Paul laid in ch 1 on the fact of election even of the weak. In ch 3, he taught that any 'building' was not to re-lay *that* foundation in Christ, but to be based on the understanding that 'you *are* God's temple and that God's Spirit dwells in you' (3:18). That they were indeed God's people was not to be judged by examining what spiritual possessions the arrogant 'wise' might have (4:7a).

We therefore take this verse as the sternest qualification of the position of the Corinthian 'strong'. Paul stated that it was simply untrue to say that all people had such knowledge. Secondly, Paul showed here and in the next few verses that in trying to make those who lack 'self-consciousness' of their position among God's people into so-called 'strong', the weak were being drawn into sin. In 10:14-22 Paul was to show that the 'strong' were already involved in that sin.

2.3.3   Proving status before God

'For food will not affect our standing before God:[163] rather if we do not eat we lack nothing (before God),[164] and if we do eat we have no advantage'. The interpretation of v 8 is important, yet problematic. Barrett assumes the first clause 'is clearly consistent with the position of

---

161 Pierce, *Conscience* 81.
162 Cf 2 Cor 7:1.
163 Robertson 170. Cf 2 Cor 4:14.
164 Ibid 170, 'τῷ θεῷ is to be understood in both clauses'.

the strong'.[165] But this is actually not so clear![166] Below, we defend our suggestion that the text is best understood as a continuation of the challenge to the 'strong'[167] who might have said something like this: 'Eating this idol food, in as much as it demonstrates that we have the gift of γνῶσις, does establish (or prove) us before God, that is, it shows that we are known by him'. Paul uncompromisingly denied this and emphasised his point in v 8b.[168] If this suggestion is correct (and our earlier caveats concerning 'mirror reading' must be borne in mind), then it is in stark contrast with the views of scholars such as Lietzmann,[169] Allo,[170] Hurd,[171] and Murphy-O'Connor,[172] who argue that the 'strong' Corinthians believed food to be adiaphorous. In support of this, some have suggested that parts[173] or even all of v 8 are a quotation from the Corinthian position.[174]

If v 8a is a Corinthian slogan, then the positioning of μὴ φάγωμεν in the first clause of v 8b only makes sense if the Corinthians believed the food to be adiaphorous. Such a view is possible, but also poses some tricky questions. Why did the weak follow the 'strong', if food was adiaphorous? If these people believed that food was an indifferent matter, why did Paul use οἰκοδομέω in v 10 (whether or not it was an ironic[175] use of the word)? If the whole of v 8 is a slogan, then v 8b sounds strange, for they might have been expected to say the opposite,[176] thus: οὔτε ἐὰν μὴ φάγωμεν περισσεύομεν οὔτε ἐὰν φάγωμεν ὑστερούμεθα.[177]

---

165 Barrett 195.

166 Fee, "Εἰδωλόθυτα" 190, 'this text is as puzzling as it is abrupt'.

167 So Lietzmann 39.

168 Barrett 195-6, suggests that Paul agreed with the sentiments of the 'strong', but wished to point out that no one was damned for being over scrupulous'.

169 Lietzmann 39.

170 Allo 204.

171 Hurd 123.

172 Murphy-O'Connor, "Food" esp 297.

173 Cf Barrett 195, says that the first clause represents the Corinthian position while 'the second and third clauses begin Paul's correction' of them. Jeremias, "Briefzitate" 152, argues that the first part of the verse is in line with Paul's view while the rest is all the Corinthian view.

174 Grosheide 194; Parry 133; inter al. Also cf Hurd 123. Morris 128 and Fee 383 say that the words are from the Corinthians but that Paul agrees with them.

175 Vielhauer, Oikodome 94.

176 Meyer 245.

177 Among textual variants notably A* has sought to avoid the problem in this way. Murphy-O'Connor ("Food" 294) says this accords better with the view of the 'strong': '... we envisage v 8 as a statement directed against the "weak"

Further, if v 8, or indeed only v 8a, is regarded as a slogan then it is difficult to see the force of the δέ at the beginning. It is unlikely that the *RSV* is correct in failing to translate it at all in v 8 and yet giving it the force of 'only' in v 9! Hurd suggests that each δέ in 8:7-9 is part of a series of criticisms of the liberal position and thus originating from Paul[178] — a point with which we concur.

A study of three important words in v 8 will help clarify why we believe this was *Paul's* statement and will allow us to deduce further information concerning the religious problem Paul believed he faced at Corinth.

Παρίστημι has a variety of meanings. 'To present a sacrifice' and 'to stand beside' are out of the question here.[179] Otherwise it can mean 'present' in the sense of 'introduce' or 'represent one to another' which would not fit the context either. The most likely meanings are 'to bring to stand before a judge' (probably as a legal technical term), or 'to prove/demonstrate/show something to someone'.[180] The forensic sense is widely accepted because the presentation is τῷ θεῷ, and the tense used is future. Héring says, 'There is a clear allusion to the Judgement'.[181] This may be supported by 2 Corinthians 4:14, although the thought is much clearer in Romans 14:10 where the 'presenting' is before the βῆμα τοῦ θεοῦ. It is difficult properly to substantiate a technical legal meaning in this context. However, some indicators make it possible.

i)   As will be seen below, the words ὑστερέω and περισσεύω are found in contexts dealing with eschatological blessings, so the judgment of the last day might be in mind.

ii)   The reference to πρόσκομμα in v 9 has to do with 'stumbling' before God, that is, failing to 'stand' in the presence of God as one of his people (see below).

iii)   When Paul considers the impact of this behaviour on the weak, he talks of 'destruction' (ἀπόλλυται - v 12) which probably looks to future judgment.[182]

iv)   Later, we shall show that 10:1-14 is further commentary on the same problem. The main message of 10:1-14 is summed up in the

members of the Corinthian community'. The textual evidence for this is poor. The reading taken by Nestle[26] and adopted by us is the 'harder reading' and supported by p[46] B 81 and various minuscules.

178   Hurd 123.
179   Cf Conzelmann 148 n 21.
180   *BAGD* 627-628.
181   Héring 73. Also cf Bengel 634; Allo 204; Barrett 195; *inter al.* Godet I 423 takes the verb as present tense with the Majority texts (so also Weiss 229). If future, he grants that the Judgment Day would be the issue.
182   Cf Rom 2:12, 15-16.

warning of 10:12 which again might relate to a 'standing' before the judgment seat.

However, a translation of 'prove', 'show', or 'establish' would also fit the context. This meaning is rarely considered except, possibly, in the use of words like 'commend' in a couple of translations.[183] But it is common in Greek and often in contexts which involve proving, showing, or demonstrating something to be true.[184] For example, in Acts 1:3 we read:

οἷς καὶ παρέστησεν ἑαυτὸν ζῶντα ... ἐν πολλοῖς τεκμηρίοις ...[185]

or in Josephus: ... βουλόμενος παραστῆσαι τοῖς ἀναγινώσκουσιν ὅτι...[186]

or: Παράστησον δὲ καὶ νῦν, ὅτι πάντα σῇ προνοίᾳ διοικεῖται.[187]

Paul has argued with the 'strong' thus far in this chapter and continues to do so in v 8. We suggest that *Paul* was the one saying 'food will not establish or prove us before God'.[188] In other words, before *God*, eating idol meat in a temple (v 10) was no indication that the Corinthians were 'known by him'. Thus Paul was completely undermining the so-called knowledge the Corinthians had. There was no religious value in causing those who were weak to eat in an idol temple because γνῶσις simply did not *function* in the way the 'strong' claimed.

Whether παρίστημι means the proving or demonstration of a case before God in a general sense or in a more technical forensic sense, the word did involve a *showing* or *proving* of someone or something.

Fee is probably correct to suggest that βρῶμα in v 8 'seems to put the argument *for a moment* into a broader framework'.[189] Perhaps Paul was being mildly sarcastic: 'eating food proves nothing about our status before God!'[190] But v 8b helps further to elucidate Paul's attitude to this food.

The *RSV* translates ὑστερέω and περισσεύω as 'no worse off ... no better off'. This is inadequate. Robertson says that, in the light of the previous sentence, Paul must mean: 'If we abstain from eating we are

---

183 *AV*; *RV*. It is not clear precisely what is meant by 'commend'. Murphy-O'Connor, "Food" 296, is probably correct in saying it represents a 'paraphrase to convey the idea that food is not a guarantee of divine approval'.

184 Cf *BAGD* 628.

185 Cf Acts 24:13; 2 Tim 2:15.

186 Josephus, *Vita* 27.

187 Josephus, *Ants* 4:47. Cf also Epictetus 2:26:4; 2:23:47 — εἴ τις τοῦτο παριστὰς βλάπτει τοὺς ἀκούοντας ...

188 Conzelmann 148: 'We have here a positive declaration on Paul's part'.

189 Fee 382 n 33 — our emphasis.

190 'proves ... status' is perhaps something of a double translation of παρίστημι but it helps convey the idea more clearly.

not prejudiced (in God's sight), and if we eat we have no advantage'.[191] Barrett, assuming the technical use of παρίστημι, believes that the 'lacking' and 'advantage' have to do with what he calls 'status' or reward and 'damnation'.[192]

Περισσεύω stands in direct contrast with ὑστερέω. Paul used this word in eschatological contexts. For him the 'fulness' of the Christian concerned the grace of God in Christ (Romans 5:15).[193] It far exceeded the blessings of the old covenant (2 Corinthians 3:9). As περισσεύω could mean the fulness of God's received grace, so sometimes ὑστερέω could indicate a 'falling short' of participation in God's glory and grace (Romans 3:23). To the 'super apostles' claiming to be greater than Paul in 2 Corinthians 10-13, he insisted that he did not have 'less' than they did.[194]

Ch 1 provides a framework for interpreting these words. In 1:5 Paul recognised that the Corinthians were enriched in speech and γνῶσις. None was lacking (ὑστερέω) any χάρισμα (1:7). The eschatological context is also clear in 1:7ff. Paul saw the richness of the gifts as part of God's blessings in the present era until the Parousia. However, it was not the gifts but the Lord who would sustain them guiltless on the Day of our Lord (v 8).[195]

Paul incorporated this perspective into his response to the 'strong' in ch 8. He was therefore standing beside the *weak* over against the 'strong' in 8:8b.[196] The contrast of ὑστερέω and περισσεύω in 12:24 further supports this view. There, in a closely related argument, Paul used the body metaphor to show that not all people had *particular* gifts, but that even the apparently inferior person remained an important part of the body. Status[197] (membership) in the body was not granted by demonstration of a particular gift of the Spirit — it could not be because people had *different* gifts.

---

[191] Robertson 170.

[192] Barrett 195, although he reaches a different conclusion from us about who is saying what to whom.

[193] Cf Rom 5:17, 20.

[194] 2 Cor 11:5; 12:11.

[195] Cf the eschatological context of ὑστερέω in Rom 3:23; Heb 4:1 and 12:15.

[196] Wilckens, "Ὕστερος" 597.

[197] The word 'status' is not used in terms of 'reward' rather than 'damnation' (Barrett 195), but in the sense of the 'standing or position of a person as determined by his *membership* of some class of persons legally enjoying certain rights' (*OED* Vol X 866-867 — our emphasis.) Hereafter, we use the word to describe the position of people enjoying the rights and privileges of being in the class of people 'known by God'. We do *not*, therefore, intend to distinguish rank among these people.

As far as we are aware, Murphy-O'Connor is the only commentator to make this specific link between spiritual gifts and 1 Corinthians 8:8. We agree with him when he says:

> The importance that the Corinthians attached to *charismata* needs no emphasis. Such gifts were of divine origin (1 Cor 12:6). Consequently, they could be used as a tangible test of one's standing before God ... This interpretation, of course, is hypothetical, but is not entirely gratuitous. It is suggested by the Pauline usage of perisseuo and remains within the category of divine approval/disapproval clearly insinuated by v 8a.[198]

However, his understanding of v 8 is different from ours. He takes the verse to mean that, although the 'strong' ate meat offered to idols, 'their spiritual gifts were in no way diminished. Conversely, abstention from such food did not produce any increase in spiritual gifts. Hence, idol-meat was morally neutral [for the Corinthians]'.[199] Murphy-O'Connor's difficulty with taking v 8 as a comment from Paul is that 'v 13, which is indisputably Pauline, contradicts v 8'.[200] However, this is not the case when v 8 is interpreted as we have suggested above. Paul addressed the 'strong', denying that food had the *religious* value that they attributed to it. This fact did not deny the possibility of food having *other* positive or negative effects on the community. In v 13 Paul summarized his position: if food were to cause someone to stumble, he would give it up. He was able to give up eating precisely because he did *not* believe that γνῶσις (seen in eating) was a mark of the Christian. V 13 was the final 'nail in the coffin' of the position of the 'strong' on this point: even the apostle Paul was prepared to give it up!

Although not regarding the problem as arising from an abuse of a gift of the Spirit, Hauck unambiguously interprets these verses in a way similar to that outlined above. He also recognises that the Corinthians did not hold an indifferent position with regard to eating 'food':

> To the "strong" in Corinth, who seem to have regarded the eating of meat sacrificed to idols as a *proof* of their Christian wisdom and *consequently as something of religious value*, Paul has to say that they do not hereby gain any advantage before God (1C.8:8) ...[201]

2.3.4   Summary

Verses 7-8 continue Paul's attack on the so-called 'strong' position, amplifying the points made in vv 1-3.

Proving a person (παρίστημι) to be 'known by God' was not through the evidencing of knowledge in eating idol-meat. The study of the word

[198] Murphy-O'Connor, "Food" 298.
[199] Loc cit.
[200] Ibid 293.
[201] Hauck, "Περισσεύω" 60, our emphasis.

συνείδησις showed that it referred to (painful?) self-awareness in relation to others. The 'weak' would therefore have been those who felt insecure in their status as Christians. The word παρίστημι may have referred to a legal 'standing' before God. That is, people felt this demonstration of knowledge would confirm their position as the elect on the Judgment Day. Otherwise, it may have simply meant a general 'proving' of, or 'showing' oneself before God as truly one of his. Either way, the *demonstrating* force of the word cannot be neglected and confirms our understanding of this passage so far. It further reinforces the fact that Paul was continuing to deal with problems raised in the opening chapters. The Corinthians felt the need to be *seen* to be God's people. The way they had chosen led to being 'puffed up' and arrogant.

If this way of looking especially at v 8 is correct, then it is worth noting that we are in agreement with Weiss, Lietzmann, and others,[202] in their suggestions that the Corinthians were *deliberately* eating this food. But unlike Weiss, we have not based our position on an analogy with later Gnostics who were determined to show their freedom. We have suggested that the problem arose *from a fundamental religious desire to be identified openly as members of the group (of Christians)*. Their experience of the Spirit's presence in giving a gift of knowledge led them to regard that gift as a marker of their community membership.

Paul's concern was to continue to show that knowledge did *not* function as the 'strong' thought it did. Eating idol meat had nothing to do with eschatological blessings; it neither brought fulness of, nor did it reduce their participation in God's grace. This message is summarised in 10:12: 'Take heed, lest thinking you stand, you fall'. That this idea of standing or falling was already in Paul's mind is evident in 8:9 with the use of πρόσκομμα. The problem with the behaviour of the 'strong' was that they might cause others to fall, while they too were in danger of falling (8:9; 10:12).

2.4   A cause of stumbling (Verses 9 - 13)

Paul's concern for the weak person is evident. With the imperative βλέπετε   Paul continued the case against the 'strong.' If the 'knowledgeable' ate this food, they would sin against their brother and against Christ (v 12). The words πρόσκομμα and ἐξουσία reflect the contrasting attitudes to what is going on. For Paul the so-called ἐξουσία of the Corinthians is a πρόσκομμα.[203]

202   Weiss 228; Lietzmann 39; Schmithals, *Gnosticism* 226-227, etc.
203   Willis 98.

2.4.1 An Ἐξουσία

The word ἐξουσία is difficult to define and is used in different ways by Paul.[204] Lietzmann[205] followed Reitzenstein[206] in suggesting a Gnostic background for the word. Others have suggested that the meaning is to be found in Stoic ideas.[207] Horsley[208] sought to demonstrate that the word ἐξουσία (among others), was derived from a Hellenistic-Jewish background of the sort especially found in Philo. Whatever its background, Willis lists three reasons why he thinks this term may have originated with the Corinthians:

i)   The word was not common in Paul's writings, but is most common in 1 Corinthians.

ii)   When discussing a parallel subject in Romans 14-15 ἐξουσία is not used.

iii)   The slogan of the Corinthian 'strong' (πάντα ἔξεστιν)[209] is said to bear an obvious similarity to the word ἐξουσία when it appears in 8:9.

This may indeed be the case, but it is the contrast between what the Corinthians called ἐξουσία and what Paul called πρόσκομμα that is of considerable significance. This may be supported by noting that ἐξουσία was emphatically the possession of the 'strong': ἡ ἐξουσία ὑμῶν αὕτη. The use of Ὑμῶν suggests that Paul was not aligning himself with this 'right'. Αὕτη emphasises the particular ἐξουσία being addressed, indicating that Paul was referring back to the Corinthian display of knowledge (8:7). In the context, therefore, ἐξουσία referred to the end result of *practising* this knowledge. Thus, it was the one who had knowledge (v 10) who caused stumbling by eating in a temple.

A single English equivalent for ἐξουσία in this context probably cannot be found. The word is often translated as 'authority', although in 8:9 it is translated by the *RSV* as 'liberty' and in 9:4, 5, and 6 as 'right'. Both 'authority' and 'right' draw on a legal understanding of ἐξουσία found in the LXX,[210] while 'liberty' is used because ἐξουσία (8:9)

---

204   Horsley, "Consciousness" 579, says 'Paul's use of the term *exousia* (authority) in 8:9 and 9:4-6, 12, 18 is quite distinctive in comparison with his other usage'.

205   Lietzmann 39.

206   Reitzenstein, *HMR* 461-462. Cf Schmithals, *Gnosticism* 224-229.

207   Dupont, *Gnosis* 301-308. For further discussion see Willis 102. He mainly attributes the word to 'popular philosophy'. Also see Conzelmann 109, who provides (n 5) interesting examples of possibly parallel Stoic formulations in the writings of Epictetus and Diogenes Laertius. Schlier, "Ἐλεύθερος" 493-496.

208   Horsley, "Consciousness".

209   6:12; 10:23.

210   E.g. 1 Macc 10:38; Ps 113:2; Wis 10:14.

appears to be synonymous with ἐλευθερία (10:29). It is clear that this ἐξουσία resulted in some Corinthians eating idol meat and then 'building up' others to do the same. Thus they asserted their freedom or rights. In ch 9 Paul contrasted an apostle's ἐξουσία with that of the 'strong'.[211] Therefore, his use of the word there may help us understand it.

In ch 9 the translation 'right' seems appropriate enough. In that Paul called on the law of Moses (v 9) for support then, possibly, a legal right was part of what was meant. Paul was also clear that his ἐξουσία concerned what he was entitled to *do* as an apostle. Perhaps, therefore, the best translation may be a phrase like 'the exercise of your legal right' (given your membership of a particular group of people). This would offer a satisfactory understanding of both 8:8 and the use of the word in ch 9. The 'strong' were exercising what they believed to be their right as those having knowledge, and Paul talked in ch 9 of a right derived from apostleship. This definition is consistent with the word's use on some occasions in other Greek literature.[212] Foerster emphasizes both the *action* involved and the *freedom* which derives from the 'legally ordered whole'. He says:

> This ἐξουσία which is operative in ordered relationships, this authority to act, cannot be separated from its continuous exercise, and therefore ... can denote the freedom which is given to the community.[213]

The use of ὑμῶν and αὕτη as noted above, dissociated Paul from the ἐξουσία of the 'strong'. An ἐξουσία was not simply a theoretical possibility but involved *practice*. In their belief that eating ἐν εἰδωλείῳ was their right, the 'strong' caused the destruction of a weak person. Thus Paul was not prepared to allow it as an ἐξουσία of the Christian community. Rather it was a πρόσκομμα. The seriousness of this

---

[211] For a defence of this understanding of the place of ch 9 in Paul's argument see ch 3 below.

[212] The word's meaning in Greek stems from the 'ability' to perform an action because 'there are no hindrances in the way', (Foerster, "Ἐξουσία" 562). The legal or political right to do something seems to predominate even when the best translation may be 'power', for that power is often understood as pertaining to the one with sufficient power to enforce his will. The following examples help to demonstrate the different meanings of the word within this category. In Plutarch we read of 'royal power' (καὶ βασιλικὴν ἐξουσίαν ἔχοντι, *Lycurgas* 3:14, cf Thucidides 6:31:4; 7:69:2) and of freedmen not receiving the 'rights of suffrage' [*Loeb*] (... ἐξουσίαν ψήφου, *Publicola* 7:8). Also cf Epictetus 1:29:11 καὶ τίς σοι ταύτην τὴν ἐξουσίαν δέδωκεν; Ποῦ δύνασαι νικῆσαι δόγμα ἀλλότριον;

[213] Foerster, "Ἐξουσία" 566. He regards this 'freedom' as exercising freedom from *Jewish* law.

accusation will be seen by examining the word πρόσκομμα, and the way Paul used the 'stumbling' theme in this epistle.

2.4.2 Πρόσκομμα

Paul's use in this letter of words such as πρόσκομμα, σκάνδαλον,[214] σκανδαλίζω, ἐγκοπή, and ἀπρόσκοπος is of considerable importance, especially in chs 8-10.[215] Like other ideas mentioned above, this theme of a 'stumbling-block' (σκάνδαλον) was introduced in ch 1. It is widely accepted[216] that the background for the use of σκάνδαλον in the NT lies in the so-called 'stone texts' of the LXX.[217] We will suggest that the same texts provide the background for πρόσκομμα in 8:9.

Lindars has studied links between the 'stone' texts and their use in NT apologetics in detail.[218] That work need not be repeated here. However, attention must be drawn briefly to certain aspects of the function of those texts that help illuminate the present discussion.

Both in OT and NT texts, the 'stone' idea is often used in discussions related to apologetics. In these cases the concept functioned in two ways. A 'stone' might cause stumbling and destruction or it might become a secure sanctuary, or foundation. The function of the stone in this respect concerned the response of the people: whether they responded in faith or not. The stone would then indicate whether a person belonged to God's people (for example, as 'remnant' in Isaiah, or κλητοί in Paul), or whether a person would be destroyed.

The word σκάνδαλον[219] was probably not used in pre-LXX Greek literature or in Philo or Josephus. Σκανδάληθρον, meaning 'trap', occasionally occurred. This was sometimes used metaphorically,[220] and could mean 'setting a trap in discussion'. In the LXX σκάνδαλον translated both מוֹקֵשׁ (snare or trap) and מִכְשׁוֹל (an obstacle to trip over). The noun πρόσκομμα[221] was also rare outside the LXX, not appearing in Philo or Josephus. It is to be found in *Historia Alexandri*

214 It is doubtful that Paul distinguishes between πρόσκομμα and σκάνδαλον. Cf Rom 9:33 and his use there of σκάνδαλον to translate Is 8:14 (LXX uses πρόσκομμα).

215 1 Cor 8:9, 13; 9:12; 10:32.

216 Stählin, "Σκάνδαλον" 344: 'Both formally and materially the NT use of σκάνδαλον and σκανδαλίζω is exclusively controlled by the thought and speech of the OT and Judaism'; Conzelmann 148 n 28; *inter al.*

217 Is 8:14; 28:16; Ps 117:22 (LXX). Cf Rom 9:33.

218 Lindars, *Apologetic* esp 169ff. Cf Stählin, "Προσκόπτω" 750; Müller, *Anstoss*; Lindblom, "Anstoss".

219 This appears twenty-one times in the LXX; σκανδαλίζω four times.

220 E.g. Aristophanes: *Archarnenses* 687: κᾆτ᾽ ἀνελκύσας ἐρωτᾷ σκανδάληθρ᾽ ἱστὰς ἐπῶν...

221 It occurs eleven times in the LXX (five are in Sirach).

Magni[222] where it refers to Δαρεῖος Μακεδονικόν whom Alexander cannot conquer and so flees. In the LXX it is used to translate different words, including מוקש, but is exclusively metaphorical, meaning a 'trap' or 'cause of destruction' brought about by sin.[223] The idea of being led to worship other gods by a 'stumbling block' is clear in Exodus 23:33 and 34:12. Thus, something which causes stumbling causes sin against God.

Two OT texts have played a key role in the development of the 'stumbling stone' and the 'foundation' and/or 'corner-stone' themes. Both Isaiah 8:14 and 28:16 were addressed to a rebellious Israel. The Israelites who 'believed' in and 'feared' the Lord were the ones who would be kept safe and would not stumble but find that the Lord was their sanctuary.

Isaiah 8:14 describes God as a λίθος προσκόμματος, a πέτρα πτώματος, and a ἁγίασμα. Though God might cause such stumbling (many would stumble and fall — πίπτω, 8:15), he was also a sanctuary. In Isaiah 28:16 God laid a θεμέλιον in Zion in which a person had to believe lest he should be 'shamed' (καταισχύνω).[224] Both texts attach the idea of testing to the stone. In Isaiah 8:14 it is a snare (פח) and in 28:16 it is a 'testing' stone (אֶבֶן בֹּחַן).[225] The question in both texts was whether those being addressed would be destroyed or whether they would find God a sanctuary. Chs 28-29 emphasise God as the basis for Israel's salvation rather than man and his wisdom, while Isaiah 8 shows what a problem such a view of salvation really was for a proud, even arrogant, Israel.[226]

In that these chapters in Isaiah face the issue of who among the Israelites were really God's people, it is perhaps not surprising that the texts were used in *Christian* apologetics. As Lindars has so carefully shown, in the NT apologetic of response, "the stone is first of all an article of belief, belief in Christ, the crucial test between belonging to the New Israel or being rejected from it".[227] This application of the texts was especially amenable as an answer to the early problem of 'response to the Gospel, and its effect in the rejection of Jews'.[228]

In Romans 9:33 Paul brought together Isaiah 8:14 and 28:16. There, in dealing with God's destiny for Israel, Paul showed it was Christ who

222 Recensio γ, Book 2:15 and Recensio ε, 16.
223 Exod 23:33; 34:12; Judith 8:22; Is 8:14; 29:21; Jer 3:3.
224 The possibility of destruction is seen in the 'shaming' and the 'falling'.
225 Whether בֹּחַן is to be translated here passively ('tested stone') or actively ('testing stone') is discussed in Hillyer, "Rock-Stone" 65. We accept with Delitzsch and Hillyer that it is active.
226 Ridderbos, *Paul* 142.
227 Lindars, *Apologetic* 177.
228 Ibid 175.

was the λίθος προσκόμματος and the πέτρα σκανδάλου. Significantly, Paul added ἐπ' αὐτῷ in v 33b: 'and he who believes *in him* [i.e., Christ] will not be ashamed'. In this way Paul faced the Jewish problem head-on. If Israel was to be destroyed, or non-Israel to be saved, the determining factor was to be found in the response to Christ the stone. Belief in him determined whether a person belonged to the people of God.[229]

Much the same sort of argument is present in 1 Corinthians 1. The point Paul stressed at Corinth did not concern the place of physical Israel in God's plans, but he did face the same basic *religious* issue of 'Who are the people of God?' or, 'What is it that identifies people as belonging to God?' The contrast Paul drew in ch 1 lay between the wisdom the Corinthians claimed to have and the Gospel message centred in Christ. This message of 'Christ crucified' was a σκάνδαλον (1:23).[230] This σκάνδαλον led to the wisdom of the wise (1:19) being confounded but also to some people 'being saved'. Both aspects of the way in which the stone functioned were 'simply variations on the no less biblical principle that God and His gifts can bring either salvation or perdition'.[231] In essence the only difference between this 'scandal' in 1:23 and the scandal/stone discussions of Isaiah 8 and 28-29 was the christological content.[232] Was their confidence 'before God' (1:29) to be found in 'wisdom' or 'in Christ'? Would they be part of the folly that God put to 'shame' (1:27-28 — the discussion of Isaiah 28:16 — καταισχύνω)? Or would Christ be their foundation stone?

---

229   These 'stone' themes occur also in 1 Pet 2:4-10. The stone was precious to believers but would cause stumbling and falling to those who were disobedient. The Israelites stumbled and fell (vv 7-8). However, the true people of God were those who had believed and had received mercy (vv 9-10). The writer employed a third OT 'stone' text (Ps 118:22) to show that Christ was that stone.

230   It is not necessary to distinguish greatly between the effect of preaching Christ crucified on Jews or Gentiles. The σκάνδαλον of the cross was that it caused a re-thinking for both Jew and Gentile (in different ways) of the area within which salvation, or God's grace, was manifest.

231   Stählin, "Προσκόπτω" 750. This arose, no doubt, from the dual function of the stone in Is 8:14. The context of Is 28:16 also discusses two responses: in one the stone becomes a θεμέλιον, in the other the wisdom of the wise is destroyed (Is 29:13; cf 1 Cor 1:19).

232   The move from seeing God as a potential πρόσκομμα to seeing Christ in this way was probably quite natural to a faith which saw Christ as fulfilling many of the functions fulfilled by God in the OT. Also note the 'law' was a potential σκάνδαλον in Ps 118:165 (LXX) and a transfer to Jesus Christ may also have been prompted by this route.

It was noted[233] that Paul's use of the building metaphor in 3:10ff gave rise to his use of the word οἰκοδομέω both there and in ch 8. We suggested that in using the metaphor Paul had a number of OT texts in mind which talked of rebuilding or 'building up' the temple and cities in the messianic era. In 3:10 and 11 the word θεμέλιον is used. Given the way Paul personalized the foundation, making it refer to Christ (see Romans 9:33), it is quite possible that Isaiah 28:16 was also in mind. Paul did not discuss the σκάνδαλον while writing about the foundation but the line of thought is similar to Romans 9:33 and 1 Peter 2:6ff where Isaiah 8:14 and 28:16 are conflated. In both Romans and 1 Peter the stone laid was the 'cornerstone' of Isaiah 28:16, and in both it resulted in stumbling and salvation.[234] This was Paul's purpose in the Corinthian epistle. He had preached Christ as the foundation of God's building. Acceptance of this foundation identified those who were God's, and Paul emphatically reminded them that they *were* God's temple and the Spirit *did* dwell in them (3:16-17; cf Psalm 117:22-24 LXX).[235]

Returning now to chs 8-10, we can make better sense of Paul's use of πρόσκομμα (8:9), σκανδαλίζω (8:13, twice), ἐγκοπή (9:12), and ἀπρόσκοπος (10:32).[236] The πρόσκομμα of 8:9, like the σκάνδαλον of 1:23, had to do with a person's response to the gospel of Christ. The end of the weak man was at stake: salvation or destruction. This is made clear in 8:11 where one 'for whom Christ died' is the subject of the stumbling. The weak were being led to worship other gods. In ch 10 Paul used the wilderness events to illustrate the danger. *The particular association of* πρόσκομμα *with the Israelites turning to other gods*[237] *may have given the word added significance in 8:9.*

For Paul the only touchstone of belonging to the people of God was 'Christ crucified'. Certainly Paul did not want anyone to stumble, but if

---

[233]   2.1.5 above.

[234]   Although much has been made of the omission of θεμέλιον in these two conflations, their reliance on Is 28:16 is clear. That both θεμέλιον and ἀκρογωνιαῖος can be used of that upon which the building takes place is evident in Is 28:16 and Eph 2:20. Hillyer ("Rock-Stone") argues that both these words refer to the base of the building. Considerable supporting evidence for this is adduced in his study of the Qumran and Mishnaic use of the 'stone' theme (70ff).

[235]   Cf 1 Pet 2. Lindars, *Apologetic* esp 179ff, shows how this verse relates to Is 28:16, suggesting that the whole metaphor of Christ as a stone depends on Ps 117:22 (LXX). Is 28:16 is then used as a comment on Ps 117:22.

[236]   Προσκοπή and σκανδαλίζω are used in 2 Cor 6:3 and 2 Cor 11:29 respectively. In both cases the idea is similar to that expressed in 1 Cor. Space does not permit a discussion of Fee's view that 2 Cor 6:14 -7:1 summarises 1 Cor 10 ("Food" 140ff.).

[237]   Exod 23:33; 34:12-13.

that were to happen, then it should only come about because people had rejected the 'placarding'[238] of Christ and certainly not because they had rejected the 'knowledge' of the 'strong'.

It has been our proposition throughout that the 'strong' Corinthians were making a deliberate 'theological' issue in their expression of γνῶσις. Paul regarded what they were doing as a πρόσκομμα. He saw their requirement of γνῶσις as a hindrance to the gospel. The irony was that causing another to stumble over the *wrong* issue was to sin 'against Christ'.

Paul's response was not just that such action was *wrong*, but to offer himself as an example of one who would never present any σκάνδαλον to anyone (v 13) except, of course, that presented in the preaching of Christ (1:23). We shall see that this is precisely the same point he made with the use of the word ἐγκοπή in 9:12, and the command ἀπρόσκοποι ... γίνεσθε in 10:32.

The contrast between the two terms ἐξουσία and πρόσκομμα is important. It was probably the Corinthians who used ἐξουσία to describe their 'knowledgeable' action in attending idol temples. This action was one of the ways they demonstrated possession of γνῶσις which they believed *functioned* as an identifier or marker of those 'known by God'. We have seen that the stumbling block concept was used in those contexts where issues of apologetics were at stake: primarily, 'Who are, or what identifies, the people of God?' Something that prevents or hinders a person from being identified with the community may legitimately be called a 'stumbling block'. If we are right in proposing this, then in this context ἐξουσία and πρόσκομμα are direct *opposites*.

Paul's contrast between γνῶσις and ἀγάπη, in 8:3, emphasized the building-up potential of love and the boastful, flaunting nature of knowledge. Parallels were seen between 8:1-3 and 3:10ff which suggested Paul was drawing on the earlier chapter — at least for his metaphor. In 8:9-10 the building metaphor was used, probably ironically,[239] as Paul referred to the wrong sort of building in which the Corinthians were involved. Christ was no longer the subject of the 'placarding' (to use Barrett's term), in fact the 'strong' were sinning against Christ and leading others towards destruction. Πρόσκομμα was, therefore, an *entirely appropriate word* for the Corinthian situation in which Paul regarded the action of the 'strong' as sinning against Christ and leading people to worship other gods. Christ's position as θεμέλιον had been usurped. Πρόσκομμα should therefore be allowed its full

---

238 Barrett 245. 'It is more important that Christianity should offend for the right and not the wrong reason, because it is a placarding of Christ crucified ...',
239 2.1.3 above.

weight in signifying that which stopped people either being identified with or actually being the people of God.

2.4.3   Sin against Christ

The use of ἀπόλλυται in v 11[240] demonstrates the full repercussions of the wrongful use of this ἐξουσία. The use of the word ἀδελφός strengthens the point. Conzelmann is correct in saying it points back to vv 1 and 3 and the discussion of love. 'Destruction' is to be seen as an opposite of οἰκοδομέω — the goal of love:

> ... by love he [Paul] does not understand a subjective feeling. Love is determined by the saving work of Christ. As a result of this work the other is brought into my field of vision as my brother.[241]

The emphasis on the 'Father' as creator of his people, *through Christ*, also reminded the reader to think about the implications for the community of any behaviour. Thus, we suggest that the work of Christ ('for whom Christ died' — v 11) was somewhat more central to Paul's debate with the 'strong' than commentators have generally realized. Not only did Paul refer to it in 8:6 (δι᾽ οὗ τὰ πάντα καὶ ἡμεῖς δι᾽ αὐτοῦ), but it was prominent throughout the introductory chapters to this epistle. A person's identity as 'brother', as a member of the community, was established on and through (8:6) the one foundation: Christ crucified (1:23; 3:11). Again, this was made clear in ch 1. The only 'boast' that a Christian could have was 'in the Lord' (1:31), because 'in Christ Jesus' (1:2) these people were 'set apart' (ἡγιασμένοις). Participation in the community of God's people was by participation εἰς κοινωνίαν τοῦ υἱοῦ ... Ἰησοῦ Χριστοῦ τοῦ κυρίου ἡμῶν (1:9). This point was developed at greater length in ch 10.[242] What Paul said in ch 8:11-13, therefore, served further to establish the full community status that even those *without 'knowledge'* enjoyed. They were indeed[243] 'brothers', and they were that because Christ died for them. To suggest otherwise of the weak was to 'sin against Christ'.

Willis may be correct when he says: 'In view of Paul's use of the "building up" imagery in the letter it is perhaps best to understand εἰς Χριστὸν as εἰς σῶμα τοῦ Χριστοῦ i.e., the church'.[244] But that point has already been made in v 11 with talk of the destruction of the

---

[240]   Robertson 172: 'The emphatic position of ἀπόλλυται, and also the tense, have force; it is no less than destruction that results'. On the structure of this verse cf Willis 106-107; Fee 387.

[241]   Conzelmann 149. This link is made by most scholars in varying degrees. Esp see Fee 388.

[242]   Ch 4 below.

[243]   Note the repetition of 'brother' three times in vv 11-13.

[244]   Willis 107.

'brother' and in v 12, 'sinning against your brethren'. Sin against Christ seems to be more than this. Perhaps Paul meant that this was specifically against 'Christ' in that it was no longer he who was at the centre of the message proclaimed by the 'strong'. That the Corinthians were tempted to remove Christ from that central position is seen in 1:29-31, where Paul sought to put the 'Lord' back at the centre. Verse 13 both concludes ch 8 and introduces ch 9. With this, Paul began to contrast *his* position with that of the Corinthians.

2.4.4 Summary

In vv 9-13 Paul continued his stand against the 'strong' in Corinth. What they had considered an ἐξουσία, he called a πρόσκομμα. It is to be noted that:

i)   this contrast reinforces our view that no division between theory and practice adequately explains the debate in these verses. Ἐξουσία has to do with *action*, not simply a theoretical possibility;

ii) the use of the word πρόσκομμα is entirely appropriate in a context in which issues of apologetics and the possibility of destruction are being discussed;

iii) Paul has still not attacked or even shown a desire to modify the views of the weak. The argument has continued to be aimed at the 'strong';

iv) the reference to eating in an *idol temple* has made it clear that this was the particular exercise of knowledge which Paul faced.

2.5   Conclusions

1 Corinthians 8 started with a problem raised by the Corinthians: eating idol-meat. We have suggested that the issue in *this* chapter was probably no broader than that mentioned in v 10: eating such meat in an idol temple.[245]

It appears that the 'strong' were eating idol-meat to prove that they had the gift of the Spirit called 'knowledge'.[246] They were 'puffed up' about this gift because they were allowing it to *function* religiously as a marker or identifier of those 'known by God' (v 3). Paul's response to

---

[245] Fee 357-361, 386 etc. strongly argues that Paul was confronting attendance at *temple* feasts rather than eating market-place food. Also Willis 76-77.

[246] Inconsistently, Fee 366 agrees that γνῶσις in 8:1 'is a gift of the Spirit' (n 34), but then dismisses Murphy-O'Connor ("Food" 297-298) when he says that the problem of spiritual gifts helps us understand v 8. Fee claims that there is a 'complete lack [sic] of mention of spiritual gifts in the context.' (Fee 382 n 35).

this situation, introduced in 8:3 and expounded in the remainder of the chapter, was rigorously to deny their assumptions at *two* levels.

Firstly, any knowledge they did have was inadequate and incomplete (v 2).

Secondly, knowledge could not be allowed to function as they wanted it to. *Love* was the indicator of those 'known by God' (v 3).

Knowledge appears to have involved the application or *practice* of some perceived truth from God. It is unlikely that either Paul or the Corinthians would have separated theory from practice. Such a separation has usually been suggested in order to help resolve apparent contradictions between what it is assumed Paul agreed with and what he actually said, for example, between vv 1 and 7, or vv 4 and 5b.

It is possible that οἴδαμεν ὅτι was part of the quotation from the Corinthians[247] rather than Paul's agreement at least with the *theory* of the 'strong'. However, even if Paul agreed that he personally shared the gift of knowledge with the 'strong', he adamantly refused to countenance the sort of *practised* knowledge to which he now addressed himself.

There is no need to separate theory and practice here in order to sustain this understanding of the text. Γνῶσις was a gift which involved a *practised* understanding of the truth. It is irrelevant to ask whether Paul would have agreed in *theory* with 'there is no God but one' (v 4). He was attacking the γνῶσις which said, 'there is no God but one *with the result that* we may eat idol meat in idol temples'. To this his response was to show that such knowledge i) was inadequate — there *are* gods and lords (v 5), and ii) could not function as a marker of those 'known by God', but might actually cause some 'for whom Christ died' to be 'destroyed' (v 11).

The distinction between vv 5b and 6 is not between what is 'subjectively' and 'objectively' true, but between what is true and what is true specifically within the community of faith which Christ brought into existence. Thus, in two ways, even v 6 is to be seen as part of Paul's argument *against* the 'strong'. Firstly, it reminded the 'strong' of the community context of God's creation of his people. They 'belonged' through his grace. He was their 'Father' just as the weak were their 'brothers'.[248] Secondly, it introduced the 'strong' to the fact that, when this Christian community was left behind and idol temples were entered, the situation of v 5 pertained. Paul expanded this in 10:1-22 but for now he simply pointed out that those who were weak (in their self-awareness in relation to that community) would be the first to realize that they had become involved directly with pagan gods — eating food ὡς

---

247   With Willis 67-70.
248   Cf Murphy-O'Connor 80; Wolff II 10.

εἰδωλόθυτον. It is interesting that in ch 10 the 'strong' actually have to be *told* that they have become involved in worshipping demons. Their assumed 'knowledge', far from indicating their status in the fellowship of Christ, had led them into another κοινωνία altogether.

Unlike those commentators who believe that Paul was correcting the *emphasis* of the Corinthians,[249] and unlike those who regard this passage as primarily a discussion about the 'predicate of Christian ethics' (γνῶσις or ἀγάπη),[250] or about the supremacy of love over knowledge, we have suggested that Paul was addressing an important *religious* problem that had to do with 'markers'. Initially, our understanding of this arose in our exegesis of v 3. There Paul's main response to the Corinthians was given: 'if someone loves God, *this person* is known by God'. The contrast was between the Corinthian position that 'knowledge' showed a person to be 'known by God' and Paul's view that 'love' functioned in this way.

Although this suggestion arose from a cautious 'mirror reading' of the text (see p 13 above), it was reinforced through further exegesis. Knowledge was causing the 'strong' to be 'puffed up' because they were showing off. The word οἰκοδομέω, in v 10, implied a deliberate policy on the part of the 'strong' to be *seen* (ἐὰν τις ἴδῃ). The use of συνείδησις as meaning 'self-awareness with respect to others' also supports this proposal. The problem for the weak was that they did not feel secure in their identity as Christians. This explains why they were apparently prepared to follow the 'strong' even into sin. Seeing the 'knowledge' of the 'strong', the weak also wanted to experience the self-confidence of security which the 'strong' were claiming. They, too, wanted to be marked out as God's people — totally secure.

Paul's contrast of ἐξουσία (the Corinthian view of their practice of knowledge) with πρόσκομμα (his view of their action) offers further support for our position. The latter word was commonly used in apologetic contexts. The so-called ἐξουσία of the 'strong' was actually something that caused stumbling and *prevented* people from being identified with those 'known by God'. Instead of 'building up' the weak in Christ, the 'strong' were leading the weak to destruction (v 11).

The emphasis in vv 11-13 of the effect of the action of the 'strong' on the relationship of both weak and 'strong' to *Christ* is important. This builds on what Paul had said in v 6. Status as one of God's people was determined by the grace of God alone and was brought about through the death of Christ. This was a point Paul had already made in the

---

249 Willis 81: 'The only γνῶσις that really counts is ... the prior one of God's call'; also Barrett 190.

250 Fee 369 n 46.

epistle.[251] The so-called ἐξουσία of the 'strong' must, therefore, be seen in this context. Love for the Father God, who had called his people into being through Christ, was *alone* what identified a Christian and would 'prove' him to God or enable him to stand before the Judgment seat (v 8).[252]

Paul was probably using Corinthian terminology when talking of ἐξουσία and this may also have been true of his description of people as 'weak'. For Paul weakness was not to be decried. Perhaps his references to the 'weakness of God' (1:25) and God's choice of the 'weak' (1:27) were making just that point. Certainly Paul identified himself with the weak in 4:10 and apparently with those who might 'stumble' (σκανδαλίζω — 2 Corinthians 11:29). If 2 Corinthians 12:9-10 and 13:4 are allowed to interpret Paul's view, we can see why Paul sided so strongly with the weak against the 'strong': it was because in weakness the grace and power of God were more readily seen. In other words, an attitude of weakness meant a person could truly 'boast in the Lord' (1:31) and thereby avoid the possibility of causing someone to stumble.

[251]   Cf the whole argument of 1:18-31; 2:2; 3:11-17; 4:7; 5:7-8 etc.
[252]   It does not materially affect our argument if παρίστημι is or is not taken as a legal technical term.

3. For The Sake Of The Gospel

Exegesis of 1 Corinthians 9

3.1 Introduction

... dieses ganze Kapitel [9], vom ersten bis zum letzten Verse, nichts anderes ist als eine anhangsweise angefügte Erläuterung zu 8:13: Paulus zeigt den Korinthern an seinem eigenen Verhalten, wie ein Christ auf ihm zustehende Rechte verzichten kann ....[1]

Jeremias' statement appears in an article suggesting that in ch 9 Paul used a chiastic structure:

Er gibt zwei Beispiele für seine Verzichtbereitschaft: 1. οὐκ εἰμὶ ἐλεύθερος; (v.1a) — ausgeführt in vv.19-27, und 2. οὐκ εἰμὶ ἀπόστολος; (v.1b) — ausgeführt in vv.1c-18.[2]

However, others suggest the subject of ch 9 is different from that of ch 8. Héring believes that 'A transition from 8 to 9 is lacking'. Therefore, ch 9 belongs to a different letter[3] — a view shared with Loisy[4] and Goguel[5] and, in part, with Schmithals.[6] Several scholars agree with Héring that the *issue* is now apostolic authority but also believe chs 8 and 9 are linked.[7]

---

1   Jeremias, "Chiasmus" 156.
2   Loc cit.
3   Héring xiii, 75.
4   Loisy, *Introduction* 39-40.
5   Goguel, *Introduction* V 14-15.
6   Schmithals, *Gnosticism* 93-95, believes 9:24ff belongs to another letter. Cf Weiss 231.
7   Dungan, *Sayings* 4-9; Barrett 200: Paul is 'ready to digress'; Conzelmann 152. Fee (392ff) contends that the chapter contains an apostolic defence linked to ch 8; Wuellner, "Rhetoric" 186-188 discusses ch 9 as a rhetorical digression.

We shall argue below that Paul's purpose in ch 9 was to challenge the belief that the practice of a person's ἐξουσία could demonstrate position or status. For Paul, ἐξουσία was to be subordinated to the call of God.

3.1.1   Structure

The first two questions of v 1 are pursued in the rest of the chapter, but the existence of a chiastic structure is not obvious, as is made clear by Schmithals' rejection of Jeremias' structure.[8] We shall see below that the first two rhetorical questions do not concern different subjects later addressed in reverse order. 9:1c-3 is not a 'defence' of 9:1b. Rather, in 9:1-12a Paul offered himself as an example of one who belonged to a group that possessed a certain ἐξουσία. However, the provision of an example to follow was not Paul's only purpose. He was also teaching the Corinthians that their view of the *function* of an ἐξουσία was wrong. Thus, apostleship and apostolic ἐξουσία became an analogy for the Christian and his ἐξουσία.

3.1.2   Rhetorical questions

Paul's style changed somewhat between chs 8 and 9. In the first twelve verses a series of rhetorical questions[9] makes the passage vivid and clear. However, many interpreters, while acknowledging a rhetorical literary device in vv 1-2, let the rhetorical questions *function* virtually as 'real' questions. The functional difference between real and rhetorical questions is that the former are 'used to elicit information' and the latter 'to convey or call attention to information'.[10] Thus, for example, Fee says that these questions 'expect a positive answer: "Of course I am; of course I have"'.[11] A question containing the particle οὐ does expect an affirmative reply but it need not be deduced from these *rhetorical* questions that Paul was attacking the Corinthians.[12] The questions

---

[8]   Schmithals, *Gnosticism* 383 agrees there is a chiasm but claims Jeremias has got it wrong. Instead it should be a) 9:1a, b) 9:1b, b) 9:1c-3, a) 9:4-23. Cf Bengel 635.

[9]   Ellingworth, "Translating" 237-238, says there are 15 in these 12 verses alone. Questions of this nature are common in the letter, e.g. 1:20; 12:19, 29-30; 14:6-9. Beekman (*Word* 230) says there are at least 100 rhetorical questions in 1 Cor.

[10]   Beekman, *Word* 231: a chapter on 'Rhetorical Questions' (229-248). Also cf *Bradley's Aids to Latin Prose* quoted in *OED* Vol VIII 672, 'Questions that do not require an answer, but are only put in the form of a question in order to produce a greater effect, ... are called rhetorical questions.'

[11]   Fee 394.

[12]   Fee 394-396 assumes the questions provide further evidence for the supposed confrontation with the Corinthians on each question raised.

themselves should be allowed to function in a truly rhetorical manner, that is, as 'strong affirmations' — without prejudice to the views of the audience.[13] It is unlikely that such questions indicate confrontation. Paul may simply have been using the questions as they were most frequently employed in the NT: 'a statement of certitude, in which he [the writer] conveys information or calls the attention of his hearers to something they already know'.[14]

3.2   Apostolic ἐξουσία (Verses 1 - 12a)

The abrupt use of the word ἐλεύθερος is unexpected.[15] The word had been used in 7:21 of literal freedom from slavery, but Paul extended this in his analogy in 7:22 — a text that can contribute to our understanding of 9:1a. There a (literal) slave is a 'freedman of the Lord' but ὁ ἐλεύθερος κληθεὶς δοῦλός ἐστιν Χριστοῦ. In 10:29 ἐλευθερία is used in conjunction with what may or may not be eaten.

In ch 8 Paul called the Corinthian ἐξουσία a πρόσκομμα and concluded by talking about his own behaviour in relation to the 'brothers'. As this behaviour was very different from that seen among the 'strong', it is incorrect to say that ἐξουσία in 8:9 is equal to ἐλεύθερος in 9:1a or ἐλευθερία in 10:29. The word ἐλεύθερος is *not* a word applied by Paul to the Corinthians. He used it, in this metaphorical way, only of himself (9:1) or *his* behaviour (10:29).[16] In 7:22 he used it *in principle* of all Christians, but carefully defined it to show that a Christian concept of 'freedom' was at variance with the norm: a slave could be a 'freedman of the Lord', and a 'freedman' could be a 'slave of Christ'.

It is possible that the Corinthians regarded the ἐξουσία which they attached to γνῶσις as their 'freedom', but Paul did not call it that. In fact, what Paul described of his own behaviour in v 13 must have sounded restrictive when compared with the position of the 'strong'. In this context, the rhetorical device, οὐκ εἰμὶ ἐλεύθερος; makes perfect sense. Paul was making a positive affirmation that stood against the appearances of *what he had just said*. Whether the 'strong' agreed in

13   Willis, "Apologia" 34 says that *because* a positive answer is expected, there can be no debate on this point with the Corinthians. For Fee to claim that Willis 'misunderstands the nature of rhetoric', when both allow the questions to *function* in a linguistically similar way, is somewhat curious! (Fee 394 n 10).

14   Beekman, *Word* 355. Thus, οὐκ εἰμὶ ἀπόστολος; can be translated: 'As you well know, I am certainly an apostle'.

15   This is not the case if ἐξουσία in 8:9 has already been interpreted as 'liberty' (*RSV*).

16   It is used of some Corinthians as a literal or legal description: 7:39; 12:13.

principle that Paul was or was not free does not affect the development of the argument. In 8:13 Paul limited himself but then in 9:1a adamantly affirmed his freedom, perhaps recalling the discussion of ἐλεύθερος in 7:22. What appeared to be true by the standards of the world was not necessarily the case ἐν κυρίῳ (7:22). As we shall see, the phrase ἐν κυρίῳ is re-emphasised in 9:2-3. In proposing his example, Paul was deliberately distancing himself from the 'strong'. For Paul, to be 'free in the Lord' was to be a 'slave' in the service of Christ — a point developed in 9:12b-23 (esp v 19).

The second rhetorical question,[17] is also unexpected, making some believe the subject has changed or that Paul has digressed.[18] Fee offers the clearest argument that, in the 'long excursus'[19] of ch 9, Paul was defending his apostleship.[20] He says:

> The second question, "Am I not an apostle?" is the one that gets immediate attention. This is the first direct statement in the letter that his apostleship itself is at stake in Corinth; but such has been hinted at several times before this (1:1, 12; 4:1-5, 8-13, 14-21; 5:1-2).[21]

There are several problems with Fee's position, and some points may briefly be made.[22] i) 1:1 is little different in emphasis on apostleship from Romans 1:1. ii) 1:12 is viewed in several different ways,[23] but it is hardly evidence of conflict, let alone *specific* conflict with Paul himself. At most, it is evidence of various divisions. iii) While something is made of Paul's authority at the end of ch 4 and the beginning of ch 5, there is little evidence of direct *conflict* with him. Some were arrogant (4:18) possibly against him specifically, but chs 4-5 as a whole suggest that the Corinthians' arrogance was in how they *behaved* on a number of different issues (e.g., 5:2). That was why Paul could still call them 'beloved children' (4:14). iv) It is unlikely that Paul would have called on those in conflict with him to 'imitate me' (4:16; 11:1) if they did not still respect him as their apostle and 'father in Christ Jesus' (4:15). v) While the earlier verses of ch 4 perhaps offer slightly stronger support for Fee's case, numerous exegetical issues arise there which indicate that *conflict* may not have been the problem. Without examining these in

17   Above n 14.
18   Above nn 3-7.
19   Fee 433.
20   Ibid 394-397.
21   Ibid 395.
22   Fee's commentary *throughout* takes the position that Paul is defending his apostolic authority. His 'basic stance' 'is that the *historical situation* in Corinth was *one of conflict between the church and its founder* ... For Paul this conflict presents a twofold crisis — over his authority and his gospel' (Fee 6, his emphasis).
23   Above ch 1.

detail, v 6 at least raises the possibility that vv 1-5 are exemplary rather than describing a specific situation in which the Corinthians 'judge' Paul (4:3). It is also important to take note of the movement between first person plural pronouns and verbs and first singular. If the conflict with Paul is so evident, why is the first plural used in 4:9-13? Perhaps this is a further indication that when the first singular is used in 4:3-4 it is a matter of Paul offering himself as an example. vi) If the historical situation 'was one of conflict between the church and its founder' it is strange that, on Fee's own admission, 9:1-2 is the 'first direct statement' of the issue. However, our exegesis does not require that 9:1-2 be read in the way he suggests.

The next two questions reinforce and define Paul's apostolate which included being a witness to the raised Jesus,[24] and being the founder of the church at Corinth. The Corinthians should recognize Paul's apostleship because they are its σφραγίς.

Εἰ ἄλλοις (v 2) may indicate the presence in the church of 'others' who contested Paul's apostleship, or the possibility that outsiders were claiming that Paul was not an apostle because he did not demonstrate the ἐξουσία expected of an apostle.[25] On the other hand, it may represent a hypothetical possibility which serves strongly to confirm Paul's apostleship as the premise for the forthcoming argument. Thus, possibly Paul was saying that in his discussion with the Corinthians this premise would not be disputed.

Two further points should be noted in v 2. Firstly, the word σφραγίς meant a seal indicating a 'legally valid attestation'.[26] In Romans 4:11 the word was used of the mark of circumcision which was the 'seal' of Abraham's 'righteousness by faith'. It thus connoted his membership of the justified people.[27] In 2 Timothy 2:19 σφραγίς was used as the 'seal' of being part of God's community. Apart from the literal use of the word in Revelation 5 and 6, it was always used in the NT of that which confirmed, or legally attested a person's membership of God's people.[28] The only exception to this is here in 9:2. However, 9:2 is not that different, for *here it refers to that which marks Paul out as a member of*

---

24   Probably a reference to the Damascus road incident. Schlatter 102; Héring 75. See Kim, *Origin passim*.

25   Fee 396-397 suggests there are indications of outsiders entering the church. He believes this may have been the beginning of the 'vigorous confrontation' in 2 Cor 10-12 (Cf Wolff II 21). He admits, however, that the general tone of the passage suggests an internal problem.

26   Conzelmann 152 n 11. Wolff II 21, 'im Sinne der Bestätigung'.

27   Fitzer, "Σφραγίς" 949.

28   Apart from texts cited, cf Rev 7:2; 9:4. The cognate verb (σφραγίζω) has a number of meanings, but compare 2 Cor 1:22; Eph 1:13; 4:30, and texts in Rev 7.

a group — the apostles. 'Authentication is the idea which is specially indicated by the figurative σφραγίς.[29] This authentication or seal of the apostleship was the church.

Secondly, as mentioned earlier, the phrase ἐν κυρίῳ is repeated.[30] For Paul, the existence of the Corinthian church validated and authenticated his apostleship because *it demonstrated the Lord's work and will.*[31] In 7:22, Paul had already shown that being 'free' depended on being 'called in the Lord'. Now his apostolic authority was also seen to be dependent on the Lord's call, and confirmed in the work done through him.

The links between ch 8 and 9:1-2 are, therefore, substantial. Paul continued to talk in the first person singular, as in 8:13. More significantly, he continued talking about authentication of membership of a group of people — albeit of a different group or sub group (apostles rather than the 'strong').[32] Also he twice emphasised the link between this authentication and the fact that it happened 'in the Lord', a point which was implied by 8:6 and by the emphasis on Christ's work (death) for the weak 'brother' (8:11).

However, granted these important links with ch 8, the question still remains as to whether Paul was actually *defending* his apostleship. Verse 3 exacerbates the problem. Paul referred to his ἀπολογία against those who would examine him (ἀνακρίνουσιν). Some say v 3 looks backward to vv 1-2 which were the defence of his apostleship[33] while others believe it looks forward. Weiss[34] and Barrett[35] consider that the position of αὕτη at the end of the sentence anticipates the defence which is to come.[36] Before this question can be answered the word ἀνακρίνουσιν must be defined.

---

[29]   Robertson 178.

[30]   Kramer, *Christ* 177-179. Meyer 253, 'out of Christ the Corinthians were no seal of Paul's apostleship'.

[31]   1 Cor 1:4-8; 2 Cor 2:12.

[32]   It is of course possible that the 'strong' regarded this group as 'super-strong'.

[33]   Godet II 5; Meyer 253; Wendland 63; Robertson 179; *et al.*

[34]   Weiss 233.

[35]   Barrett 202.

[36]   Also Robertson, *Grammar* 703. But cf Lietzmann 40 who says that the more formal nature of the verse suggests it is an introductory statement in an argument. Cf also Allo 210; Fee 401; Nickle "Apologia" 68.

3.2.1 Judging and evaluating

'Ανακρίνω rarely appears in the NT outside this epistle.[37] The whole subject of 'judging', 'examining' or 'discerning' things or people seems to have been of importance at Corinth. Elsewhere in this epistle Paul also used the words συγκρίνω,[38] διακρίνω,[39] and κρίνω. [40]

In 2:14 Paul developed the subject of discernment (ἀνακρίνω) as an important spiritual issue. The χαρισθέντα had to be 'understood' (ἵνα εἰδῶμεν — 2:12).[41] The precise meaning of 2:13 is problematic with both the interpretation of συγκρίνω and πνευματικός causing considerable difficulties.[42] The former word is used elsewhere in the NT only in 2 Corinthians 10:12, a passage that is somewhat similar in subject matter to that being dealt with here: the standing of Paul compared with others. In that context the word seems to denote an evaluative comparison, but it is not clear that it can mean 'evaluate' or 'compare' in 2:13. Most commentators opt for translating συγκρίνω by 'interpret', in the light of the use of the word in the LXX for interpreting dreams.[43] For example, Conzelmann believes that the issue concerns the 'criterion and possibility of judgment' and so suggests 'interpreting spiritual things in spiritual terms'.[44] Reitzenstein and Lietzmann[45] both suggest it means 'comparing spiritual gifts with spiritual gifts'. In this view συγκρίνω means the same as it does in 2 Corinthians 10:12. Our own view of 2:13 is that the emphatic position of πνευματικοῖς leads into the comparison with the ψυχικός of v 14, where a 'non-spiritual' *person* does not receive the gifts. Thus we take πνευματικοῖς as masculine.

As regards συγκρίνω, we believe that 2 Corinthians 10:12 offers a better indication of its meaning than the LXX for three reasons. i) The subject matter of 2 Corinthians 10:12 is somewhat similar to this passage and is addressed to the same church. It is, therefore, likely that Paul used the word in a similar way. ii) In the LXX the use of συγκρίνω as 'interpret' is applied only to dreams, which are not an issue in 2:13. iii) Συγκρίνω *is*, however, used also in the LXX for evaluative judging

37 2:14; 2:15, 15; 4:3, 3, 4; 9:3; 10:25, 27; 14:24. Cf Lk 23:14; Acts 4:9; 12:19; 17:11; 24:8; 28:18.

38 2:13.

39 4:7; 6:5; 11:29, 31; 14:29, and διακρίσις, 12:10.

40 2:2; 4:5; 5:3, 12, 12, 13; 6:1, 2, 3, 6; 7:37; 10:15, 29; 11:13, 31, 32.

41 Barrett 75: 'The Spirit thus enables inward apprehension of profound divine truths'. Οἶδα here probably means 'understanding' in the sense of experiencing inwardly the true purpose of the gifts; Dunn, *Spirit* 235.

42 Robertson 47 lists various interpretations.

43 Cf Gen 40:8, 16, 22. Dan 5:7 etc.

44 Conzelmann 56; 57 n 7; 67; so Barrett 76.

45 Reitzenstein, *HMR* 430; Lietzmann 13-14.

or comparison.[46] In view of the emphasis on discernment and comparative judging or evaluation in 2:14-15, this seems a more reasonable translation. Thus Paul appears to have been saying that those 'taught by the Spirit' (2:13) should have been able properly to 'evaluate' the function of the gifts for God's people (the πνευματικοί). By way of contrast (v 14) the 'non-spiritual' person was unable spiritually to 'judge' (ἀνακρίνω) them.

Although there is some debate about the meaning of ψυχικός,[47] the contrast with the πνευματικός is so strong that it probably refers to those who were not Christians at all.[48] When Paul specifically talked about the inadequacy of the *Corinthian* position he used the word σαρκικός. It is possible that he did not use the word ψυχικός because he wished to distinguish between the Corinthians who were *acting* like non-Christians (and thus to be treated as 'babes') and actual 'non-Christians' or 'non-spiritual' people.[49]

In 1 Corinthians the word ἀνακρίνω usually connotes a judicial searching or investigation.[50] The idea of a 'spiritual' discerning or judging is also present in most contexts. In 2:14-15 the ability to 'understand' (γνῶναι) depends on the ability to carry out the 'spiritual judging or investigation' (ἀνακρίνω). The nature of the 'judgment' concerned seems to be forensic. In 4:3-4 the forensic element of the word is clear. Judgment comes at the return of the Lord (4:5) and until then the Corinthians should not make such judgment on others.[51] Paul talked of standing before God on the judgment day and showed that by being 'reckoned' (λογίζομαι — 4:1) in the way he was by the Corinthians, there was a danger that they would find him wanting in ways that only Christ could judge. Therefore, they should not 'judge' (κρίνω — v 5) in this manner before Christ comes.[52]

The context of 4:1-5 makes it clear that Paul's concern in this passage remained similar to that in ch 2 and 3:1-3. A 'non-Christian' (ψυχικός — 2:14) was incapable of 'judging' another person, while the one who judged and understood was 'spiritual', properly evaluating all things (ἀνακρίνει πάντα — 2:15).

---

46   Num 15:34; Wis 7:29; 15:18; 1 Mac 10:71.

47   See discussion in Conzelmann 67-68; Bultmann, *Theology* 1 203-210; Ridderbos, *Paul* 120-121; *inter al.*

48   Beker, *Paul* 218: 'The distinction between the *psychikos* ... and the *pneumatikos* ... simply marks non-Christian from Christian life'; but cf Horsley, "Pneumatikos".

49   *Contra* Lincoln, *Paradise* 41: 'ψυχικός ... becomes synonymous with σάρκινος and σαρκικός.'

50   Cf Büchsel, "'Ανακρίνω" 944.

51   See discussion of 4:4 in Ziesler, *Righteousness* 156ff.

52   Cf Davis, *Wisdom* 128.

The problem Paul had with the Corinthians was that they showed no evidence of proper evaluation or judgment and therefore, although 'brothers', they had to be be addressed οὐκ ... ὡς πνευματικοῖς ἀλλ' ὡς σαρκίνοις (3:1). If the forensic spiritual meaning is established, then we may deduce that the Corinthians were prematurely adjudging others as ones who would 'fall' on the day of the Lord. In effect, they were excluding 'brothers' from the community of the elect — obviously a 'fleshly' and 'non-understanding' assessment! In view of Paul's emphasis on properly evaluating the spiritual gifts for spiritual people, it seems likely that wrong judgments about people were being made because a wrong evaluation of people's gifts was taking place.

This last point is further supported from Paul's example in 3:5ff, which was centred on himself and Apollos. Both were called by God, so their work was *God's* and they would not boast in themselves. In 4:7, Paul's criticism of the Corinthians indicates that he probably still had in mind the Corinthian abuse of the gifts received from God.[53] They were not to be 'puffed up' (φυσιόω — v 6)[54] because all they had, they had 'received' (v 7). The implication is that Paul was facing, as in ch 8, the flaunting of gifts of the Spirit, as if *those* would distinguish some Corinthians from others. Paul simply asks a rather sarcastic question: 4:7 — 'For who can judge you? [After all], what do you have that you did not receive [from God]?'

To return, then, to the use of ἀνακρίνω in ch 9, three points of contact with chs 2 and 4 are immediately noticeable.

i)   In ch 9 Paul expected 'evaluation' of himself to take place.[55] In chs 2-4 Paul began to apply the problem of judging and evaluating people to himself and Apollos.

ii)   The context of ch 9 is the discussion of ch 8 where Paul had argued that the 'strong' did not understand correctly their so-called ἐξουσία. They were 'puffed up' and boastful against each other, a characteristic described in ch 4. Also in ch 8 Paul had talked of flaunting the gift of γνῶσις and a distinction between the 'strong' and the weak that even led to destruction. In this context Paul presented himself as an example. In both chs 2 and 4 Paul offered himself as an example of the problems encountered in making distinctions between people on the basis of their gifts.

iii)   Ἀνακρίνω in 4:3-4 is forensic in meaning. It is possibly so in 2:15a and more probably in v 15b. Given the use of the word ἀπολογία in 9:3,

53   Fee 171.

54   See above on 8:1.

55   Ἀνακρίνουσιν — Possibly a 'futuristic present' (Dana, *Grammar* 185). Cf Robertson, *Grammar* 869-870; Willis, "Apologia" 34.

which normally has forensic connotations, it is probably also forensic here too.

Thus it seems that either a) Paul was indeed 'in the dock' and in direct and full conflict with the Corinthians,[56] or b) Paul was putting himself there in order to make his example personally vivid to the readers. After this brief examination of chs 2 and 4, we believe that b) is more likely. In 4:6, Paul actually said that he held himself and Apollos up 'for your benefit' (δι'ὑμᾶς). In neither ch 4 nor ch 8 is there evidence of specific charges being laid against Paul.

However, the use of ἀνακρίνω does point to Paul's desire that they should fully 'evaluate' or 'judge' him. Paul's ἀπολογία was, therefore, his argument defending his own behaviour (not his apostleship), that is, defending his approach to his ἐξουσία. He was not so much confronted by an opposition as deliberately driving the Corinthians into admitting that, on their basis of making judgments, he must himself fail. He did not flaunt his ἐξουσία in the way that they expected. He was to be seen as 'weak'.

Certainly the religious problem that Paul faced provided fertile ground for strong opposition to Paul. By the time Paul wrote 2 Corinthians 10-13 that opposition had materialized, but a caution must be voiced about reading that situation back into chs 2, 4 and 9 of 1 Corinthians. Rather, we believe, Paul used himself as an example to force people into the realization that if they were to evaluate or judge (ἀνακρίνω) people on the basis of their gifts, and how they were used — their ἐξουσία (ch 8) — Paul himself would not survive.

3.2.2   An analogy from Apostleship

In our discussion of the word ἐξουσία above, it was suggested that it might best be paraphrased as 'the exercise of your legal entitlements'.[57] These rights belonged to people who were members of a particular group. The 'strong' felt that certain entitlements were theirs *because* they had knowledge. Paul had already denied the ἐξουσία of the 'strong' and offered his own behaviour as an example (8:13). He continued with the discussion of ἐξουσία (esp 9:4ff), but he did this by defining a *different group* within which certain legal entitlements pertained. This was why he emphasised the *commonly accepted fact* that he was an apostle. What he was about to describe was an ἐξουσία that pertained to the apostolate. Unless he established the premise of the discussion — that he was indeed an apostle — the ensuing argument would fail. It was necessary that the Corinthians accept his apostleship and its accompanying ἐξουσία (vv 4-12a) if he was to be able to

---

56   So Fee.
57   Above 2.4.1.

demonstrate how an ἐξουσία should *function*. As might be expected in the light of 8:11-13, Paul was to argue that even the apostolic ἐξουσία was subordinated to the proclamation of the Gospel.

Paul thus obliged his readers to face up to the issues raised in ch 8 by ensuring that they applied their understanding to *him*. If they were to accept his view that their ἐξουσία was a πρόσκομμα, then they would have to reach a 'judgment' about Paul himself. It must not be forgotten that this section ends in 11:1 with Paul's command that they imitate *him* as he did Christ.

Paul was using his own position of apostle as an analogy. This was not an analogy that directly concerned different attitudes to idol meat.[58] Nor was Paul simply asking the 'strong' to behave like him in their use of their ἐξουσία.[59] Rather, we are suggesting that the example begins by taking Paul's apostleship as an analogy of group membership that carries a particular ἐξουσία. The Corinthians were *Christians* who believed that demonstrating their particular ἐξουσία authenticated their membership of that group. Paul was also a Christian but to have made a comparison with the 'strong' on this level would have laid himself open to a dispute about γνῶσις and gifts of the Spirit. Therefore, he produced a *non-controversial* analogy.[60] Paul was an *apostle*, and all at Corinth acknowledged that fact. They would have admitted that with apostleship came ἐξουσία. This enabled Paul to address the problem of how ἐξουσία should be allowed to function, *without* castigating the 'strong' still further, and *without* disputing further about γνῶσις itself. This perspective on Paul's argument is demonstrated in a diagram at the conclusion of this chapter. The analogy is profound:

just as an apostle's ἐξουσία *does not authenticate apostleship, so a Christian's* ἐξουσία *does not authenticate those who are God's.*

We shall suggest below that this scenario is supported by further exegesis of the chapter and, ultimately, by providing a reasonable understanding of the way ch 9 links up with chs 8 and 10.

3.2.3 The right to support

In vv 4-12a Paul presented a series of proofs that apostles, as a group, have certain entitlements. The detail of his argument is interesting but

58   *Contra* Dautzenberg, "Verzicht" 220.
59   Morris 131; Prior 150.
60   Gale (*Analogy* 101-116) discusses the individual analogies of the soldier, ox, etc. in 1 Cor 9 but makes no comment on the greater analogy (from Paul to the Corinthians or apostle to Christian).

need not concern us here.[61] His points are clear and assumed to be obvious to the readers, given the continuing rhetorical questions. Each statement takes up issues of the apostolic 'right to support'.[62] Some have analysed Paul's appeals as being to common sense (v 7), the OT (vv 8-10), religious life (v 13), and to the words of Jesus (v 14).[63] Whether or not such a structure was deliberate, the recognition of these different appeals does draw attention to the cumulative impact of Paul's case, in which he was not seeking 'to establish that he has such rights'[64] but was restating the *fact* of that ἐξουσία as strongly as possible. This helped to create the strongest possible impression when he stated, in v 12b, that he had given it up.[65]

That the Corinthians would have granted an apostle's right to material support has recently been given support by several scholars. Their work provides further evidence that Paul was probably not indulging in self-defence before the 'strong'. Some of this evidence is examined below when we discuss the nature of the possible ἐγκοπή (v 12b) that Paul imagined he might cause.[66]

3.2.4   Summary

Links have been established with ch 8. We have argued that the rhetorical questions indicate that the Corinthians would have *agreed* with Paul. The basis of the analogy had to do with how a group's ἐξουσία functioned. While the 'strong' were expected to behave like Paul and were expected to apply what Paul said to the issue of idol meat,

[61]   Many have discussed how Paul used (or abused) the 'Law' in vv 8-10, cf Kaiser, "Crisis"; Johnson, *Old Testament* 39-51; Lee "1 Cor 9:9"; Malan, "Use" 150ff; cf Bauer "Uxores"; also Gale, *Analogy* 101-116.

[62]   The way v 5 (ἀδελφὴν γυναῖκα) fits into the theme of 'support' is disputed. Probably Calvin 185 is right in assuming the wife of an apostle would also be supported by the church. Cf Héring 77.

[63]   Cf Murphy-O'Connor 86; Fee 400; Savage, *Power* 113.

[64]   Weiss 233. *Contra* Fee 400.

[65]   We agree with Willis, "Apologia" 35: vv 4-14 are 'a statement of the obvious ... Paul has established his rights so strongly so that *he can make something* of his renunciation of them!'

[66]   Sect 3.3.2. Especially note there the work of E A Judge, R F Hock, T B Savage, and B W Winter. Theissen (*Setting* 27-67) assumes that Paul is scorned by the Corinthians for renouncing support. This causes a problem for understanding 1 Cor 9 where Paul seems to be arguing *for* the right. Theissen's response draws on his assumption of a distinction between the 'charismatic itinerant asceticism' required of early missionaries (Mt 10:40-42) and 'community organizers'. Paul, he says, reinterprets the requirement of 'charismatic poverty' and expounds it as a 'privilege'. This argument has little textual foundation. Cf the criticism of Theissen in Senft 118, 120.

the real issue concerned the 'judging' of people on the basis of an
ἐξουσία. This was the argument Paul proceeded to develop.

3.3   Τὸ εὐαγγέλιον ἀδάπανον (Verses 12b - 18)

This section of text introduces a number of ideas that need to be
examined if Paul's analogy is properly to be understood. We shall see
that Paul firmly established a part of that analogy with the use of the
word ἐγκοπή. We shall briefly examine the recent work of historians to
see what factors, working on the consciousness of the Corinthians, may
have made the taking of financial support a particularly appropriate
analogy. A study of καύχημα will reveal that it was an appropriate term
for an analogy that concerned 'markers' or external 'proofs' of
membership in a group.[67] Finally, we shall contend that it was the
internal 'divine commission' (ἀνάγκη) which Paul considered to be the
proof of his apostleship rather than any intentional (ἑκών) outward acts
on his part.

After such a long series of statements about the right of support, the
repeated ἀλλά of v 12b creates a strong impact. Even though vv 13-14
revert to a further statement of legal entitlements, v 12b is the crux of the
argument. Verses 15-18 are a further exposition of v 12b. Here, as so
frequently in Paul's letters, the apostle's thought and action were centred
on the 'gospel of Christ'. Not even a commonly acknowledged apostolic
ἐξουσία would be allowed to interrupt or interfere with that message.[68]

3.3.1   Ἐγκοπή and πρόσκομμα

The meaning of πάντα στέγομεν is not entirely clear, but the context
indicates that Paul probably had in mind enduring the hardships of
physical labour and perhaps even hunger.[69] It should also be noted that
πάντα στέγει in 13:7 forms part of the definition of love which Paul
considered to be the 'marker' of God's people.[70] But what was meant by
the word ἐγκοπή, and how might taking material support become an
ἐγκοπή?

Earlier it was noted that ἐγκοπή is part of the recurrent 'stumbling'
theme in chs 8-10.[71] In the NT the noun is used only here in 9:12,

67   An incidental aspect of this study may be to draw the attention of English
readers to Bosch's work ("*Gloriarse*"), which is an exhaustive treatment of the
subject of 'boasting'.
68   Paul's Εὐαγγέλιον is defined in 15:1-11. It is the content of faith. Also
cf 1:18-31. See esp Schütz, *Authority* 53-78.
69   Allo 219; Héring 79.
70   Above on 8:3.
71   2.4.2 above. Cf Dautzenberg, "Verzicht" 219.

although the related verb is employed on five occasions.[72] Paul used the verb to refer to Christians being stopped from carrying out their tasks.[73] In 1 Thessalonians 2:18 Paul said Satan 'stopped' him from seeing his readers face to face. Similarly, in Galatians 5:7 someone evil had 'stopped' or 'prevented' them from obeying the truth, while in Romans 15:22 Paul's own work elsewhere had prevented him visiting Rome.

Ἐγκόπτω is sometimes translated as 'to hinder' since it apparently referred in early Greek to a *temporary* impediment to a person's work. Stählin suggests this indicates a certain distinction between ἐγκόπτω and the words πρόσκομμα or προσκόπτω which referred to a more permanent obstacle. But he admits that this distinction was fading by the first century AD.

There are very few uses of ἐγκοπή in extant Greek literature with which to compare Paul's use of the word. The so-called parallels in Job 19:2 (LXX) and Isaiah 43:23 (LXX) are not helpful;[74] neither are other uses of ἐγκοπή sometimes found in medical discussions.[75] Of more interest is the statement in Diogenes Laertius 4:50, τὴν οἴσιν ἔλεγε προκοπῆς ἐγκοπήν. [76]

In view of the use of the word to mean an impediment to progress, it is not surprising to find it used by Paul as part of a metaphor of the racing track employed in Galatians 5:7. In 1 Thessalonians 2:18-19, the mention of a 'crown' probably indicates that ἐγκοπή is again part of a racing metaphor. The ἐγκοπή is an obstacle which prevents a person receiving the reward in the end.[77] It is possible this metaphor lay behind 1 Corinthians 9:12 but was not fully developed until 9:24-27.

The *functional* parallel between ἐγκοπή and πρόσκομμα in ch 8 should be noted. If Paul were to place an ἐγκοπή in the way of the Gospel (as the 'strong' had placed a πρόσκομμα before the weak) then, firstly, those to whom Paul was preaching would not hear the Gospel and would not be 'saved' (v 22) — a similar thought to ch 8 where the

---

72   Ac 24:4; Rom 15:22; Gal 5:7; 1 Thess 2:18; 1 Pet 3:7.
73   Stählin, "Ἐγκόπτω" 856-857.
74   The word 'weary' is the correct translation of ἔγκοπον (not ἐγκοπή).
75   Here the word seems to mean 'fracture'. Cf Soranus Ephesius, *de Signis Fractuarum*, 1:1.
76   'Pride is a hindrance to progress [in life].' Cf also *Historia Alexandri Magni* (Recension a, 32:6):... παραγενόμενος ἐξεφόβει τοὺς ἐργαζομένους, καὶ ἐγκοπὴν ἐποιοῦντο ἔργου διὰ τὴν τοῦ ζῴου ἐπέλευσιν.
77   Stählin, "Ἐγκόπτω" 856. Stählin does not give other references in Greek literature (apart from the Pauline) where ἐγκοπή is used with this metaphor. Perhaps a somewhat similar use is found in Diodorus Siculus I 32:8, where a river hits rocks as it rushes and 'because of the obstacles, remarkable whirlpools are formed' [Loeb] ... καὶ πολλάκις διὰ τὰς ἐγκοπὰς ἀνακλωμένου πρὸς ἐναντίαν τὴν καταφορὰν συνίστανται δῖναι θαυμασταί.

weak might be 'destroyed'. Secondly, Paul himself would not receive his reward (vv 17-18) or prize (v 24) and would not 'stand the test' (ἀδόκιμος — v 27) — a similar thought to ch 8 where the 'strong' themselves are seen to be sinning (8:12).[78]

This functional similarity between πρόσκομμα and ἐγκοπή[79] and the meaning of ἐγκοπή as an obstacle in a race suggests it is correct to link the word to the theme of 'stumbling'. Stählin rightly says, 'Formally the 3 phrases διδόναι ἐγκοπήν (1 C.9:12), διδόναι πρόσκοπήν (2 C.6:3), and τιθέναι πρόσκομμα (R.14:13) can have the same sense'.[80] Thus, Paul's analogy in ch 9 demonstrates that his ἐξουσία could not be allowed to function as an ἐγκοπή to the Gospel. But was there a situation at Corinth that would have made the taking of material support a more prominent ἐγκοπή for them and therefore a particularly appropriate analogy?

3.3.2   The issue of financial support at Corinth

Savage seems to assume that Paul did not accept financial support at Corinth, while he did in some other centres of his ministry.[81] However, Paul's attitude to support from the Thessalonians[82] was similar to that in 1 and 2 Corinthians. Paul *did* receive support from the Macedonians but clearly for work *elsewhere*, not in Macedonia (2 Corinthians 11:9). He also received support from the Philippians, but again this was apparently for work *elsewhere*.[83] There is no evidence that Paul took financial help from any group while preaching *in their centre*. When he did involve people in his support it was after they were established as a church and it was designed to help him in his missionary work in other centres (2 Corinthians 11:8). In this way Paul allowed churches to share with him in his work of proclamation and to benefit from the 'increase in fruit' (Philippians 4:7). Thus, Paul probably followed the same practice at Corinth with regard to financial support that he followed in most areas where he was laying the foundations of the church.

Some scholars have turned to sociological and historical reconstructions of the Corinthian society to explain attitudes to finances. Bachmann suggested that some Corinthians were too poor to pay any

---

78   Cf Dungan, *Sayings* 16.

79   Cf also 2 Cor 6:3 with 1 Cor 9:12.

80   Stählin, "Ἐγκόπτω" 856 n 4. Cf Agrell, *Work* 110 n 64. 'In its context ἐγκοπή is analogous to πρόσκομμα (8:9), σκανδαλίζειν (8:13) ... Thus the word introduces Paul's σκάνδαλον — theology'.

81   Savage, *Power* 97, 117-118. For more detail on this subject cf Agrell, *Work* 106-115; Dungan, *Sayings* 3-40; Hock, *Context passim*.

82   1 Thessalonians 2:5-8.

83   Phil 4:14-16. Cf Dungan, *Sayings* 32.

money and were thus prevented from entering the community.[84] However, passages like 1 Corinthians 1:26-28, which may imply poverty, must be balanced against Paul's appeal for money for the Jerusalem Christians in 16:1-3 and 2 Corinthians 8:13-15. The Corinthians were still relatively prosperous in comparison with others.

It is contended by some that Paul wanted to distinguish himself from various contemporary itinerant preachers or philosophers. Hock suggests that Paul did not want to be seen to be like the Cynic travellers who lived in public buildings and supported themselves by begging. The Cynics saw this as a way of attacking the greed for which the Sophists were renowned.[85]

Judge[86] and Winter[87] believe that Paul wished to dissociate himself from the Sophists. These people often charged for their work and there is some evidence that manual work was depreciated: For example, in Plutarch we read: "Labour with one's own hands on lowly tasks gives witness in the toil thus expended on useless things, to one's own indifference to higher things".[88] Thus Winter argues that Paul was despised by the Corinthians for *not* being like the Sophists in that he worked with his hands.[89]

Recently Savage has challenged some of these assumptions concerning the prevailing attitude to work and the so-called 'greed' of the Sophists. He goes so far as to say, 'It could be well argued, therefore, that Paul *does* fit the mould of the hellenistic missionary.'[90] Inscriptions, he says, reveal a different attitude to labour. Numerous tombstones pay tribute to all manner of tradesmen.[91] The deduction Savage makes is that

---

[84]   Bachmann 325, '...Ärmere von dem Eintritt in die Gemeinde abschrecken konnte'. Cf Stählin, "Ἐγκόπτω" 857; Dungan, *Sayings* 30, who cites 1 Cor 1:26, 2 Cor 11:9, and 12:14 as evidence for poverty.

[85]   Hock, *Context* 54-56. Cf also Malherbe, "Nurse" 216-217. But see criticism in Judge, "Society" 32-34.

[86]   Ibid 32.

[87]   Winter, *Sophists* ch 7. 'The discipline and self-control Paul exercises over his own appetites in vv 23-27 contrast starkly with the self-indulgence of the sophists with their life-style'.

[88]   Plutarch, *Pericles* II 1. [Loeb]. See also refs from Lucian, Plutarch etc cited in Hock "Tentmaking" 563; cf Cicero and Lucian in Savage, *Power* 101.

[89]   Op cit. Cf Georgi, *Gegner* 110-112 who believes these travelling philosophers help explain the situation Paul faced in 2 Corinthians. But cf Betz, *Paulus* 108-109, followed by Savage, *Power* 99.

[90]   Savage, loc cit.

[91]   Ibid 102-103; n 148 lists fourteen such inscriptions. He also refers his readers to nos 7366-7817 in *Inscriptiones Latinae Selectae* (Berlin: 1902, ed Dessau, 3 Vols).

... the common man's perception of his handwork differed markedly from Cicero's or Lucian's or Seneca's. In fact we may conclude that only gentlemen of high education depreciated the trades; the rest ... worked the trades and were proud of it. It is therefore highly unlikely that the Corinthians objected to Paul's refusal of support on grounds that it forced him to enter a demeaning profession'.[92]

Interesting as these inscriptions are, Savage's conclusion moves beyond the evidence he offers. They say nothing about what the normal worker would have expected of a preacher/philosopher. He might well have lived with a view that what was worthy, good and right for him to do, was not worthy or right for a philosopher.[93] In fact, the evidence of the text in 2 Corinthians 11-12, which is the central concern of Savage's thesis, supports exactly what we are saying. Paul seemed to agree with the Corinthians that he had 'abased himself' in working so that the Gospel might be presented 'without cost' (2 Corinthians 11:7). It appears that in their attraction to the pseudo-apostles who 'put on airs' the Corinthians did expect more of a leader than of themselves, especially in terms of wealth (12:20).

Strangely, after discounting the view that the Corinthians spurned Paul for working with his hands,[94] Savage proposes that the Corinthians would not accept an *'impoverished* leader'. Although Savage's separation of the 'Humble Handworker' from the 'Impoverished Leader' seems unlikely, his discussion of the possible expectations the Corinthians had is useful.

Drawing on Judge's discussion of *P Oxy* 3273,[95] Savage shows that a leader would have expected to be εὐπόρου καὶ εὐθετοῦντος and not ἄθετος καὶ πενιχρός.[96] This was particularly likely to be the case in Corinth which was 'great and wealthy',[97] and 'exciting envy'.[98] Given that wealth was a sign of status, it may be that the Corinthians would have been offended that Paul lacked this status while refusing their

---

92   Loc cit.

93   Modern examples of this are easily found in a class-conscious society like England. Yorkshire miners are proud of their work underground but they would think it affected, abnormal, and even demeaning to see their local church minister working in the mine for his keep. Such attitudes are part of the society. It is simply impossible to deduce from these Greek inscriptions that these workers would not have condemned Paul for doing something that they considered to be 'noble' for themselves to do.

94   What Savage calls the 'Humble Handworker' approach.

95   Judge, *Rank* 14-16.

96   Translated by Judge and Savage *Power* 104 as 'financially sound and fit' ... 'unfit for service and poor'.

97   Strabo 8.6.23.

98   Dio Chrysostom, *Orationes* 37:36. For these and other refs see Savage, *Power* 48-50 esp n 166; Wiseman, *Corinthians.*

financial support. The prominent display of wealth and an emphasis 'on personal power and self-boasting' were the common way of life. Savage continues, 'The Greeks were men of eyes, and they sought to authenticate status visually'. Thus, when Corinthians wished to evaluate an orator or even an apostle like Paul 'they looked for the same evidence of personal wealth and glory that they prized for themselves'. To support *their* apostle would have allowed them to boast about *their* man and *their* part in his ministry.

Savage's work addresses primarily the issues of 2 Corinthians 10-13.[99] However, with the evidence available, it seems reasonable to assume that the Corinthians

i)   would have expected Paul to establish himself as a high-ranking member of the community,

ii)   would have desired this for him so that they could be proud of their leader and boast in their generosity, and

iii)   (*contra* Savage) might have regarded manual labour as demeaning for a *leader* and as reflecting badly on them. Assuming this, then the ἐγκοπή that Paul so feared was probably that the Corinthians would be led into boasting in *their* own generosity, shown through the high life style of *their* apostle. They would lose sight of God's grace and provision.

However, while the background suggested by Winter, Savage, and others provides possible clues as to *why* Paul chose his apostleship and its accompanying ἐξουσία as an analogy (the Corinthians felt an apostle should be flaunting his ἐξουσία and were concerned that Paul was not doing this), that background is not clear in the text. For example, there is no reference in ch 9 to contemporary secular attitudes to leadership. The Corinthians may have had good reason for being dismayed that Paul was refusing their support but the situation needs further clarification from the text.

In verse 18 Paul indicated why taking financial support might become an 'obstacle'. He did not want anyone to think they had to pay to hear the 'gospel'. This would have denied the fundamental gospel concept of *grace*.[100] If people had perceived Paul to be charging for his message then they might have been thwarted by this ἐγκοπή. In terms we used earlier, people would have encountered an additional barrier to entering the community of God's people. As well as the need to 'love God', they would have had to pay money.

Further, as we shall see below, taking support would have obscured the fact that this preaching of the gospel was by divine commission (ἀνάγκη). Thus the exercise of Paul's apostolic ἐξουσία, here

---

[99]   Savage, *Power* 112-116 has a brief section on 1 Cor 9.

[100]   Bachmann 325. Cf Wendland 65-66; Barrett 207; Fee 411; *inter al.*

specifically defined as the right to material support, could not be required of him as evidence or proof of that apostleship. Rather, to have used this right would actually have been a *denial* of his calling rather than a 'marker' of its authenticity.

3.3.3   Paul's καύχημα

Verse 15 continues the thought of v 12b. Paul has not made use of any of these arguments for support.[101] Verse 15c introduces five sentences which begin with γάρ. Each further amplifies the sentence preceding it. But v 15 contains an anacolouthon that renders it hard to translate. It was probably the enthusiasm of Paul's warming to his argument that caused the problem.[102] Perhaps this emotion is best caught in Omanson's translation, 'For I would rather die than — no one shall make my boast an empty one!'[103] However, what did Paul's καύχημα have to do with relinquishing his ἐξουσία?

The noun καύχημα appears only in Hebrews 3:6 outside the Pauline corpus.[104] The cognate noun καύχησις and verb καυχάομαι are also almost exclusively Pauline in the NT.[105]

Boasting and self-pride were common-place in the Hellenistic era.[106] The flaunting of a person's prowess, wealth, or civic status is often to be noted both in literary and inscriptional sources and was apparently encouraged.[107]

---

101   Τούτων may refer to τούτων ἐξουσίων, although Paul nowhere in chs 8-9 uses the plural of ἐξουσία. But see Weiss 239 '... "eines dieser" Rechtsgründe (darauf geht der Plural: die ἐξουσία ist nur eine ...'. Also Dungan, *Sayings* 21 n 2, points to the parallelism between τούτων and ταῦτα (i.e. the 'proofs' Paul has just written down). But see the parallel structures shown in sect 4.4.1 which may suggest 'these rights'.

102   Conzelmann 157.

103   Omanson, "Comments" 138-139.

104   In the Pauline corpus it appears ten times.

105   Καύχησις appears eleven times in Paul's letters (eight times in the Corinthian epistles). Καυχάομαι occurs twice in James and 31 times in the Pauline corpus (eighteen times in the Corinthian epistles).

106   Apart from Savage (esp *Power* 64-75) and others cited in the previous section, for discussions of Paul's boasting and its relationship to the hellenistic era see also Genths, "Kauchasthai"; Bultmann "Καυχάομαι"; Betz, *Paulus*; Dowdy, *Meaning*; Fahy, "Boasting"; Forbes, "Comparison", and especially see the work of Bosch "*Gloriarse*".

107   Philo, *Det* 32-35 allegorises the OT figure of Cain to refer to the self-seekers of his day who are proud of their learning, wealth etc. Also see Plutarch, *De Laude Ipsius*, for his treatise on proper and improper self-glorification. Plutarch demonstrates an ambivalence with regard to self-praise. On the one hand he talks of τὴ ἀηδίαν τῆς περιαυτολογίας [the odium of self-praise —

However, an examination of the word καυχᾶσθαι in Greek literature reveals that the word usually carried a pejorative denotation. Bosch's examination of the word makes this clear.[108] He cites four reasons for disapproval of boasting in the contexts where the verb or its cognates are used: a) because it is offensive to gods, b) because it is offensive to men, c) because it sounds bad in company,[109] d) because the basis of the boast is not considered worthy.[110]

A wider examination of the use of the καυχᾶσθαι group of words seems to confirm Bosch's work. For example, it is interesting that in spite of his *De Laude*, even Plutarch uses καυχᾶσθαι only in a negative sense.[111] Diodorus Siculus also employs these words only in a pejorative manner.[112] From earlier times, Bosch[113] cites Aristotle who talks of people being attacked because of boasting.[114] This idea is also developed in different ways in Aesop's fables.[115] In Herodotus, boasting (καυχωμένου — genitive participle) appears as something in which the person mentioned has no right to participate.[116] Another use of καυχωμένου in Strabo[117] seems to have been missed by Bosch, as do

Loeb] (also cf 539.C), and on the other hand he talks of a right place for περιαυτολογίας as when the truth about oneself must be told (539.E), or when avoiding self-pity (541.A-B). This last section offers an extreme contrast with the apostle Paul's 'boast' in his misfortunes in 1 Cor 4:8-13 and 2 Cor 11:21-30 — a far cry from Plutarch's approval of 'self-glorification' when avoiding self-pity. 'So the man cast down by fortune, when he stands upright in fighting posture ... using self-glorification to pass from a humbled and piteous state to an attitude of triumph ... strikes us not as offensive or bold, but as great and indomitable' (Loeb translation of 541.A-B).

In similar vein, see the study of the hellenistic view that comparison of oneself with those who are greater helps develop self-knowledge, (Forbes, "Comparison" 2-8). Savage sums up the mood of the day: 'Not surprisingly, personal glory, δόξα, became the ideal' (*Power*, 27).

108 Also Bultmann, "Καυχάομαι" 646.
109 "... por ser malsonante en sociedad".
110 Bosch, "*Gloriarse*" 4.
111 Cf *De Laude* 539.C; 539.E; *Aemilius Paulus* 27.6.
112 Diodorus Siculus: 4.16.2; 4.74.3; 5.29.5; 15.6.1-3; 16.70.2; 17.101.2; 20.36.3. In each case boasting is 'despised', 'false', 'punished by gods' etc. Only the last ref cited might possibly be understood in a neutral sense.
113 Bosch, "*Gloriarse*" 9-24.
114 Aristotle, *Politica* 1311b.
115 Aesop's fables nos 33.2; 263; 241.1.
116 Herodotus, *Historia* 7.39.
117 Strabo, *Geography* 13.1.27.

various references in the *Historia Alexandri Magni*.[118] In each, the word is used in apparently negative contexts.

Further criticism of the boasting of the Sophists is found in Diogenes Laertius.[119] Philo uses the word group twice,[120] and Josephus once.[121] Only on one occasion did Philo employ καύχημα in a positive way and that was derived from the LXX.[122]

Bosch cites only Athenaeus as using the word in a positive way on one occasion.[123] There Archilogos rightly boasted in his ability to settle civil disputes before recalling his gifts in poetry. In fact, Athenaeus uses the word group three other times, once negatively,[124] and twice in an apparently more positive way.[125]

From the above, it seems reasonable to conclude that, even if the Corinthians looked for evidence of a person's membership of a group in proudly flaunted actions, they would still have recognised the word καύχημα (or καυχᾶσθαι) as *pejorative*. This is significant for understanding both ch 9 and 2 Corinthians 10-12. The ironic and sarcastic contrast Paul made between himself and the Corinthians would have been quite clear if the word Paul chose normally connoted something distasteful.

Unlike the idea in other Greek works, in the LXX 'boasting' is sometimes considered positively.[126] Bultmann outlines the use of καυχάομαι in the LXX in the following way:

> In many passages it is regarded as the basic attitude of the foolish and ungodly man (Ps. 52:1; 74:4; 94:3). For in it we see that man desires to stand on his own feet and not to depend on God, that he builds on that which he himself can accomplish and control. Hence 'to boast' can be synonymous with 'to trust' ..., Ps. 49:7.[127]

In his more detailed examination of the LXX, Bosch subdivides the negative uses ('usos desaprobados') into different categories: a) those

---

118   E.g., In Recensio B 1.2.7; 1.40.10; 2.20.40 etc. Access to the *Historia* has been through *TLG*.

119   Diogenes Laertius 10.7: εἶχε γὰρ ἐκεῖνος ὠδίνων τὴν ἀπὸ τοῦ στόματος καύχησιν τὴν σοφιστικήν, καθάπερ καὶ ἄλλοι πολλοὶ τῶν ἀνδραπόδων.

120   Philo, *Congr* 107.5; *Spec Leg* iv.164.

121   Josephus, *Ants* 8.372: τοῦ ... μὴ καυχᾶσθαι δεῖν ἀποκριναμένου.

122   Philo, *Spec Leg* iv.164. In this text, apparently missed by Bosch, a ruler takes pride (καύχημα) in God's Law.

123   Bosch, *"Gloriarse"* 21, citing Athenaeus, *Deipnosophistae* 14.627e.

124   Athenaeus, op cit 2.39e.

125   Ibid 6.273d; 14.655f.

126   Dowdy, *Meaning* 33.

127   Bultmann, "Καυχᾶσθαι" 646.

where pagans or sinners boast against God;[128] b) those where a person boasts in something altogether vain.[129] He subdivides the positive uses into three categories: a) the 'glory' (boast) of God;[130] b) the boast of the people of God;[131] c) the boast of the righteous.[132] Bosch believes that it is the 'boast' or 'glory' of the people of God which lies at the heart of the word as it is used in the LXX. The texts combine to show 'una "gloria" del pueblo y cómo el pueblo se gloría en la gloria de Dios'.[133] God has called his people to be a 'glory' to him, thus they can 'boast' in his grace to them. If this develops into a boast in their own wisdom, power etc, he withdraws that grace.[134]

In the LXX, approval is given to boasting that arises out of a loving response to the gracious God. Thus it is not surprising that people can actually boast in God himself or in his 'name', nor that the context in which the concept most regularly occurs is *apologetic* for, ultimately, it is God's name that is at stake. Three texts help make these points clearly:

In Psalm 5:10 the psalmist speaks against God's enemies and concludes (v 12): καὶ καυχήσονται ἐν σοὶ πάντες οἱ ἀγαπῶντες τὸ ὄνομά σου.

In Deuteronomy 10 we read that the Lord requires love of his people. They are to 'circumcise their heart' (v 16) and, because he has made them a nation, God is to be their καύχημα (v 21).

---

[128] Bosch, *"Gloriarse"* 39-45. E. g. Ps 93:3-4 (LXX); Jer 50:11 (LXX — 27:11); Jer 12:13 (LXX); Judges 7:2 etc.

[129] Ibid 45-55. E.g. riches or power, (LXX: Ps 48:7; Jer 28:41), or wisdom (Jer 9:22-23), or idols (Jer 27:38) etc.

[130] Ibid 55-64. He discusses texts such as Ps 95:5 (LXX); 1 Chron 16:27; 1 Chron 29:11, 13. Here καύχημα is an attribute of God and Bosch observes (p 56) that *kabod* (δόξα) could just as easily have replaced *tipheret*. It is worth noting that in Spanish the verb 'gloriarse' means 'to boast'. The connection that Bosch makes between this concept in the LXX and the concept of God giving his people glory (δόξα) is well communicated by the use of 'gloria' in Spanish.

[131] Ibid 64-78. The people of Israel were a καύχημα because they were called by God (Deut 26:18-19; Jer 13:11 — Bosch 59). From this, he says, arises the pride of the people (cf LXX: Ezek 16:12, 17, 39) and boasting in the God who chose them (LXX: Ps 105:47; Ps 149:5 — note the 'boasting' in the δόξα).

[132] Ibid 78-86. The main passages cited here are from Sirach and Proverbs (e.g. Sir 1:11; 10:22; 25:6; Prov 17:6).

[133] Ibid 64.

[134] Ibid 64-78. Bosch's conclusions come from an examination of numerous texts. The most significant are, we believe, those mentioned above in Ezek 16 where the boasting of Israel in the beauty etc that she has been given by God has become a boasting not in God's gifts but in herself. Thus God takes away his gifts so that she can no longer boast (cf also LXX Ezek 23:26).

Finally, in Psalm 88 God's gifts and covenant faithfulness to his people are recalled (vv 1-14) so that people praise God who is τὸ καυχήμα τῆς δυνάμεως αὐτῶν (v 18).

In 1 Corinthians 9:15-18 Paul presupposed a right and positive use of 'boasting'. In his discussion about what gave the right to boast (v 16), we may recall Plutarch's *De Laude*. However, Plutarch only ever used καυχάσθαι pejoratively. The idea may perhaps be similar (there is a right and a wrong pride), but the vocabulary is not. This must be born in mind as we now examine Paul's own use of the word.

In this epistle Paul first used καυχάομαι in 1:29, 31, where he presented both a negative and a positive boast, concluding with a quotation from Jeremiah 9:22-23[135] — a passage which clearly demonstrates the contrasts between 'boasts'.[136] In Jeremiah 9 man is told that, however wise he may be, he must not boast in his own wisdom or riches but rather ἐν τούτῳ καυχάσθω ὁ καυχώμενος συνίειν καὶ γινώσκειν ὅτι ἐγώ εἰμι κύριος ... for the Lord 'carries out justice and righteousness in the midst of the earth'.

Paul had been making just that point. Man could not boast in his own wisdom, for God was carrying out all his purposes through his call. The paradox is this: no flesh may boast because everything is ἀπὸ θεοῦ (1:30), but one who 'understands and knows God' can boast in God himself, who has provided salvation 'in Christ'.

In ch 1 the boasting mentioned was ἐνώπιον τοῦ θεοῦ. The Corinthians were flaunting their 'wisdom' and apparently suggesting that this wisdom, which Paul called κατὰ σάρκα, indicated their standing 'before God'. For Paul, a person's standing before God was dependent upon God's electing choice (1:26-29). No one could boast, therefore, in wisdom. Rather, the only boast possible was in Christ ἐξ αὐτοῦ δὲ ὑμεῖς ἐστε (1:30).[137]

The problem with this, for a people concerned to flaunt their membership in the κοινωνία τοῦ Χριστοῦ (1:9), was that membership depended on something internal. 'Love', mentioned in 8:3 as a marker, fundamentally concerns a change of heart. It has its outward manifestations but they are the opposite of boasting in one's own

135 LXX also 1 Sam 2:10.
136 Cf 1 Clem 13:1.
137 'God' is the referent of ἐξ αὐτοῦ. It was 'from him' ('on the basis of God's choice') that the Corinthians were distinguished as being 'in Christ Jesus'. ὑμεῖς ἐστε does not refer to creation and existence *per se*. The clause reemphasises God's action in choosing, as did v 28. Paul here was describing the election and calling of the Corinthians by God. (Conzelmann 51; Klauck 27; *inter al.*) The antithesis continues between God's choice of some and destruction of others. Cf Godet, I 115, and our understanding of 8:6, above. Calvin 45 suggests both creation and new birth are indicated.

attributes or gifts. The relationship to outward boasting of this change of heart, involving the 'love of Christ which controls us', is made clear in 2 Corinthians 5:11-15. Paul was concerned to explain his behaviour to the Corinthians so that they might in fact boast (καυχήματος) in the apostles despite appearances. They had to learn the basic distinction between pride in outward appearances and inward realities.[138] Pride in the latter was, for Paul, pride in God who had effected the inward change. The Corinthians needed to confront those who boasted ἐν προσώπω (in what is seen) rather than ἐν καρδίᾳ (v 12).

A basic desire to boast in a badge or mark of membership in a group is frequently to be seen in the religious sphere of life. In many ways Paul's use of the καυχᾶσθαι word group reflected his concern to move back from such matters to the preaching of the cross of Christ, and a recognition that only this εὐαγγέλιον led to true membership in the community of God. Three other examples from Paul's writings demonstrate that this question of standing in the community was always at the heart of his problem with 'boasting'.

In Galatians 6 Paul confronted Jews who insisted on and 'boasted' in circumcision. This they did 'to make a good demonstration' (εὐπροσωπῆσαι — v 12) to others. For Paul the only ground of boasting was to boast in 'the cross of our Lord Jesus Christ' (Galatians 6:12-14). Circumcision counted for nothing (v 15). The only marker of community membership was to be found in Christ crucified.

In Romans boasting is linked to the other main Jewish marker of community membership — the law. Strict adherence to the law caused Jews to boast of their relationship with God. Paul pointed to their inconsistency in keeping the law[139] and argued that what went on in the heart in fact authenticated status: the true Jew 'is one inwardly, and real circumcision is a matter of the heart, spiritual not written' (2:28-29).[140] Boasting was excluded because of the law of faith (3:27). This theme is taken up again in Romans 5 where 'legitimate' boasting is discussed. Here Christians boasted (v 2) in sharing God's glory which was given διὰ τοῦ κυρίου ἡμῶν Ἰησοῦ Χριστοῦ. They 'stand' in this grace. [141]

In Philippians 3 Judaizers were the subject of Paul's attack. Confidence in the flesh (ἐν σαρκὶ πεποιθότες — v 3) was wrongly

---

138   So Lütgert, *Freiheitspredigt* 53-55.

139   Rom 2:17, 23.

140   Cf also Rom 4:2. The words 'marker' or 'demonstration' do not imply that Jews believed they *earned* their status with circumcision and law-keeping. Rather they indicate the presence of a sign that shows something that already exists to be true. Circumcision etc. were, we believe (with Sanders *PPJ et al*), regarded as the required evidence of the sphere in which grace was at work. They *authenticated* the presence of saving grace. This is what Paul denies.

141   Cf Rom 5:1, 2, 11.

placed. 'For we are the circumcision', said Paul, 'the ones who worship God in spirit and who boast (καυχώμενοι) in Christ Jesus' (v 3). Faith in Christ (v 9) was the basis of status yet to be obtained (vv 12ff.) and already obtained (v 16). Paul's membership (being found in Christ — v 9) depended on righteousness ἐκ θεοῦ.

Paul's use of Jeremiah 9 in 1 Corinthians 1:31 was, therefore, quite in accord with the way he understood boasting elsewhere in his epistles. It could have a positive function or negative. This approach to the concept is derived from the LXX rather than other Greek literature.

This is not to say that the two backgrounds can be completely separated, but the almost exclusively pejorative meaning in Greek literature is not so prominent in the LXX or in Paul. In the LXX and Pauline corpus the focus of all boasting is to be seen in terms of a person's relationship to God, which is rarely the case in Greek literature.

In summary, we suggest that Paul's use of 'boast' in the Corinthian correspondence probably had a dual purpose: a) given its normally pejorative connotation, it would have served to emphasise Paul's displeasure with their arrogant behaviour; b) its use in a way similar to that found in the LXX helped further to define the difference between the self-centred pride of the 'strong' and the God-centred pride which arose from the love for the one who had died for them.

This background provides help in understanding Paul's somewhat enigmatic use of καύχημα in 9:15, 16 which he linked directly to 'the gospel'.[142] His καύχημα would 'be emptied' (κενώσει) if he stopped preaching the gospel.[143] And yet v 16, introduced with an explanatory γάρ, makes it clear that Paul did not consider his preaching *per se* to be his boast (οὐκ ἔστιν μοι καύχημα). Rather, he had to preach because ἀνάγκη had hold of him. As we shall see, his 'boast' was in fulfilling the divine commission laid on him.

3.3.4   Ἀνάγκη, ἑκών, and ἄκων

Käsemann's masterful discussion of ἀνάγκη[144] has shown that Paul used the word to describe his belief that he lived under a divine compulsion to preach the gospel. This is not to be interpreted ethically[145] or psychologically:[146]

---

142   Note the repetition of the verb εὐαγγελίζωμαι and its cognate noun: v 12; twice in v 14; twice in v 16; three times in v 18.

143   A point summarised in 9:23a. Cf Bosch, "*Gloriarse*" esp 218-220; 312-313.

144   Käsemann, "Amor" 228-230, summarises succinctly the different positions taken on the subject.

145   Ibid 228. For those holding this view with whom Käsemann takes issue see nn 61, 66, 67. Since Käsemann's article (original 1959), we note that

The ethical and psychological interpretations clearly pay no heed to the fact that our passage professes to concern itself with a compulsion exercised on Paul from outside.[147]

Käsemann contends that the eschatological connotation of the 'Woe' of the next sentence indicates that Paul was talking of God's 'power in action' in grace or in wrath. The Ἀνάγκη showed that, under God's control, Paul was destined to preach the gospel.[148]

Verse 17, also introduced by γάρ, expresses the same idea as v 16[149] but this time Paul's metaphor is 'reward' or 'pay' (μισθός). The contrast between ἑκών and ἄκων is normally understood as a contrast between what Paul might have done 'voluntarily' and what in fact he was obliged to do 'involuntarily'.[150] Some scholars suggest that Paul distinguished himself from apostles who had 'voluntarily' followed Jesus while he, Paul, had been forced to do so.[151] However, it is hardly conceivable that Paul would have understood that those 'voluntarily' obeying the call of God somehow earned the right to 'pay', while he did not. After all, in v 14 he had argued that *he* had that right, even though he did not use it.

We believe it is incorrect in this context to translate ἑκών as 'voluntarily'. The contrast Paul was making with his use of ἀνάγκη was between doing something as God's will and doing it as man's will — the ground of the LXX and Pauline distinction between a right and a wrong type of boasting. The wrong type of boasting was one centred in man's own actions rather than in God's grace.

Paul posed this contrast in v 17. a) Paul may preach ἑκών, that is 'intentionally'[152] — from within himself — or b) he may preach ἄκων,

ἀνάγκη is treated as a psychological or ethical obligation by Prior 158 and Morris 136-137.

[146]   Loc cit. See nn 62-65.

[147]   Ibid 229.

[148]   Possibly Paul viewed his ἀνάγκη as similar to a prophetic calling (Jer 20:9; Amos 3:8). Cf Barrett 209; Wolff, II 29.

[149]   Didier, "Le Salaire" 236.

[150]   Senft 122; Bosch, "*Gloriarse*" 219; Héring 80; Dungan, *Sayings* 23-24 n 1, *inter al.* See Didier, "Le Salaire" 232-234 for a discussion of Roman Catholic exegesis of this in support of works of supererogation.

[151]   Godet, II 30; Thrall 79; Käsemann, "Amor" 233 is correct to insist that 'It is not the model of the humble earthly Lord that keeps him [Paul] from exercising this right ... The attempt to solve the problem by taking a diversion through Christology is therefore impermissible'; cf also Munck, *Paul* 22.

[152]   The difference between 'voluntarily' and 'intentionally' is largely one of connotation. Both words in English imply that the individual himself willed to do something. We use the word 'intentional' to indicate clearly the purposeful action that we believe Paul had in mind (cf *RSV* 'of my own will'). However, we cannot simply compare 'of my own will' ... 'not of my own will' (*RSV*) as this fails to make the connection with ἀνάγκη, and with οἰκονομίαν πεπίστευμαι.

that is 'under God's compulsion' (ἀνάγκη).[153] The first would bring him his reward (ἔχω — present indicative). That is, if this were the case,[154] *he could receive his pay from the church for his task performed and boast in the fact.*[155] The second possibility, which was actually the case, was that Paul did what he did *because God had called him to it as a 'steward' or 'slave'* (οἰκονομία) *with a job to do.*

The issue, we suggest, is somewhat similar to that found in Matthew 6, where Jesus distinguished between outward and intentionally self-flaunting acts (ἔμπροσθεν τῶν ἀνθρώπων) of hypocrites and the quiet work of the righteous. The former 'receive' (present) their 'reward' (μισθός), while the Father 'will reward' (future) the righteous.[156] That is, the latter will be rewarded at the judgment day, while the hypocrites receive immediate reward in the attention they draw to themselves.

The comparison is better rendered (slightly paraphrased), 'But if I do this from my own intention ... but if not from my own intention but from the commission God has given me, then what is my reward?' This is the punctuation taken by Bachmann 331; Munck, *Paul* 22; Barrett 209; *NIV*.

The idea of deliberate intention arising out of man's purposive self-will is seen in connection with the word ἑκών in a number of places. Cf Plutarch, *Moralia* 972.E: καὶ περιπλεκόμενος οὐδὲν οὔθ' ἑκών οὔτ' ἄκων ἔβλαψεν, '... and coil about her without doing her any harm at all, either intentional or accidental' [Loeb]. Euripides, *Daughters of Troy* 709, οὐκ ἑκὼν γὰρ ἀγγελλῶ, 'I shall not intentionally announce ...'
Herodotus 7:104, ἑκών τε εἶναι οὐδ' ἂν μουνομαχέοιμι. εἰ δὲ ἀναγκαίη εἴη... 'of my own will I would not even fight with one: yet under necessity ...' Also cf Herodotus 8.116; Plato *Gorgias* 499C. Note the discussion of man's will and his exercise of it in Plato, *The Laws* 646.B: εἰ δεῖ ἑκόντα ποτὲ ἄνθρωπον 'of his own free will a man ...'
θαυμάζοιμεν ἂν ποτέ τις ἑκὼν ἐπὶ τοιοῦτον ἀφικνεῖται; 'Should we be surprised if a man of his own free will ever got into such a state?' [Loeb]. Also see *LS* 449; Hauck, "Ἑκών" 469; cf Rom 8:20.

153 Surely not 'unwillingly'! (nn 150-151 above.) The anacolouthon, and emotion of v 15 speak against the view that Paul could ever have been an 'unwilling' recipient of God's ἀνάγκη. Cf Acts 21:13; Gal 2:9-10; 6:7-10; Phil 1:18-24 etc. Cf Ellicott 164.

154 Although the conditional clause (εἰ + pres ind) normally states a real condition, it does not appear to do so here. Rather, the first clause is balanced against the second which states the true condition (Barrett 209; Conzelmann 158; Fee 419 n 35).

155 Preisker, "Μισθός" 699, 'The term μισθός is here assimilated to καύχημα in content'. Also see Fee 421 (following Käsemann "Amor" 231-232), who says 'the way the argument is structured implies that his "pay" and his "boast" refer to the same reality, preaching the gospel without accepting support so as to put no hindrance before the gospel'. So also Calvin 193; Meyer 267; Moffatt 120-121; *inter al.*

156 Matthew 6:1-6, 16.

If we are correct to place Paul's argument into this type of religious framework, then support is offered to those who believe μισθός, in v 18, refers to an eschatological reward.[157] In passing, we should also note that 'love' (for Paul the community 'marker') was firmly linked to the concept of μισθός within the dominical traditions of Matthew and Luke.[158] This may be further evidence that Paul's use of the word in ch 9 was not far removed from its eschatological use in parts of the Gospels.[159]

Apart from the links with an eschatological use of the word in the Gospels, there are four other indicators that μισθός is here to be understood eschatologically:

i)   Paul had just used the word 'Woe' which, we noted above, had strongly eschatological overtones.

ii)   The two other occasions in this epistle (3:8; 3:14) where μισθός is used both have an eschatological reward in view.

iii)   These two verses are the *only* two other metaphorical uses of the word in Paul,[160] which may suggest that his use here in 9:18 was similar.

iv)   Paul later (vv 24-27) spoke of his eschatological 'prize' and possibility disqualification.

Arguments against taking μισθός in this way are twofold:

i)   In v 17a it is obviously a *present* reward. Some believe that this sets the context of μισθός for v 18a.

Our interpretation of ἑκών has led us to view v 17a as not just a hypothetical condition but a conditional clause that is fundamental to Paul's analogy. This refers to the κατὰ σάρκα approach to preaching. If v 18 follows from the ἄκων conditional clause then that, we suggest, refers to Paul's 'spiritual' approach to preaching (obedience to the divine will). It is thus perfectly feasible that in v 17a the μισθός was immediate while in v 18a an eschatological reward was contemplated.[161]

ii)   Verse 18 also appears to be talking of immediate reward.

Certainly if 'boast' and 'reward' refer to the same reality, then Paul has already acknowledged he *has* a 'boast' and will not give it up (v 15)! However, his argument seems to be rather more subtle than that. It is true that in one sense Paul's reward lay in making the gospel 'free' (ἀδάπανον) to people[162] but v 18 was not the end of Paul's argument. His boast and hence his reward was ultimately in the fact that he was under God's ἀνάγκη to present the gospel. Thus he was a 'fellow-

---

157   E.g. Meyer 267; Goudge 76; Allo 222 says the reference is 'indirect'.
158   Cf Mat 5:46 and Lk 6:35.
159   *Contra* Preisker, "Μισθός" 699-700.
160   Paul used μισθός with a literal meaning in Rom 4:4; cf 1 Tim 5:18.
161   *Contra* Conzelmann 158 n 30.
162   Robertson 190; Conzelmann 158 n 28; Dungan, *Sayings* 23; *inter al.*

partaker' (συγκοινωνός) in the benefits (*RSV*) of the Gospel[163] and looked towards a 'prize' at the end. Verses 24-27 look forward to an eschatological reward and must not be separated from the rest of Paul's argument.

To conclude, we suggest that if there was any 'ground of boasting' (*RSV* — v 16) for Paul, it lay in God who had called and, in this case, who had enabled him to preach without having to 'abuse'[164] his ἐξουσία (v 18). What he did in preaching the gospel was not some self-initiated job bringing pride and demanding a salary, it was the work of a slave — a point discussed in more detail in v 19. As Paul preached the gospel, knowing that he presented no stumbling block (9:12), he knew that he himself would not be disqualified (v 27).

3.3.5   Summary

We have seen that in vv 12-18 Paul was concerned to show even apostolic ἐξουσία was subject to God's call. With this perspective no-one could diminish Paul's reason for 'boasting' (v 15b). His ἐξουσία would not be a 'stumbling block' or 'hindrance' in the way of the gospel (v 12b). This made the link with ch 8 quite explicit, contrasting his perspective with that of the 'strong' who were becoming a πρόσκομμα to the weak.

This ἐγκοπή was a good example to use with the Corinthians because probably they both expected an apostle to take money and to be able to 'boast' in support of him. Equally, they expected Paul to boast, like the wandering philosophers, in the status his apostleship brought him. His material support would therefore have been a 'marker' to the Corinthians of his apostleship. However, Paul's rejection of his ἐξουσία was radical. He did not simply say that he turned down support because that was better behaviour. In fact, to use this ἐξουσία as the Corinthians expected would have been *wrong*. It would have obscured the fact that his apostleship was authenticated through the preaching of the gospel demanded of him by *God's* call, by ἀνάγκη.

Paul would not use his ἐξουσία for to do so would have implied that he was preaching of himself (ἑκών). Rather, he redefined the idea of 'boasting' along the lines of the LXX.

His boast, his 'marker of apostleship', lay not in the outward deployment of his ἐξουσία but in his submission to God's will.

---

163 'Benefits of the Gospel' is defended below.

164 The use of καταχράομαι in this way, as 'abuse' or 'misuse' is discussed in detail in Fee 421, who cites Dungan, *Sayings* 24 n 1. Dungan refers to an 'antithetical parallelism' between this word and χράομαι in v 15.

As Käsemann puts it, Paul's ἀνάγκη 'is the ultimate distinguishing mark of this Christian and apostle'.[165] 'Enduring everything' (v 12b) was part of that submission to God's call and will for his life. Doing this brought both a present reward, in that he knew he was doing right in making the gospel free (vv 15b and 18), but also the prospect of the eschatological reward for which he was striving (vv 24-27).

3.4   All things for the sake of the Gospel (Verses 19 - 27)

These verses have been scrutinized for information concerning Pauline ethics. This has led to debates about whether Paul was inconsistent in his teaching about accommodation in 1 Corinthians 9, given his apparently contrary action in dealing with Judaizers in Galatia.[166] Bornkamm argues that these verses provide an indication of Paul's "missionary stance",[167] while Fee suggests that in these verses Paul's argument 'now broadens in scope considerably' and turns from the narrow subject of 'accepting patronage' back to the broader defence of his apostolic conduct.[168] Fee's position highlights the problem of the relationship of these verses to what precedes them.

In examining these verses, we shall suggest that Paul's 'freedom' and 'slavery' can be understood only in the light of the previous discussion of ἀνάγκη and the issues raised in 6:12 and 7:17-24. We shall also suggest that Paul's central concern remained one of discussing the place of ἐξουσία in the light of God's call.

3.4.1   Paul's freedom and slavery

Before looking at the whole of this text three issues must be addressed. What did Paul mean by i) ἐλεύθερος, ii) by 'enslaving' himself, and iii) by 'saving some'?

Most commentators recognize that Paul's use of ἐλεύθερος looks back to 9:1. Lietzmann sees this as a direct continuation of 8:13 and 9:1 and regards what lies between as an excursus. Thus Paul 'kehrt zu dem Thema von 8.9-13, der Rücksichtnahme auf die Schwachen, zurück'.[169] Although we have not regarded 9:1-18 as an excursus, support is given to the link with ch 8 by the reference in 9:22 to the 'weak', but that verse also highlights a point of discussion: in vv 19-23 was Paul speaking about Christians or non-Christians? The use of the two verbs κερδαίνω

---

165   Käsemann, "Amor" 230.
166   Cf Richardson, *Ethic*, and "Inconsistency", with the response in Carson, "Inconsistency".
167   Bornkamm, "Stance".
168   Fee 423.
169   Lietzmann 43-44.

and σῴζω might suggest he now refers to non-Christians, but his mention of the 'weak' in v 22 suggests Christians.

In section 3.2 we argued that ἐλεύθερος in 9:1a needed to be understood in the context of 7:22-24,[170] that Paul was free ἐν κυρίῳ (7:22) and that freedom was *contrary* to appearances. However, 6:12 is also significant in helping to interpret Paul's meaning here in 9:19. In 6:12, as in 10:23, Paul quoted a Corinthian slogan: Πάντα μοι ἔξεστιν, and he used the verb ἐξουσιάζω for the first time. The verb reappears twice in ch 7 and the noun is used eight times in chs 7 to 9.[171] Most commentators have pointed to an apparent 'play on words' in 6:12 between ἔξεστιν and ἐξουσιασθήσομαι,[172] but they have overlooked the possibility that οὐκ ἐγώ ἐξουσιασθήσομαι lays the basis for Paul's discussion of ἐξουσία in chs 8 and 9.[173]

The ἔξεστιν of the catch phrase in 6:12 and 10:23 is less dogmatic than the ἐξουσία of chs 8 and 9 but already in 6:12 Paul was looking at the religious problem he faced in Corinth:[174] the danger of becoming 'enslaved' or 'overpowered' by insisting on an ἐξουσία. Both chs 8 and 9 make good sense in the light of the phrase οὐκ ἐγώ ἐξουσιασθήσομαι. In ch 9 Paul's analogy, as we have analysed it, shows an apostle refusing to be enslaved by what people expect of him. If an ἐξουσία were allowed to function as a 'marker' of membership, a person would be 'enslaved' to it. That is, without it they would not be *seen* to be members of the group. What started off as 'being permitted' for a 'free' person has become an object of enslavement. Ellicott summarises 6:12 well:

What the Apostle says is, that the ἐξουσία of the Christian must never so be used that the matter or practice to which it extends prove in the sequel to

170 Cf Bornkamm, "Stance" 196.

171 Also 11:10; 15:24.

172 E.g. Godet I 305; Allo 141. Most note the repetition of the phrase in 10:23 without developing the links.

173 But cf Bachmann 259; Richardson, *Ethic* 54. Fee 252, establishes a link between 6:12 and chs 8-9, but once again stresses that this is part of the confrontation between Paul and the Corinthians. This is not the 'crisis of authority' Fee suggests. Cf Barrett 216: Paul 'addresses his readers as ... one who stands with, not over against them'.

174 Dupont, *Gnosis* 282-321 examines the relationship between ἐξουσία and ἐλεύθερος, and the possible backgrounds for the concepts. On 6:12 he concludes: 'La formule ... de 1 Cor., VI, 12 suffirait à montrer combien Paul est au courant des thèmes de la morale populaire; il en connaît la terminologie et il en pénètre l'esprit'. The evidence for this position is considerable and much of it appears in other commentaries. Cf Conzelmann 108-110, 158-159 etc; Weiss 243. But see criticism of Dupont and Weiss in Schmithals, *Gnosticism* 230-233.

be of over-mastering influence; the free, must not become the fettered, will.[175]

Whether Paul had in mind men or things in his use of ἐκ πάντων in 9:19 is not clear. Either alternative makes sense. On the one hand Paul is free from men who wish to see him exercise his ἐξουσία, on the other, he is not enslaved by his ἐξουσία, but is able to subordinate it to the calling. A comparison with 7:17-24 also leaves the matter open. There Paul exhorts the Corinthians not to become δοῦλοι ἀνθρώπων, but the context shows that Paul means no one should be enslaved to the ideas of men — such as the necessity of circumcision. Each person should remain in his 'calling' (7:17-18).

Paul's 'freedom' in 9:19 is best understood in this light.[176] His 'enslaving' himself thus has to do with his calling, that is, with the divine ἀνάγκη to which he referred in the previous verses. His calling forbids his becoming a slave to men and their ideas, but insists that all be done to further the proclamation of the Gospel (vv 16b-18, 23). His enslavement to 'all men' (v 19) is, therefore, very carefully qualified. It is not that he will do whatever they demand of him — the whole point of the analogy is that he will not — but he is willing to accommodate himself in 'practical conduct'[177] in order to 'win' more people.

Of the verb κερδαίνω Fee says, 'Such language, as the interchange with "save" in v 22b makes clear, can only refer to evangelizing'.[178] Similarly, Bornkamm believed that vv 19-23 were an indication of Paul's 'missionary practice'.[179] But does κερδαίνω, or even the corresponding σῴζω (v 22), require that Paul be talking about his behaviour among *non*-Christians? Daube's work on this has been influential.[180] He argues that κερδαίνω refers to conversion. However, after study of the possible Hebrew background to the word, he acknowledges that the usual meanings are 'gathering in', 'gaining advantage', 'profit', and the 'gaining by God of men whom he had cast

---

[175]   Ellicott 103. Cf Ruef 49.

[176]   This freedom neither concerns Paul's Roman citizenship (*contra* Morris 138), nor his freedom from people gained by 'plying a trade' (*contra* Hock, "Tentmaking" 558-559). Parallels between Paul's use of the concept of freedom and popular philosophy or Stoicism have been examined in detail elsewhere. Our concern here is to see how freedom, slavery etc. function in this part of *Paul's* correspondence, rather than examining how current such concepts may have been in popular philosophy. (See n 174 above. On popular philosophy of freedom see Freidrich, "Freiheit".)

[177]   Bornkamm, "Stance" 203.

[178]   Fee 427. Wolff II 31: 'κερδαίνω ist Ausdruck der Missionssprache', also Weiss 243.

[179]   Bornkamm, "Stance" 194-198.

[180]   Daube, *Judaism* 336-351.

away'.[181] He suggests κερδαίνω came to mean 'convert' via Aramaic, but he offers no clear evidence of any background to κερδαίνω which implies the conversion of *outsiders*.

In Matthew 18:15 the word is used of winning back God's people, while in 1 Peter 3:1 it may refer to the conversion of non-Christian husbands. However, it seems to us that in 1 Corinthians 9 commentators have over-emphasised the division between these two ideas. The context concerns an analogy centred on apostolic ἐξουσία. In vv 15-18 Paul had shown that he subordinated everything to the proclamation of the gospel — the very point made by the summary of vv 19-22 in v 23a. This was the apostolic commission, but that work was never just a matter of conversion. The very existence of Paul's epistles demonstrates that part of the commission consisted in building up those already converted. The message of Christ crucified did not simply demand some existentialist decision but, as Paul showed very clearly in the Corinthian correspondence, it had to form the basis of the on-going life of the church.[182] We suggest that in the context of apostolic work, therefore, κερδαίνω can be understood to refer *both* to initial entrance into the community (conversion), *and* to the continuing process of winning people from inadequate ideas to a deeper Christian consciousness.[183]

This possibility becomes even more likely, later, when we examine 10:31-33. The parallels with 9:19-23 are clear. Paul's aim (v 33) was to seek the benefit (σύμφορον— cf 6:12) of the many (τῶν πολλῶν) ... ἵνα σωθῶσιν (cf 9:22b). But when we look at the groups which Paul had in mind, they included Jews and Greeks (10:32; cf 9:20, 21), but *also* the ἐκκλησία τοῦ θεοῦ.[184] Finally, it must also be noted that 'salvation' for Paul was a much broader concept than conversion alone — a point that requires no further development here.[185] .

3.4.2   Paul's accommodation to others

The structure of vv 19-23 has been discussed in detail by Bornkamm.[186] It is not chiastic[187] but vv 19 and 22b-23 enclose the

181   The Hebrew words he examines are *'Kanas'* (Op cit 352-354); *'Qana'* (354-355); *'Sakhar'* (355-360).

182   Cf Murphy-O'Connor 91.

183   Cf Carson, "Inconsistency" 14.

184   Cf Richardson, *Israel* 123.

185   Paul's use of the words σωτηρία and σῴζω demonstrates that 'salvation' concerned the eschatological destiny of the people of God, as well as initial conversion. Cf 2 Cor 1:6; 6:1-3; 2:15; 1 Cor 1:18-21; I Thess 5:8-9; etc. Cf Bornkamm, *Paul passim*, esp ch IV and 196-200; Furnish, *Theology* 122-135; Sanders, *PPJ* 447-474; *inter al.*

186   Bornkamm, "Stance" 194-195.

187   *Contra* Willis, "Apologia" 38.

section by stating in both places the thrust of Paul's argument that, for the sake of the gospel, he became 'all things to all men'[188] in order to 'win/save' people. The play on the word πᾶς stresses his point.[189]

In vv 20-22a Paul lists three groups of people:[190] Jews, those outside the law, and the weak. In each case a ἵνα clause shows Paul's purpose in accommodating to them. There is no need to distinguish between 'Jews' and 'those under the Law' as we shall see. The latter is part of Paul's immediate and necessary qualification of what he has said.

Dodd asked how Paul could 'become as a Jew' (v 20) when he was already a Jew[191] and believed that v 20b removed the ambiguity. Paul distinguished between voluntarily submitting to the Jewish Torah,[192] which he was prepared to do when preaching the gospel, and Jews who were obliged to obey the Torah. Paul had relinquished that obligation in accepting the freedom of the gospel.

Conzelmann says of v 20 that Paul 'is able as a Jew to practice Jewish customs, without teaching that the Law is a way of salvation'.[193] But, following Sanders *et al*, we consider this an inaccurate assessment of Jewish theology. Salvation was not attained by Law but *evidenced* through obedience to it.[194] However, Dodd and Conzelmann are right to

---

[188] On this text cf Chadwick, "All Things".

[189] V 19: ...πάντων πᾶσιν. V 22b ...πᾶσιν ... πάντα, ἵνα πάντως ... V 23 πάντα ...

[190] So most commentators, e.g. Dodd, "Ἔννομος Χριστοῦ" 134-135; Murphy O'Connor 89; Black, "Weak" 240; Fee 428-429.

Some argue for four separate groups. Ruef 84: 1) Jews (not Christians). 2) Those under the Law (Jewish Christians). 3) Those outside the law (Gentiles). 4) The weak (Gentile Christians with a pagan world view). Cf Olshausen 151; Richardson, "Ethics" 95.

[191] Dodd, "Ἔννομος Χριστοῦ".

[192] Ibid 134-135. Dodd says that νόμος in v 20 can only mean Torah.

[193] Conzelmann 160.

[194] It is clearly impossible to discuss Jewish soteriology here. However, Sanders (*PPJ* 33-59) *et al* have forcefully insisted that the Protestant-Lutheran assessment of Judaism has been misconceived. This view has argued that Judaism taught that salvation was achieved through 'works'. Sanders (*PPJ* 147-182) considers this pattern to be incorrect. Rather (p 180) 'The pattern is this: God has chosen Israel and Israel has accepted the election. In his role as King, God gave Israel commandments which they are to obey as best they can. Obedience is rewarded and disobedience punished. In case of failure to obey, however, man has recourse to divinely ordained means of atonement, in all of which repentance is required. As long as he maintains his desire to stay in the covenant, he has a share in God's covenantal promises, including life in the world to come. The intention and effort to be obedient constitute the *condition for remaining in the covenant*, but they do not *earn* it'. Also cf Moore *Judaism* esp II 94-95; Sandmel, *First Century*; Montefiore, *Judaism*; Wright, *MPG* 89ff.

say that Paul's caveat, μὴ ὢν αὐτὸς ὑπὸ νόμον, has to do with the way he allows the law to *function*. The word ὡς is important in v 20. Paul distinguished between being '*as* under the law' and not himself actually *being* under the law.[195] The issue is, as we have suggested throughout our exegesis of chs 8 and 9, a *religious* one. Paul was not 'under the law' as an obligatory *religious* demand.[196] This becomes clear if we recognise that 'Those under the law' (v 20b) is a further description of 'the Jews'. Paul no longer *had* to be a Jew to be one of God's people. The important issue is the law.[197] Paul no longer has a 'relationship to God which is *evidenced* by *possession* of the law'.[198] He can and will 'enslave' (δουλόω — v 19) himself to the Law when among Jews, but will not allow it to function as a compulsory 'marker' of his relationship with God. In this sense he is not *under* the Law, but rather the Law is at his disposal to use *appropriately* to further the cause of the gospel.[199] Paul is, of course, *under* Christ — a point he makes in the next verse. Thus his illustration of what he does among Jews is easily understood. 'Paul no longer recognises as such the *religious* positions of the groups described',[200] but is free deliberately to change his practice rather than hinder the gospel.

Several commentators have drawn attention to the fact that Paul is carefully handling a *religious* problem in vv 19-23. Conzelmann, Dodd and Bornkamm have been mentioned, and Fee says that Paul 'had no problem with Jews' continuing to follow Jewish practices 'as long as they were not considered to give people a right standing with God'.[201] Whilst agreeing with these scholars, we believe they have misunderstood the *nature* of that religious problem. Paul was not objecting to Jews achieving salvation by law — although he would have done so if confronted by it — rather he was stating that the law was not

---

Sander's work has been criticised (cf Neusner "Judaisms") but see also his "Puzzling". On the subject of religious ideas in Judaism in NT times see Green, *Approaches*; Kraft, *Judaism* (esp the Introduction and the article by Saldarini: "Reconstructions" 437-477).

[195] 'The context shows clearly that νόμος here means the Mosaic law', Robertson 191; Barrett 212; (cf 9:8-9). It is possible that proselytes are in mind, cf Robertson loc cit; Lietzmann 44.

[196] Cf Black, "Weak" 240.

[197] Fee 427.

[198] Sanders, *PPJ* 550 (his emphasis).

[199] We note with Bornkamm, ("Stance" 197-198) that 'The freedom of his service is not a matter of his discretion; it is a matter of his obedience to the gospel, so much so that his own eternal salvation is at stake'.

[200] Ibid 196 (our emphasis).

[201] Fee 428.

a 'marker' of salvation, just as taking money from the Corinthians was not a marker of apostleship.

His next example about conduct among Gentiles is necessary, if only to make the previous point more strongly. Paul is also prepared to be τοῖς ἀνόμοις ὡς ἄνομος (v 21). Conzelmann asks, 'Why does Paul not say, "to the Greeks?". (This would balance τοῖς Ἰουδαίοις in v 20.) His observation is important and suggests that Paul may not have simply been offering parallel examples of his different behaviour. We suggest that his choice of ἄνομοι rather than Ἕλληνες was deliberate because his concern was with the *law*. To those without or outside *the law* he became as (ὡς) one of them. He lived as one who did not regard Mosaic law as a religious requirement for salvation. Again, however, Paul needed to qualify his statement. He did so through an interesting word-play on νόμος and insisted that he was μὴ ὢν ἄνομος θεοῦ (balancing μὴ ὢν αὐτὸς ὑπὸ νόμον — v 20) but he was ἔννομος Χριστοῦ.

The meaning of ἔννομος Χριστοῦ is much debated, but Paul was not attempting to define the phrase here. Rather, the phrase provides his response to the potential accusation of complete lawlessness — *the mark of pagans*. Paul would not have his Christian status *defined* by his being ἄνομος, any more than he would by being ὑπὸ νόμον. He was not 'without God's law'. Paul was happy not to be identified by the Torah when among the Gentiles but would not thereby like to be identified as a *pagan*![202]

It is evident that Paul was neither *properly* Jew nor Gentile in the light of the two μή clauses. In fact, Paul took a third position which was defined by his allegiance to Christ (v 21b). Paul could be 'like' either group in order not to put up unnecessary barriers to the gospel, but he would not do anything that made the possession or lack of possession of the law the determinative marker. He was always to be seen to be ἔννομος Χριστοῦ.

Dodd maintains that ἔννομος Χριστοῦ refers to a 'law of Christ' which is not against the Torah but is a different expression of the 'law of God'.[203] To be under the law of Christ is to carry out 'the precepts which Jesus Christ was believed to have given to his disciples'.[204] However, this is too restrictive and, as Conzelmann[205] and Fee [206] both note, seems to be out of line with Paul's normal use of νόμος. More probably Paul was still thinking of the ἀνάγκη, the compulsion to serve by preaching.

---

[202] Dodd, "Ἔννομος Χριστοῦ." 135 n 2, is right to draw attention to the 'wider sense' of the word ἄνομος and compares 1 Tim 1:9 where 'It is equated with ἀνυπότακτος and explicated in a typical list of heathen vices and crimes.'

[203] Ibid 137. Cf Rom 8:2; Gal 6:2.

[204] Ibid 147.

[205] Conzelmann 161 n 27.

[206] Fee 430 n 44.

The gospel centre is Christ. Christ is also the goal or end of the law for Paul.[207] It is possible that, mindful of ideas like this, Paul was thinking quite broadly about obedience to Christ in his day to day service,[208] an obedience evidenced in love.

Thus, we suggest that in vv 20-21 Paul was primarily concerned to show the parameters within which he was prepared to accommodate both Jew and Gentile. The play on the word νόμος highlights this, especially given that both caveats (the μή clauses) have to do with the law. Paul would accommodate his behaviour to the Jew under the law and to the Gentile with no law *but*, when doing this, he would not allow either νόμος or ἄνομος to become a marker to the community of his status before God.

It is for this reason that, in the next verse, Paul was able to say without caveats that he was 'weak to the weak'. The weak were those who recognised the possibility of stumbling, or who had stumbled, on some marker (such as γνῶσις — ch 8) to which others had insisted they conform.[209] As such demands were considered ill-founded by Paul, he was *always* going to be on the side of the weak. If this is correct, then it means that Paul rejected antinomian, libertarian behaviour (ch 8), because the 'strong' Corinthians believed it demonstrated that such people were 'known by God' (8:3). It also means that Paul was able, *consistently* with this, to reject Judaising practices in which Torah obedience and circumcision were believed to function in the same way. Paul undoubtedly had other criteria for rejecting certain behaviour,[210] but this was an important aspect of his religious understanding.

Verse 22 speaks of the weak, linking Paul's application to the discussion of ch 8.[211] The word ὡς is omitted and there is no caveat entered.[212] The three groups are therefore not grammatically parallel.

---

207 Rom 10:4. Barrett 213-215, writes extensively on this phrase, linking the 'law of Christ' with love (Rom 8:2; 13:8-10), and with Paul's view of Christ as the 'end of the law'.

208 So Kümmel 180: 'die Formulierung ἔννομος Χριστοῦ ist durch den Parallelismus verursacht und besagt nur "Christus gegenüber zum Gehorsam verpflichtet"'. Cf Conzelmann 161 n 27. Kümmel's criticism of Lietzmann 44 (that thoughts of a new covenant are 'alien' to the text) is unwarranted.

209 This much about the weak is reasonably evident given the continuity of subject matter in chs 8 and 9. We have not tried to argue above that these weak were of Jewish origin, not yet emancipated from legalism (Barrett 215). They were unlikely to be 'non-Christians, presumably of Jewish origin' (Dodd, Ἔννομος Χριστοῦ 134).

210 See later Paul's rejection of eating idol meat in idol temples.

211 A link is further suggested by the repetition of πάντα.

212 Various mss (ℵ2, C, D, F, Maj. *inter al*) have added ὡς to bring the text into line with vv 20-21. Its omission has strong support from p46, ℵ*, A, B, *inter al*.

This, we suggest, is because Paul did become 'weak to the weak' in a way that was not *directly* parallel to his behaviour mentioned in vv 20-21. Bornkamm rightly says, 'Significantly, Paul cannot say to the "strong" that he became strong'.[213] Verse 22 thus appears to be fundamental to what Paul was saying in chs 8-10. In ch 8, Paul sided with the weak *against* the 'strong', and so also here in 9:22. Paul had indeed been 'weak to the weak'. This was the stance of an apostle who would never put a stumbling block in the way of the gospel.

In the light of this discussion, we are further convinced that Paul was using κερδαίνω and σώζω in a broader sense than simply 'conversion'. Paul's practice of accommodation suited his work among Christians as much as it suited his work among pagans. But, from ch 8, the weak are more readily identified as Christians ('the brother'— 8:11).[214] It is surely possible that Paul's use of κερδαίνω and σώζω in v 22 had *this* stumbling and destruction in mind.[215] The weak needed to be won from the potential results of the teaching of the 'strong': destruction (8:10). Paul identified with them entirely in their rejection of the teaching of the 'strong' but, unlike him, they remained vulnerable to being persuaded (8:10).

While ch 8 was written against the 'strong', the analogy of ch 9 does speak indirectly to the weak as well.[216] Paul showed that an apostle's ἐξουσία was subject to his calling. The '*strong*' had to learn that this was how an ἐξουσία always *ought* to function. However, the weak were offered a theological underpinning to their position. In this sense Paul could 'save' them from destruction, not by having them become 'strong', but by showing them *why* they had no need to be tempted by the 'strong'. They did not *need* to regard spiritual gifts like γνῶσις as requisite markers. They had no need of boasting in such prerogatives.[217] They were members because of their *calling* — after all, they were weak when called (1:27b-31).[218] Paul was thus prepared to be identified as 'weak' (cf 4:10) in a way that he was not prepared to be identified as 'under law' or 'lawless'.

---

213   Bornkamm, "Stance" 203.

214   See Olshausen 152; Wendland 68; Murphy-O'Connor 90-91.

215   *Contra* Black "Weak" 241.

216   Παντῶς (v 22) may mean 'at any rate'. Cf *P Wisconsin* 55.1 cited in *New Docs* 2 92: ἀλλὰ πάντως σήμ[ε]π[ον].

217   Bornkamm, "Stance" 197.

218   Conzelmann 160: 'every man is addressed by God as the man he is in his κλῆσις, "calling"'.

The summary statement of v 23a could not be clearer,[219] but the purpose clause ἵνα συγκοινωνὸς ... (v 23b) is more ambiguous.[220] The previous six purpose clauses in vv 19-22 have to do with Paul's purpose concerning *others* being saved, while this one seems to be more self-interested. Schütz suggests that Paul has in mind sharing 'in the gospel's *own* work' and his reward 'comes in sharing in the effectiveness of the gospel'.[221] This clearly shows a link with the preceding purpose clauses, where Paul wanted to see people saved. In the last clause he wanted to share in the work of the gospel: they 'are two ways of saying the same thing'.[222]

However, most scholars agree with Godet, that this clause means something like 'partaking with all other believers in the blessings which it confers, and in those which it promises'.[223] Paul here stood with his readers.[224] He did not anticipate participating with them in the gospel blessings because of some particular ἐξουσία, but because of his submission to God's calling. If we have understood correctly the religious problem Paul faced in Corinth, then the word συγκοινωνὸς makes good sense. The problem of the 'strong' lay in their belief that they were assured of 'joint participation with others' in the present and eschatological blessings of the gospel. Paul's analogy demonstrated that the basis of assurance cannot be the implementation of a particular ἐξουσία. In v 23 Paul showed that actually giving-up his ἐξουσία was leading to this συγκοινωνία.

The analogy is now complete. Unlike the 'strong', Paul had no false sense of security based on his own ἐξουσία, rather he was obedient to the divine will which was seen in his love for those among whom he ministered. His accommodation was not unconditional but sought to avoid putting a stumbling block in the way of the gospel. The next four verses remind the readers that Paul himself had to work hard at fulfilling his call correctly if he was to reach the eschatological 'reward'. We shall see that vv 24-27 emphasize the work needed to implement the lessons learned from Paul's analogy.

---

[219]   διὰ τὸ εὐαγγέλιον means 'for the sake of the Gospel', Barrett 216. That is, Paul does all things on account of the divine commission laid on him to preach.

[220]   Weiss 246 believes the ἵνα clause may be 'von einem Sammler und Redaktor'.

[221]   Schütz, *Authority* 52.

[222]   Loc cit.

[223]   Godet II 42. Cf Bornkamm, "Stance" 197; Robertson 193; *RSV*; *NIV*.

[224]   Barrett 216.

3.4.3   An imperishable crown

In vv 24-27 Paul summarised and applied his message. The Corinthian 'strong' seemed to assume that they all 'shared in the gospel' and would receive the prize. They believed they were secure in their possession of γνῶσις.[225] While it is clear that Paul wanted the Corinthians to apply this metaphor of the race to themselves (οὐκ οἴδατε ...), the continuing use of the first person singular in vv 26-27 reveals that he was still referring to the analogy of the earlier verses[226] and his personal struggle.

The metaphors from the games have been discussed elsewhere.[227] In vv 24-25 they form the background for Paul's imperative: τρέχετε.[228] The picture is clear. There is an 'imperishable' prize for which all should strive, as Paul himself has done.[229] Paul's readers needed to realize the difficulties in exercising self-control. For Paul this had meant giving up the ἐξουσία that appeared to be attached to the calling. On this verse Pfitzner is correct in saying that it is 'Not the thought of maximum exertion but rather the theme of self-restriction ... [that] dominates in Paul's mind'.[230]

Paul's example came from apostleship and its ἐξουσία. He was not suggesting that the 'strong' copy him in specific actions. But they should have the same attitude to *their* ἐξουσία as he to his. They must not be enslaved by it (cf 6:12), but should 'exercise mastery over'[231] themselves in all things (πάντα — v 25). The use of πάντα suggests the link with vv 19-23. The 'race' was not just about good moral behaviour but about completing what had been started. It does seem at least possible, therefore, that this metaphor arose out of the use of ἐγκοπή which we discussed earlier. In section 3.3.1 it was noted that ἐγκοπή could refer to an obstacle in a race. It clearly contains the idea of something being stopped from attaining its goal.

---

[225] It is commonly held that these verses in ch 9 must be understood in the light of Corinthian over-confidence in the *sacraments*. There is no evidence for this unless the subject changes most suddenly. Among those mentioning a problem with sacraments in these verses see Barrett 217; Whiteley, *Theology* 172-173; Fee 432. Willis, "Apologia" 39, mentions 'over-confidence' but does not, at this point, attribute it to the sacraments.

[226] See discussion of μισθός, above 3.3.4.

[227] Weiss 247-248; Pfitzner, *Agon* esp ch 5; Wolff II 34.

[228] Pfitzner, *Agon* 83 regards ἐγκράτεια as the 'central point of the image'. This depends on taking τρέχετε as indicative rather than imperative.

[229] Πυκτεύω can be used for boxing and gladiatorial combat (see *New Docs 4* 19).

[230] Pfitzner, *Agon* 87; *Contra* Weiss 248.

[231] Barrett 217.

The 'imperishable crown' is an eschatological prize.[232] Paul's 'pommelling' of his body recalls the πάντα στέγομεν of v 12b. Thus again Paul may have been referring to difficulties experienced in giving-up the apostolic ἐξουσία of material benefit or, more broadly, to the troubles listed in 4:9-13. In view of our understanding of μισθός (above) and the argument of 9:15-18, Paul was probably still addressing his own personal goal that had to be achieved without his ἐξουσία and in response to the ἀνάγκη. The ἀνάγκη was to preach, and it was to this that he returned at the end of v 27. The metaphor has changed, but his 'disqualification' (ἀδόκιμος) recalls the thought of the 'Woe' of v 16.

Chapters 8-9 have indicated that if the 'strong' caused others to stumble, the weak were in danger of destruction. Paul also maintained that the stumbling block the 'strong' put up would lead to their own sinning. As a climax to this application, in 9:27 Paul showed that if he failed to carry out his commission by putting obstacles in the way of the gospel, then even he could be disqualified. Paul thus ended this section where he began in 8:13 — talking of his own behaviour, not defensively, but offering it as an example.

3.5   Conclusions

Discussions about ch 9 have often centred on the nature of Paul's ethic of accommodation. Just how Paul practised the ideas presented in vv 19-23 is interesting but tracing this has not been our purpose. Ours has been limited to seeing how his argument progressed, how it related to chapter 8, and how the analogy functioned.

In ch 9 Paul discussed the place and function of an ἐξουσία in the life of a community. For Paul it had to be subordinate to God's calling. This subject was raised in ch 8 and many ways have been noted in which ch 9 is an extension of that argument. Chapter 9 is neither misplaced, nor properly called an 'excursus'.[233]

The suggestion that Paul was involved in direct confrontation with the Corinthians is unpersuasive. The *rhetorical* questions indicate a position that would have been accepted by the Corinthians. They affirm two main points:
i)   Paul was indeed an apostle and 'free'. That freedom was ἐν κυρίῳ and thus did not lead to indiscriminate behaviour.
ii)   Paul therefore had apostolic ἐξουσία defined here in terms of material support. Paul stressed both these points as the premises for the analogy that he wished to make.

---

232   Cf Fee 437: 'the Christian's "crown" is not some specific aspect of the goal but the eschatological victory itself'.
233   3.1 above.

It is possible that the subject matter of the analogy was particularly appropriate to the Corinthians who wished to 'boast' in their apostle as he flaunted his status. It was undoubtedly appropriate in that it clarified what Paul meant when he talked of a 'hindrance' to the gospel. Taking pay would have obscured both the message of *grace*, and the divine origin of the message preached through ἀνάγκη.

Unlike those who see this section as an example of Paul relinquishing things to which he was entitled, or as a simple contrast between the behaviour of the inconsiderate 'strong' and that of the 'loving' Paul, we believe Paul was concerned with a) the *function* of ἐξουσία and b), the truth about community authentication. For this, he needed a strong and widely agreed proposition so that the Corinthians would follow his logic. We suggest the analogy is to be seen in the following way:

i)   the background: the Corinthians were 'spiritually' evaluating each other 'before the Lord comes' (4:5)[234] and were doing so by looking at the ἐξουσία derived from a person's γνῶσις.[235] This, they believed, authenticated their standing before God.[236]

ii)   the illustration: Paul was an apostle and possessed a consequent *apostolic* ἐξουσία.

Therefore, he asked the Corinthians to judge him and evaluate his position. He began by offering an ἀπολογία for his apostleship. This he did by showing that he had a certain ἐξουσία. In other words, he appealed to his ἐξουσία (which the Corinthians granted he had) in order to confirm his apostleship. This was a *Corinthian* style of argument (ἐξουσία confirming status). The point of this became clear in 9:12ff, when Paul demonstrated the fallacy of the argument with regard to apostleship and thus pointed towards the fallacy of such an argument with regard to normal Christian life.

Diagrammatically we can show the position of the 'strong' like this:

1.   Corinthian Christians with gift of γνῶσις
                        ἐξουσία from γνῶσις

                                │

                        eat idol meat

                                │

                therefore are *proved* to be Christians
                    (will 'stand' before God)

---

[234]   An evaluation that, in effect, disbarred people from full community privileges.

[235]   See interpretation of 8:3 above.

[236]   See interpretation of 8:8 and 10 above.

To this Paul responded with an analogy that he built up in vv 1-12a and
vv 13-14:

2.   Paul with gift of apostleship
                     ἐξουσία from apostleship

                              |

                     takes material support

                              |

                therefore is *proved* to be an apostle

In v 12b and vv 15ff, Paul showed that such a pattern was unacceptable
in the case of apostleship. It was therefore *also* unacceptable as a
religious pattern for the Corinthian 'strong'.

Paul's position, (below) was that he was an apostle by divine
commission. He was not preaching the gospel of his own accord — from
within himself (ἐκών). His 'boast' was actually in his ἀνάγκη (which is
ἄκων) which comes from God. Rather than taking pride in human
possessions or achievements, Paul took pride in what God had done.
This better explains what Paul said than trying to make the ἐκών —
ἄκων contrast into a 'voluntary' or 'involuntary' submission to God.

Diagrammatically we can portray Paul's own position like this:

3.   Paul *called* to be an apostle

                              |

                compelled by God to preach the gospel
                           (ἀνάγκη)

                              |

                therefore is *proved* to be an apostle

                              |

                     ἐξουσία from apostleship
                     can take material benefit

                              |

                ἐξουσία always subordinated to calling

In interpreting vv 19-21 we have suggested that the three examples
employed are not directly parallel. Paul's accommodation to the first two
groups was hedged with the word ὡς and important caveats. The point at
which Paul would not accommodate further was precisely at the point
that he had been driving towards throughout this chapter — when certain

actions or life-styles took on a *religious* significance. If Paul found himself *defined* as being 'under the law' he would insist he was not. If some began to *define* him as ἄνομος, he pointed to the law he was under. However, to the weak he really was weak. His behaviour to them was one of love and care, but more than that: their recognition of 'stumbling blocks' was theologically correct. Paul agreed with the complaint of the weak. He did not urge them to become 'strong', because the 'strong' were wrong. At most Paul wanted them, in their weakness, not to be vulnerable to the temptations of the false teaching of the 'strong'.

This interpretation allows us to do full justice to Paul's understanding that the call to a Christian life is a call to the way of the cross — a call to weakness (1:26-31; 2:3-5; 3:18-21; 4:9-13; 2 Corinthians 4:7-12, 17-18; 11:29-30 etc). It was thus Paul's weakness to the weak, his love for them, that was evidence of his participation in the community formed by the gospel. Paul's introduction of the word συγκοινωνός demonstrated that community aspect of the message he preached.

The last four verses of this chapter are a reminder that 'he has applied all this to himself for the benefit of the Corinthians' (cf 4:6). Just as Paul had to work out the relationship of his apostolic ἐξουσία to his calling in difficult situations, ensuring that he did not become 'enslaved' to the ἐξουσία (cf 6:12), so the 'strong' would have to do the same. Paul had to do it lest he suffer disqualification. This very possibility of disqualification was acute for the 'strong' (cf 8:12), so in ch 10 it is that specific issue which is addressed.

4. Let Him Who Thinks He Stands Take Heed ...

Exegesis of 1 Corinthians 10 - 11:1

In moving from 1 Corinthians 9 to ch 10, some source critics have argued that there is a change from letter B (ch 9 — or parts of it) to letter A (ch 10:1-23).[1] Below it is argued that ch 10 follows logically from both chs 8 and 9.[2] The issue of status in the community of God's people, and how such standing is authenticated, remains the primary concern of Paul's message. This is indicated in v 12 which is the central challenge of the text. As noted, in chs 8 and 9 there is a problem with the 'strong' who 'think they stand'. They think this, we have argued, because of their possession of God's spiritual gifts, especially γνῶσις.

The narrative of the Israelites in the wilderness was an excellent example for Paul to use. Like the Corinthians, the Israelites had relied on God's *gifts*. They thought they were 'standing' but, in fact, fell and were destroyed. The example was even more satisfactory given that the point at which the Israelites 'fell' had to do with idolatry — the 'stumbling block' of ch 8.

An exegesis of vv 1-2 leads into questions about the function of the Exodus events in Paul's argument. An examination of the WT in pre-Christian Jewish literature helps resolve these questions. We turn to those traditions for two purposes. Firstly, they offer a background for understanding specific words and phrases such as 'our fathers' and 'in the cloud'. Secondly, and more importantly, we examine the traditions in a deliberately *broad* overview. This reveals that they have a surprisingly consistent *paraenetic* function. It is the *functional* parallels between 1 Corinthians 10:1-14 and earlier accounts of the WT which prove a most satisfactory aid in the interpretation of the Pauline text.

---

[1]   Cf Weiss; Schmithals, *Gnosticism*; also others mentioned in ch 1 above. Cf Hurd 45.

[2]   Cum Robertson, Barrett, Conzelmann, Fee, *inter al.* Willis, *Apologia* 39, shows how many 'word links' there are between chs 8, 9 and 10, e.g. ἐλεύθερος, ἐξουσία, πάντες, μετέχειν etc. He also lists some thematic links.

4.1   Typology

Paul's approach to Scripture is raised in the text itself with his use of the word τύπος (vv 6, 11).[3] The framework surrounding this approach is to be seen, in part, in the passage. Firstly, for Paul there was a definite and providential correspondence between the old and the new events (πρὸς νουθεσίαν ἡμῶν — v 11).[4] Secondly, he saw the significance of the relationship between old and new as for those 'upon whom the ends of the ages have come' (v 11). The OT was being viewed by Paul from the perspective of the messianic age — the age of Christ, 'the wisdom of God and the power of God' (1:24).[5] From this perspective 'hidden' realities were revealed (2:9-12, 16), for it was the age of the 'new covenant' in which the 'veil' was removed — even from the reading of the 'old covenant' — through Christ (2 Corinthians 3:6, 14-16).

Paul saw a correspondence between the attitude of the Israelites and that of the Corinthians towards the gifts God had given them. Thus Paul may be said to have used the OT as an 'example', or 'warning'. But these words fail adequately to convey Paul's attention to the providential, historical framework of revelation. From Scripture Paul showed a correspondence between old and new that was visible because God had now revealed how he worked in redemptive history. Paul's generation had received the revelation of Christ and, through him, was able to discern a deliberate purpose for the *present* of events providentially overseen by God in the past. All upon whom 'the ends of the ages have come' needed to learn from these events in the OT. This understanding was 'spiritual'.[6]

The Jewish view of history recorded in Scripture was dynamic. God was at work in and revealed himself in that history. That the Israelites in the wilderness were expected to see beyond their hunger and thirst *was* important — that is why many were destroyed in the wilderness.[7] It was also important for later generations that they, too, should respond correctly to God who still talked to them through those past events (Deuteronomy 8:1-3).

This process of interpretation is frequently termed 'typological' but that can mean little more than 'allegory'. Two principles of interpretation must not be neglected in this discussion. The first is that the original events, such as the Exodus, were important in themselves as

---

3   The problem also arises with Paul's use of the word 'spiritual'. See 4.4.1 below.
4   Cf Amsler, "Typologie" 118.
5   Hanson, *Studies* 97.
6   n 3 above.
7   Cf Num 11:1-23, 32-35; Deut 8:1-3 etc.

evidence of God's redemptive purposes among his people.[8] They should not be regarded as of 'secondary' importance.[9] The second is that later revelation from God was not always to be seen as a straight forward *application* of the events to a later generation in some 'spiritual' manner. Rather God revealed more about how things actually *were.* This new understanding of what happened *then* could now be shown providentially to parallel events of the day in which the reader lived. Woollcombe suggests that this is particularly evident in the Pauline corpus:

> Paul proceeded to show that the events ... directly corresponded to the events which he and his contemporaries were experiencing *because Christ was the prime mover in both* ... the historical pattern of the Old Covenant exactly corresponds to the historical pattern of the New Covenant, because both are the work of the Word and Wisdom of God.[10]

Goppelt argues likewise, 'Paul believed that the meaning of Scripture is only unlocked by faith in Christ'.[11] Goppelt calls this 'unlocking' 'typology' but says this of it,

> ... with Paul, typology is not a hermeneutical method to be used in a technical way ... It is a spiritual approach that reveals the connection ordained in God's redemptive plan between the relationship of God and man in the Old Testament and that relationship in the NT. ... Each points to the other and is interpreted by it, and thus they describe man's existence under the gospel.[12]

This somewhat general definition of 'typology' is well borne-out by 1 Corinthians 10. Our use of the word 'typology' must refer more to an *attitude* or approach to Scripture than to any particular *application* of Scripture.

This is an attitude that expects new revelation — through Christ himself in the NT — to reveal a greater understanding of events as they really *were.* It is not just an understanding that these events have a symbolic or analogical use for us today. Thus, for Paul, his understanding of the WT, as we shall see below, showed him that Christ was present in the wilderness and gave gifts to the people but that they were still rejected. Once this has been understood, as for example in v

---

[8] Although, of course, the people often failed to recognise this or 'forgot' what God had done.

[9] *Contra* Ellis who says, 'Although the "type" has its own historical value, its real significance typologically is revealed only in the "anti-type" or fulfilment' (*Use* 128).

[10] Woollcombe, *Essays* 66: a position similar to what Ellis (*Prophecy* 166) calls 'covenant typology'.

[11] Goppelt, "Apocalypticism" 219.

[12] Ibid 223.

4c, *then* application may be made of this to Paul's generation. For Paul, even the writing down of these events had been overseen providentially so that people might be instructed.

It seems evident, therefore, that, in using the word τύπος (v 6) and τυπικῶς (v 11), Paul regarded the WT as more than an 'example' or 'pattern'[13] and more than simply a 'warning'.[14] After all, ταῦτα δὲ also looks *backwards* to vv 1-4 which are hardly 'warnings'.[15] The correspondence which Paul saw between the covenants must be reflected in our translation of the words concerned. This is why some have translated τύποι as 'types' (v 4).[16] While this word can have a variety of connotations when used in English, it remains perhaps the best translation if its content is understood bearing in mind the points made above.

Verses 1-13 reveal a structured piece of writing, possibly 'composed prior to its use in its present context'.[17] Some scholars regard these verses as 'midrash'.[18]

A definition of the term 'midrash' is also somewhat elusive. It can relate to a particular *genre* of literature or to a general attitude to Scripture. Both Wright[19] and Patte[20] have appealed for more specific definitions of both the word and *genre* than those found in Bloch's early work on the subject.[21] Patte describes two uses of the term 'midrash':

> a) at the *convictional level* where it will refer to the attitudes towards Scriptures, i.e., the hermeneutical axioms; b) at the '*symbolic*' level where it will refer to literary genres.[22]

When 'midrash' is defined as broadly as a 'written meditation on the significance of a passage of Scripture with a view to bringing out its full meaning',[23] then we are operating at Patte's convictional level, and apparently nothing is being said about *genre*. Used in this manner, 10:1-13 has to be 'midrash'.

13   *RV*; Robertson 203; Grosheide 223.
14   *RSV*; Hanson, *Jesus* 174; Ridderbos, *Paul* 419.
15   Davidson, *Typology* 253.
16   Amsler, "Typologie" 120; Schoeps, *Theology* 233; Goppelt, "Τύπος" 251-252; Ellis, *Use* 126; Murphy-O'Connor 95.
17   Meeks, "Midrash" 65.
18   Ellis, *Prophecy* 156 n 36; Hanson, *Studies* 206ff; Goppelt, *Typos* 218ff; Longenecker, *Exegesis* 118ff; *inter al.*
19   Wright, "Genre" 138.
20   Patte, *Hermeneutic* 315ff.
21   Bloch, "Midrash" 1265-1266, says that a midrash, as a means of communication, starts with Scripture, is homiletical, attentive to the text, practical in its goal, and adapted to the present.
22   Patte, *Hermeneutic* 316.
23   Hanson, *Studies* 205.

Ellis uses the word in both of Patte's senses.[24] He regards the *midrash* of 1 Corinthians 10 as 'Implicit midrash' and discerns a specific pattern:

"Implicit Midrash" (1-5, cf Ex 13.; Num 14,20) + Application (6) + Additional Text (7=Ex 32,6) + Exposition/Application, alluding to the preceding midrash and other texts (8-13).[25]

This view of the structure as beginning with 'Implicit Midrash' and leading to application and exposition is, we believe, adequate and is used as a basis for our exegesis.

Paul structured the paraphrased conflation of Scriptural texts in vv 1-5 around the emphatic use of the word πάντες. This is contrasted with the repetitive use of τινες in vv 6-10. The application section can be divided into two units (vv 6-10 and 11-13), each referring to the exegetical assumptions involved in the application. Verse 6 shows that the texts are relevant to contemporary events because they are τύποι ἡμῶν. Various allusions and one important additional text are then applied to the present situation. Verse 11 re-emphasises the 'typological' assumptions of the exegesis before making a more general application in vv 12-13.

In summary, this text is structured in a way that is commonly described as 'midrash'. The phrase 'typological midrash', therefore, adequately describes 1 Corinthians 10:1-13. By this we mean that there is apparently a formal style in a structured text, and that a particular approach to Scripture is indicated. This approach was not new for it had been seen in other Jewish literature, but it was new in that the revelation in Scripture was to be understood *in Christ* who brought the 'wisdom' to understand. The examination below of the word πνευματικός will confirm and clarify some of the points made above.

4.2   Cloud, sea and baptism (Verses 1 - 2)

Still addressing the 'strong',[26] Paul turned to biblical evidence to make his case that even they could stumble and fall. The first two verses are primarily intended to establish the fact that *all* the Israelites, to whose story Paul appeals, were indeed covenant community members.

---

[24]   Ellis, *Prophecy* 151-162ff, esp 151-152. He refers to interpretative renderings of the Hebrew text as 'implicit midrash' and to formal "text+exposition" patterns as 'explicit midrash'. Under the former Ellis includes the LXX and the Aramaic Targums, under the latter, the rabbinic commentaries. Also *Use* esp 139ff.

[25]   Ellis, *Prophecy* 156 n 36.

[26]   A point borne out throughout the exegesis.

4.2.1   Our fathers

The litotes, 'I do not want you to be ignorant, brothers', draws attention to the subject matter.[27] Γάρ indicates the link with ch 9.

Some conclude that Οἱ πατέρες ἡμῶν refers generally to Christians in Corinth[28] whom Paul regarded as 'sons' of the OT men of faith.[29] Others believe this phrase is evidence that the 'strong' were comprised of converted Jews who were still being addressed in ch 10, as they had been in chs 8-9. 'Our fathers' would thus be racial in intent. There is no parallel in Paul's writings to such a statement. Σπέρμα Ἀβραάμ[30] together with the hope of salvation involved in the expression, is of a different order from the reference here in ch 10 to 'fathers ... most [of whom] were destroyed'.[31] Nevertheless, Paul probably took the phrase over from earlier Jewish WT where the phrase is common.[32] It certainly suited his purpose in accentuating the covenantal correspondence he was to develop between the Exodus events and the Corinthian church.

4.2.2   Through the sea and under the cloud

The phrases 'coming through the sea', and 'under the cloud' refer to the crossing of the Red Sea and God's protection which was seen in the cloud, but the clause 'they were baptised into Moses'[33] is problematic and has no Jewish parallels. The question asked by Gander, 'Parle-t-il du baptême?' is therefore appropriate.[34]

---

27   Cf 12:1; 2 Cor 1:8; 1 Thes 4:13.
28   Weiss 249; Lias 111.
29   Cf Paul's discussion of 'sons of Abraham' in Rom 4 and 9.
30   Rom 9:7.
31   So Meyer 281.
32   Sect 4.3 below.
33   A minor problem arises with the textual variant: ἐβαπτίσθησαν (aorist passive) and ἐβαπτίσαντο (aorist middle). ℵ and A and various Byzantine minuscules support the former, while a corrected p[46], B, and Maj support the latter. The textual evidence possibly is superior for the former. It is also more in tune with Pauline usage of the verb. (*Contra* Barrett 220, but with U B S, Nestle[26], and Metzger, *Commentary* 559).
34   Gander, "Baptême?". Gander's answer to his own question is that Paul is using an Aramaic text. A hellenistic scribe had wrongly read עמד ('baptise') when he should have read עמר ('to pass'). Thus vv 1-2 are parallel. 'Into Moses' has been added by analogy to 'baptised into Christ'. According to Gander this should have read '*sous la conduite* de Moïse, ils ont tous passé par la nuée et par la Mer (Rouge).' Gander's argument depends on Paul's reliance upon an Aramaic text. It is highly speculative in nature and, in view of Paul's use of the LXX in the same midrash, we believe it is unlikely to be correct. On Moses in this text see Démann "Moïse"; Jones, *Apostle*; Hanson "Moses". Also cf Teeple, *Prophet*.

There is widespread scholarly consensus that here 'baptism' refers to an OT 'type' of the NT 'sacrament'. In view of the discussion of the Lord's Supper in vv 14-22, it is assumed that the issue Paul faced was false reliance on the sacraments.[35] Therefore, in the example Paul used, some have suggested that 'passing through the Sea' and eating 'spiritual' food were regarded as sacramental types. It is argued that Paul showed that sacraments could not save because they did not save in the OT. Our own examination of the text suggests an alternative understanding of the passage.[36]

There is little doubt that the phrase 'baptised into Moses' was arrived at by analogy with 'baptism into Christ'.[37] But it is our view that uppermost in Paul's mind was not the sacrament and its abuse but the *result* of the initiatory rite: a community of people to which *all* belonged. This view is supported in a number of ways. Firstly, the emphasis given by the repeated πάντες in vv 1-2 suggests that Paul's concern was that the Corinthians should understand that *all* the people were identified as a single *community*.[38] Secondly, the phrase 'into Moses' quite specifically identified a particular group of people. This group *all* had the same experiences of God's protection through Moses and *all* received the same gifts. Thirdly, the experiences of being 'under

[35] Argued in detail in Bengel 638-639, and forcefully by Fee 442ff. The latter provides an interesting example of how much an understanding of vv 14-22 can be read back into vv 1-5 (e.g., 446 n 27). The following explain the opening verses in terms of sacramental typology of one form or another: Ellicott 174-176; Weiss 250; Meyer 281; Lietzmann 45-46; Schlatter, *Bote* 290; Allo 233; Senft 128-129; Barrett 220, 223-224 etc; Ridderbos, *Paul* 411; Bornkamm, "Herrenmahl" esp 317; von Soden, "Sakrament" 345-354; Conzelmann 165-167; Murphy-O'Connor 94-95; Käsemann, *Essays* 113-114, 116ff; Whiteley, *Theology* 172-173; Héring 84-85; Roetzel, *Letters* 85; *inter al.* Also see Dunn, *Baptism* 124 n 25.

[36] Thus we join the few commentators who also reject a sacramental interpretation of vv 1-5. Cf Schmithals, *Gnosticism* 394, who admits to a typological portrayal of sacraments but forcefully denies that 'sacramentalism' was the problem; Dunn, *Baptism* 124-127, denies there were sacraments for the Israelites but concludes: '*we* can regard them as "sacraments"' (127 our emphasis). Cf Willis 140-141; Malina, *Manna* 96-97 (who regards the 'sacramental' interpretation as a 'gratuitous assumption'); Sandelin *Nourisher* 161-172. Also cf Grosheide 218-223.

[37] Weiss 250. Moses is not a 'type' of Christ in this text.

[38] Possibly Paul was drawing on Jewish proselyte baptism which may have been linked with the wilderness period (cf Murphy-O'Connor, 94). But this is speculative deduction from anachronistic rabbinic material. Further on proselyte baptism in Jeremias, "Johannestaufe" 318-319; "Paulus als Hillelit" 90-91; Gavin, *Antecedents* 26-58. Cf Bandstra, "Interpretation" 6, also Friedrich, "Προφήτης" 837-838.

the cloud' and 'passing through the sea' both related to the *identification* of the children of Israel as a people now separated from Egypt, and under God's protection.[39]

Further, our case can be argued negatively. The 'sacraments' have not been an issue thus far in the letter.[40] The arrogance and over-confidence noted seems to have centred on the demonstration of an ἐξουσία — primarily, we have suggested, that related to γνῶσις (8:3). Also, as Massie indicates, there are several features of this section which 'are not quite harmonious with the alleged design of parallelism' with sacraments. For example, he mentions that there is no water or 'rock' in the Supper, and that in v 4 the idea that Christ=rock=living *water* is not present in the Supper.[41] As Malina rightly observes,

> the whole point of the ... proof in 10,1-11 is to point up the *kelal* principle in v 12 ... which is a variant of the same idea expressed in 9,27 — which is what Paul set out to prove in the first place.[42]

Thus, in using the phrase 'baptised into Moses', Paul was more concerned with the result of the rite than with the process of sacramental theology. 'Baptism' demonstrated allegiance and membership of a group. By using this term Paul emphasised not the sacrament but the parallel situation between two groups of people identified in a particular way.

It seems to us, therefore, that the emphasis of vv 1-2 sets a premise for Paul's argument: *all* were members of the group. Paul will contend that the 'strong' are in danger of falling. The emphasis on πάντες will not

---

[39] Ex 14:19-31; Ps 105:39. Also Neh 9:16-20; Ps 78:13-16; Wis 10:17. Cf Ruef 90.

[40] The word 'sacrament' is widely used by commentators on this text to refer to baptism or the Lord's Supper. However, the word is anachronistic and demonstrates a tendency by some commentators to assume links between these two rites and the mystery religions.

'Baptism' was mentioned in 1:13-15. There again the emphasis seems to be on the *identification* of some people with a particular group or leader. It is, of course, possible that the mystery religions and their understanding of initiation and cultic meals provide a background to a Corinthian view of 'baptism' or the 'Lord's Supper' (see pp 7-8, 17-19 above). However, even if such sacramental rites were of great importance to the Corinthians, the subjects of arrogance and feelings of security have not been related thus far in this epistle directly to those rites. Thus, in what follows, we do not deny the *possibility* that Paul was concerned about their 'sacramental rites', rather we argue that that was not his main concern in ch 10. In 12:13 'baptism' has a greater sacramental significance, but again the context stresses the result — a group of people called there a 'body'.

[41] Massie 201-202.

[42] Malina, *Manna* 96.

allow the 'strong' to claim that only the *weak* fell. As we shall see, Paul argued that in this group in the wilderness *all* were community members (in Moses) and *all* had gifts. Therefore, they provide a useful illustration for the 'strong'.

4.2.3   The cloud and sea in Jewish traditions

Neither the phrases 'in the cloud' nor 'under the cloud' are developed at any length in Jewish sources.[43] The pillar of 'cloud' figures only occasionally as a 'wonder' or 'sign', which the people needed to remember.[44] The cloud and sea are rarely directly linked in the traditions but, when they are, it is usually Exodus 14:19-22 that is recalled. There, as noted below, the cloud moved from a position of leadership to a protective rearguard position. It separated the Israelites and the Egyptians until the crossing of the Red Sea achieved the final separation of two nations. This is alluded to in Joshua 24:7 and possibly in the reference to the 'covering cloud' and the departure from Egypt in Psalm 105:37ff. In Wisdom 10:17 it is likely that the 'protective shelter' (σκέπη) accredited to Wisdom is an allusion to the cloud. As in Exodus 14:19ff, this tradition refers to protection *prior* to the Red Sea crossing. The same is true in Wisdom 19:7 where the cloud itself is mentioned as 'overshadowing' (σκιάζω) the camp as a protection. The order is the same as in 1 Corinthians 10: cloud protection - sea parting.

Philo illustrated the theme of separation of good from evil by an allegorical reference to the cloud in the wilderness. It came *between* the Egyptians and Israel[45] giving darkness to the Egyptians and light to the Israelites. An 'extraordinary sign' occurred as the cloud went to the back of the Israelites keeping them safe but causing the Egyptians to turn back in confusion. This allowed the Israelite women and children to cross the sea safely.[46] Again the 'separating' work of the cloud and its integral part in the Israelites' crossing of the Sea is prominent.[47]

The 'passing through the Red Sea' figures more prominently in the traditions. In Exodus 14:21-31 the sea destroyed the Egyptians while God, 'in the pillar of fire and cloud', looked on.[48] This event was special because it provided the basis for the people to 'believe in the Lord and his servant Moses'.[49] In Exodus 23:31, the Sea became a permanent

---

43   4.3 below.
44   Deut 4:9-14, 32 ff; Ps 78:14ff; Neh 9:9ff; etc.
45   Philo, *Quis Her* 202-204.
46   Philo, *Mos* i 178-179. Cf *Mos* ii 254.
47   Cf *Mekilta I* 226ff esp 239-240, where the function of the cloud and the sea was primarily to cause the separation of Israel into a separate nation.
48   The cloud indicated the presence of God. Cf Exod 24:15-18.
49   Also Ps 106:7-12.

boundary between Israel and Egypt. God's 'holy land' awaited the people following the destruction of the Egyptians.[50]

In Philo it was the 'nation' that made its passage 'through the sea' (διὰ θαλάττης) and the sea was a source of salvation to one party and destruction to another,[51] while, in Josephus, salvation and liberty from tyranny came to the Israelites διὰ θαλάσσης.[52]

4.2.4   Summary

The main emphasis of the phrase 'baptised into Moses' and the mention of 'sea' and 'cloud' in vv 1-2 was one of *separation* and group identification. The importance of the word 'baptised' therefore lay not in the introduction of new subject matter (sacraments), but in establishing the fact that the first community reflected the latter in its identification as a group separated from others by God. The comparison between the old and the new is 'covenantal'. The Israelites were identified as God's covenant community, separated by cloud and sea. For the new covenant people the word 'baptism' epitomised that process. Ruef summarises the argument: 'the basis of the analogy is best seen, not in the act of baptism itself ... but in the result of the act'.[53] Conzelmann also notes: 'The interpretation is focused in the first instance entirely upon the collective people of God'.[54]

This understanding of the text does not deny all 'sacramental' thought in the passage, but neither does it lay the emphasis there. There is, therefore, no need to ask how the crossing of the sea on *dry* land was a 'baptism'.[55] Although God's presence is manifest in the cloud, the particular combination of being 'under the cloud' and 'in the cloud' with 'through the sea' recalls the separation and nation-forming aspects of the events when seen *together*. It is possible to search for times when the Israelites were really 'under' a cloud[56] but this is unproductive. In the wilderness a 'people of God' existed, separated from other nations and led by a man of God — Moses. An analogy with initiation into the Christian people of God by 'baptism' sprang to Paul's mind. Possibly this occurred through proselyte baptism links with the Red Sea, or through thinking about the waters of the Red Sea. The mention of Moses

---

50   Ps 78:53-54.
51   Philo, *Mos* ii 254-255; *Vit Cont* 85-86.
52   Josephus, *Ants* 345-347.
53   Ruef 90.
54   Conzelmann 165.
55   The preposition διά was used by both Philo and Josephus in reference to a *dry* crossing of the Red Sea. Thus there is no need to suggest that the phrase was formed in light of a desire to stress the 'baptism' *through* waters — an issue of no significance to Philo or Josephus.
56   Cf Ellis, *Prophecy* 209 n 1. See Wis 19:7.

may indicate Paul was especially thinking of 'the initiation of the fathers into the sphere of the Law and its teaching'.[57] More likely, we believe, it was simply that Paul had in mind the end result of Christian baptism — a 'collective people of God'.

4.3   The function of the Wilderness Traditions in Judaism

In this section we shall examine the *function* in Jewish literature of those aspects of the WT which Paul used in 10:1-5. We shall limit our discussion to material generally thought to have been written before the end of the first century AD. This examination deliberately adopts a 'broad brush' approach to the traditions. This can be justified on the literary and thematic links that we demonstrate below between the WT and 1 Corinthians 10. However, it is also important to note, in an era so influenced by analytical linguistics and critical literary analysis, that for people in the first century AD, it often seemed to be an overall 'impression' of the stories of the past which spoke to the needs of the present. Support for this broader method has also come from recent studies in the field of social theory, where some have argued for the formative role of this wide-base approach in the establishment and maintenance of a given community's historical self-understanding.[58]

In this section of 1 Corinthians, the wilderness events are believed by many to *function* in a new, sacramental way. Paul viewed the manna and water as Israelite 'sacraments'.[59] We shall argue that Paul used these traditions in a similar way to the way they functioned in other Jewish literature. There they served mainly two broad purposes: i) to show God's gracious *gifts* to his covenant people, and ii) as a warning to later generations of the judgment that awaits those who become arrogant after receiving the gifts. We shall suggest that it was a false security generated by 'gifts' received from God that caused the problem Paul faced.

4.3.1   The traditions in Exodus and Numbers

A description of the wilderness wanderings first appears in the biblical narrative in Exodus 12ff and Numbers 9ff. In Exodus 13 the feast of unleavened bread is described. The traditions were to be retold: 'By strength of hand the Lord brought us out of Egypt, from the house of bondage' (vv 8, 14). The Israelites embarked on their journey by the Lord's command. He led 'in a pillar of cloud' and a 'pillar of fire' (vv 18-22). On arrival at the Red Sea (ch 14), the Israelites, trapped between land and sea, complained against the Lord and Moses (vv 10-12). God intended the 'salvation of the Lord' (v 13) to be seen, so the

---

57   Sandelin, *Wisdom* 166.
58   Cf Ricoeur, "Science"; Ellul, "l'idéologie".
59   So Senft 129; Morris 142; *inter al.*

cloud moved to separate Egyptians and Israelites and Moses divided the sea (vv 16-21). The Israelites were saved and the people believed in the Lord and Moses (v 31).

In Exodus 16 manna is mentioned for the first time in this narrative.[60] In the wilderness of Sin a lack of meat caused the Israelites to murmur against Moses, but the Lord brought quails and manna. The tradition emphasises the miraculous nature of the manna that Yahweh gave them to eat (vv 4, 8, 12, 15, 32, 35), and the murmurings which Moses said 'were not against us but against the Lord' (vv 7-12). The sabbath theme in the chapter may, as Malina suggests, point to the fact that the 'God of creation ... is the same God responsible for the new creation of the Exodus and its results'.[61]

A further lack of water is recounted in Exodus 17. The people again murmured[62] against Moses who responded by asking: 'Why do you put the Lord to the proof?' (πειράζω).[63] At the Lord's command, Moses struck the rock at Horeb and produced water. Therefore the place was called Massah (πειρασμός).

In Exodus 19 we read that the Lord offered Israel a covenant because 'You have seen what I did to the Egyptians, and how I brought you to myself'. The Law was given (ch 20) and the Lord 'proved' the people (πειράζω — v 20). Later, in Exodus 32, the incident of the Golden Calf is recounted. The Israelites held a feast to the Lord, offered sacrifices, 'and the people sat down to eat and drink and rose up to play' (v 6 — quoted by Paul in 10:7). God desired to destroy them (vv 8-10), because they were a 'stiff-necked' people (a key motif[64] of Exodus 32-34). Verses 25-29 describe the contrast between the faithful few, to whom blessing came (v 29), and the disobedient many. The theme of 'curse' and 'blessing' seen here recurs throughout the traditions. The key issue was 'who is on the Lord's side?' (v 26).

The traditions were also recounted at the celebration of the Passover (Numbers 9). The cloud or pillar of fire 'continually' travelled with the Israelites (9:16). But the people craved (ἐπιθυμέω) meat (ch 11) rather than the continued manna (11:4) and this led to their destruction (v 34). The miraculous nature of manna is alluded to in the vivid description of its appearance and taste (11:7-9).

---

60   The question of sources for this material does not impinge upon our argument as we are concerned with the final redactions most probably available to Paul. On possible sources of Exod 16 cf Malina, *Manna* 2-19 and others cited there.

61   Ibid 20.

62   LXX: γογγύζω. Cf 1 Cor 10:10.

63   Cf 1 Cor 10:9.

64   Moberly, *Exodus* 87.

In Numbers 20 the Israelites again blamed Moses for lack of water. Moses used his rod to bring water from the rock. The harshness of the Egyptian rule experienced by 'our fathers' (v 15) was recalled. At Shittim (ch 25) the Israelites committed acts of immorality with the Moabites and offered sacrifices to other gods (Baal Peor), so God destroyed many.[65]

In these passages there is a continuous interplay between the people's rebelliousness and the great power of the Lord. The tradition of the Red Sea crossing was used to indicate the separation of the Israelites from the Egyptians, and to demonstrate God's redeeming power. His presence was experienced in three ways: i) through the cloud and pillar of fire; ii) through the miraculous events of the Red Sea, and the gifts of water, manna and quails when needed; iii) and through the words of Moses whom the Lord used to bring his salvation to the people. The Israelites were to keep the Lord's covenant. Allegiance and faith were the two parallel issues confronting the Israelites. Both should have remained constant, but when this did not happen the Israelites were judged.

As we shall see later, the major themes of 1 Corinthians 10:1-14 are present in these traditions. For now we simply draw attention to i) the separating action of the cloud and the Sea distinguishing between the Israelites and Egyptians, ii) the Lord's faithfulness in his providing gifts of manna etc, and iii) the 'testing' of the people leading to blessing or judgment.

4.3.2   The traditions in Deuteronomy

Here a much briefer description of the WT is given primarily as a background to covenant renewal.

In Deuteronomy 1, murmuring against the Lord is recalled. Even though the Israelites had evidence of the Lord's blessings: 'Yet [they] did not believe in the Lord [their] God' (v 32). They 'were presumptuous'. The incident at Baal Peor is recounted in ch 4 as an example of God's destruction on those who were not faithful to the Lord. Therefore the Israelites were not to forget the covenant by making any graven image, for God is a jealous God (vv 23-24). If, however, they obeyed God, they would demonstrate their 'wisdom' and 'understanding' before the world. If, having sinned, the Israelites were to 'search after the Lord God with all their heart and with all their soul', they would find him faithful to his covenant with their fathers (1:30-31). The mighty signs were performed so that they 'might know that the Lord is God; there is no other beside him' (4:35, 39).

---

[65]   1 Cor 10:8 is probably a reference to this.

Following the review of the Law (ch 5) the people were reminded that they were not to *test* (ἐκπειράζω) God, who was a jealous God, as at Massah (6:14-17).

In Deuteronomy 7 complete separation from the inhabitants of Canaan was required. The Israelites were a holy people, chosen by the loving grace of the Lord (vv 6-8). This grace showed God to be a 'faithful God (θεὸς πιστός) who keeps covenant and steadfast love' with those who love (ἀγαπάω) him (v 9). When there was any doubt about this the WT were to be recalled (vv 17-26).

The testing of the Israelites was to be 'remembered'. In 8:2-3 they were to remember the manna, given so that God 'might make you know that man does not live by bread alone, but ... by everything that proceeds out of the mouth of the Lord' (v 3).[66] They were warned of the temptation to 'forget' God after he had blessed them and they were 'full' (vv 11-13), and they were warned of becoming overconfident. Their temptation would be to say 'My power' has achieved all this (cf also 9:4) and then to turn to other gods (8:19-20), which would result in destruction.

The difference between this use of the WT and that in Exodus/Numbers is at once apparent. Moses' role in the narrative diminishes and the issue is more clearly one of allegiance to the God of the covenant. The WT are somewhat 'spiritualised', serving as descriptions of the gracious gifts and blessings of the covenant, and of the curses that come as a result of arrogance and idolatry. The signs should have been the cause of belief (Deuteronomy 4:35) and not have resulted in disbelief (1:32). God's faithfulness was not to be 'tested' (6:16).[67] As a holy and chosen people, the Israelites were to remember the WT for *one* major purpose: so that having seen how God blessed the people, leading them through testing and humbling, they would understand that what they possessed had come from the Lord. Neither *their* power nor *their* righteousness had achieved what they had been given. There was no room for arrogance (8:17). The Israelites were to 'learn' and to know — a process (8:3, 5) that concerned how God dealt with his people and was designed to evoke a 'heart' response of 'love' to the faithful covenant God (7:6-9: 8:5 etc).[68]

At the covenant renewal ceremony in ch 29, the same ideas were expounded. The Israelites were judged because the 'heart' that would

---

[66]   Von Rad, *Theology I* 282, says of the giving of the manna: 'The event comes to have typological significance — God gives to each according to his need'.

[67]   Ibid 283: 'Israel's chief sin ... mentioned in an almost stereotyped fashion ... consists in her "tempting Jahweh"'.

[68]   On knowing God leading to a heart response cf Deut 4:9-10, 29; 5:29; 6:4-6; 8:2; 10:12 etc.

'understand' (εἰδέναι) was lacking (v 4). Thus, again, the blessings and curses (29:19-21) of the God of the covenant (v 12) were laid before the people. Recalling the WT should have evoked love for and obedience to God (30:6, 10). God's faithfulness and his covenant blessings and curses are prominent in chs 29-30.

Deuteronomy 32 is important for our purposes. We suggested that it might have been in Paul's mind in 1 Corinthians 8: he quoted from it in 1 Corinthians 10:20-22. Here covenant renewal was extolled in a song which the Israelites were to learn to sing (31:19). God's greatness was proclaimed (vv 1-3) as were his faithfulness and justice (vv 4-9). God was called 'rock', emphasising the permanence and faithfulness of the God who chose them (cf vv 15, 18; Is 44:8). This was contrasted with the imperfection of the people (v 5) who forgot that he had 'created' (קנה) them — an allusion to the Exodus and the 'creation' of the people of the Lord.[69]

The Israelites were obliged to 'remember' in order to 'meditate' on God's goodness to them in the wilderness (vv 10-14). Poetic hyperbole describes honey coming from the flinty rock. Again God's curses are seen beside his blessings, for Jeshurun grew fat and resisted God. The application was direct: 'You grew fat ...' (vv 15-18). They forgot the God who bore them and scoffed at the rock of salvation, causing him to be 'jealous' through sacrifices to 'demons' (δαιμονίοις). Because of the unfaithfulness of God's 'sons and daughters', God became jealous and brought judgment on them (vv 19-27). It is interesting to note (vv 28-33) that again judgment came because Israel did not *understand* (συνίημι) nor *discern* (φρονέω) the works of God (v 29) — either in blessing or in judgment. The question of 'discernment' in God's dealings with his people is, as we shall see, at least one of the levels on which these traditions function similarly in Deuteronomy 32 and 1 Corinthians 10.

As earlier in Deuteronomy, the theme of God's blessing and curse is prominent. The traditions were used to remind the people of their 'creation' as God's people and how they had taken advantage of God's goodness, 'scoffing' at the rock and going after other gods. Their very prosperity should have pointed the Israelites back to God who was the giver. Again they were to take to 'heart' and apply the lessons of the wilderness (v 46).

---

69   On קנה see Driver, *Deuteronomy* 354. We suggested above that this reference to 'father' and 'creation' (v 6) lay behind Paul's argument in 1 Cor 8:6.

4.3.3   The traditions in Nehemiah 9 (2 Esdras 19)

In Nehemiah 9, 'our fathers'[70] were 'presumptuous', 'stiff-necked', and disobedient (v 16). They forgot God, in spite of the law given on Sinai and the bread and water which God had given ἐξ οὐρανοῦ (v 15). The golden calf incident is recalled. God also gave τὸ πνεῦμά σοῦ τὸ ἀγαθόν to instruct them (v 20). He gave so much that they were 'filled' (ἐμπίμπλημι) and 'became fat' (v 25). But in their presumption they rebelled, and were handed over to their enemies (vv 26-29). Again there is a stress on the faithfulness of God[71] which has been present in all the texts we have examined thus far. This is also an interesting aspect of Paul's argument in 1 Corinthians 10:13.[72]

4.3.4   The traditions in the Psalms

We briefly examine three psalms that recount the WT.

Psalm 78[73] is a 'mashal'[74] — revealing 'mysteries' of the past to learn lessons for the present. The addressees were not to be like 'our fathers ... whose heart was not steadfast' (vv 5-8). They suffered for 'not keeping God's covenant' and 'forgetting the miracles he had shown them' — the Red Sea, cloud, fire, water (vv 13-16). Vivid hyperbole describes the streams from the rock (vv 15-16, 20). The sin of 'testing' God through 'craving' (v 18) was interpreted as having 'no faith in God and not trusting in his saving power' (v 22). Therefore, the Israelites were judged because 'despite his wonders they did not believe'. They tested God in their hearts (v 18) even after they had been 'filled' (v 29). But in their punishment the people 'remembered God', their 'rock' and 'redeemer' (v 35). Yet again, though, they 'were not true to his covenant' (v 37) and they provoked God to jealousy with their images (v 58).[75] However, God still remained faithful and then he later chose David (vv 67-72).

The origin of the manna as God's gift from heaven is clearly stated. It 'rained down' through the 'opened doors of heaven' and is called the 'bread of angels' (vv 23-25). With this emphasis on what God had given them, the contrast with the faithless Israelites, who always wanted more and even turned to idols, is all the more effective.

In Psalm 95[76] the Lord is also addressed as 'rock'. He was the 'rock of [their] salvation' and hence to be worshipped. The wilderness was a

---

70   2 Esdras 19:9, 16, and 32.
71   Vv 7, 17, 20, 22, 28, etc.
72   See below.
73   LXX: 77.
74   Used to utter 'indirectly taught lessons' (חידות), cf BDB 295.
75   Cf 1 Cor 10:22.
76   LXX: 94.

place of rebellion in which 'your fathers tested me' even 'though they had seen [God's] works.' Therefore God judged them. Heart commitment (vv 8, 10) to the Lord who made them (as the people of Israel — vv 6-7) was required. Their response was crucial: did they worship him (v 6) and know (γινώσκω) his ways, or were they to be cursed (vv 10-11)?

Psalm 106[77] also refers to 'our fathers' who rebelled, not understanding or discerning (συνίημι) the wondrous works (v 7). A marked stress was laid on how much God had given the Israelites, who had rebelled and 'forgotten' God in their 'craving' and sin. Although water and manna are not mentioned, they are probably assumed in v 15 where 'God gave them what they asked' in their 'craving' (v 14). They tempted God and worshipped other gods but, in spite of their disbelief, God, in his 'steadfast love, remembered his covenant' (vv 45-46).

Other psalms contain allusions or references to the wilderness,[78] but it is the consistency of the *function* of the traditions in these examples that is notable. The sin of the people in forgetting God's gifts to them, in 'craving' more, and in turning to other gods, led to judgment. Lessons had to be learned and in that learning the faithfulness of God to his people was recalled.

4.3.5   The traditions in the Prophets

The wilderness experiences mentioned in the prophets provided lessons for people by emphasising that Israel was rebellious and was judged by God.[79] An understanding emerged that Israel would have to return to the wilderness as a judgment on those who had broken covenant.[80] However, once back in the wilderness God would again speak to his people, and renew the covenant in steadfast love. The people would respond in faith.[81]

Ezekiel was charged with describing to the elders of Israel the 'abominations of their fathers' (20:4). To do this, he used the WT, highlighting God's choice of the Israelites, the Exodus, and the injunctions against idolatry. Their disobedience was then outlined (vv 5-10). God's faithfulness was seen in 'giving them the law and the sabbaths'. For 'his name's sake' the Lord repeatedly refrained from destroying them completely, although he did judge them apparently by

77   LXX: 105.
78   Ps 29:8; 66:6,10-12; 80:8; 81:5ff; 99:7,8; 105:16ff; 107:4-11; etc.
79   Mauser, *Wilderness* 44.
80   Hos 2:3, 8ff.
81   Cf Hos 2:16-23.

causing his law to be distorted.[82] Idolatry and defiling sacrifices were regular sins (20:27-31). The picture given of the time in the wilderness is now almost entirely negative.[83] However, in the author's time God would bring the people into a new wilderness experience, where he would judge them (v 36). The 'covenant' sanctions would be renewed and a purging would take place (v 37). A purified group would then worship God, 'loathing' their past sins and being thankful for God's faithfulness. God's *gifts* were the giving of the law and sabbaths, to the end that people might 'know God' and have life (vv 11-12).

In Isaiah chs 40ff the WT become a symbol of the exodus from Babylon through the wilderness, which would pass without trouble (Isaiah 40:3-5). The Jews would have water from the rock (48:20-21) and the wilderness would become a garden (51:3). God's graciousness is thus the dominant theme. The redeemer's steadfast love remains and he makes 'an everlasting covenant' with them (54:10; 55:3; 61:8). Notably, this will happen through the giving of the Holy Spirit who, as he did in the wilderness under Moses, will once again bring water and rest (63:7-19). The elaboration of earlier traditions is interesting, for in ch 43 the image of the gift of water in the desert is a picture for future covenantal blessings (vv 18-21). In 44:3 the supply of water in the desert has become a picture for the blessings of the Spirit[84] being poured on the chosen people. The people's response was to be an admission of belonging to Yahweh, the rock (44:5, 8). They had to discern truth and be committed in heart[85] to the saving God who made covenants with them (44:18-22; 57:11ff), for they had felt secure in evil and their wisdom had led them astray (47:10).

Many themes from the WT are present in Isaiah. The need for understanding and acknowledging the Lord in the heart is prominent. An interesting development concerns the work of the Holy Spirit in giving gifts. This action is described as water being poured on thirsty lands. This is an aspect of the tradition which, we shall suggest, may have been in Paul's mind. The application of the WT now stresses God's future covenantal blessings or sanctions. The curses of the covenant play a less prominent role but are still used to warn people not to be misled by their own wisdom which is described as foolishness.

---

[82]   Cf 20:25-26. These verses are sometimes believed to be later textual additions.

[83]   For a discussion of the reasons for this see Von Rad, *Theology I* 283-285.

[84]   Note the parallel structure: 44:3a, b.

[85]   In the LXX καρδία is used many times (in amplification of the Masoretic text). Cf Is 46:8; 65:14, 16, 17 etc.

4.3.6   The traditions in the Qumran literature.

The Qumran covenanters regarded themselves as the wilderness community of the last days.[86] Settled in, or on the edge of the wilderness, they were part of a new covenant, separated from other sinners, awaiting the Messiah(s), while being 'tested' as 'exiles of the desert'.[87]

The wilderness was not regarded fearfully but as a place of testing. In the face of rebellion, God's faithfulness to a remnant of the people figured prominently. The sins of the wilderness were to be recounted so that the covenanters would obey the law, and listen to their Teacher.

Regularly covenanters appealed for pardon 'for the sake of the covenant'. In 4QDib Ham 2-5 there is an appeal in this form: the rebellions of 'our fathers' are recounted, but the marvels of the wilderness are remembered — especially the law-giving planted in the heart. The congregation found itself 'growing' through famine, thirst, and pestilence and the 'sword of [God's] covenant' because they were God's chosen people. During times of blessing the people 'were satisfied and grew fat' and turned to 'other gods', forsaking 'the fount of living waters'. But God remained faithful to his people, as he did to the covenanters, who also had 'wearied the rock with sins'. He gave the Holy Spirit to bring blessings.

The 'wilderness', then, was a place of testing for adherence to the covenant. Did the covenanters obey the Law, or walk 'with stubborn hearts'? If they did not obey the Law, or the Teacher, they were cut off as had happened in the wanderings. However, covenanters were expected to pass the test (CD3).

In 1QS 8:13-17 the new community member was 'tested' by going 'into the wilderness to prepare the way of Him ... This is the study of the law'. He had to obey the law and prophetic revelation from the Spirit. The Council of the Community would be composed of such people and would be the 'precious cornerstone' (Is 28:16). Priests at Qumran had to recite the evidence of God's grace to Israel ('our fathers') and list their rebellions. In spite of these rebellions, they emphasised that God remained faithful (1QS 1-2:1).

The application of the WT to this community was very important, but the material was handled similarly to that seen earlier. The covenanters were to avoid the arrogance shown by the first wilderness community to God's gifts of the law, sabbaths, etc. (CD 3). The gift of water (the well the princes dug) became a metaphor for the law which contained all

---

[86]   Stegner, "Wilderness" 18. Talmon, "Desert Motif" 57, points out that this is not because the desert is an ideal, but because of its 'transition-and-preparation motif'. Also cf Mauser, *Wilderness* 58-61.

[87]   CD6:19; 1QM1:2; 1QS2:21; 1QS8.

wisdom and God's mysteries.[88] Possibly following Isaiah, emphasis was laid on the Holy Spirit as the one who brought covenant blessings even when God, the rock, had been sinned against. People had to repent in their hearts and obey the covenant if they were to be covenant members. Somewhat like the accounts in Ezekiel 20, the first events in the wilderness are seen in a very negative light. The covenanters must be faithful where the Israelites had failed.

4.3.7   The traditions in Philo

Philo's use of the WT was distinctly allegorical. However, the development of the allegories was closely connected with the canonical material.[89] The wilderness still brought blessing and judgment. Trust in God was required. He had bestowed gifts on[90] and protected his people with the 'mighty works' of the Red Sea, cloud, manna, etc.[91] The need for a response to these gifts meant that the wilderness still 'tested' that faith.[92] Blessings and curses attached to the WT were seen in the good and evil that accrued to the soul on entering a 'wilderness'.[93]

Manna was the highest of gifts from God, representing the word of God[94] and wisdom for the soul.[95] Of particular interest, in the light of our understanding of 1 Corinthians 8-9, is the fact that Philo regarded it as 'proof' ($\tau\epsilon\kappa\mu\acute{\eta}\rho\iota o\nu$) of God's work among his people.[96] It was one of the 'various forms of knowledge ... not bestowed by the word of bodily sense but by God,' and it was to be properly discerned.[97]

The waters poured out in the desert[98] indicated the Spirit had been given, which was one of $\tau\grave{\alpha}$ $\grave{\alpha}\gamma\alpha\theta\acute{\alpha}$ that God gave. The rock was the 'wisdom of God'.[99]

The 'testing' aspect of the wilderness was apparent as the Israelites had to get used to a new way of life — in a desert away from the evils of the cities and with only God's law to guide.[100] Here the wilderness was an evil place in which the people were 'unexpectedly' given 'the clearest

[88]   CD3; the water brought life. Cf 1QS 4.
[89]   *Contra* Mauser, *Wilderness* 53, although Philo's emphasis on the evil cities is distinct.
[90]   *Mos* i 204.
[91]   *Mos* i 176-180; *Quis Her* 202-204.
[92]   *Congr* 170.
[93]   *Leg All* ii 84-85.
[94]   *Leg All* ii 86; *Quis Her* 79.
[95]   *Quis Her* 191; *Leg All* iii 169; iii 173.
[96]   *Leg All* iii 175.
[97]   Ibid iii 179.
[98]   *Leg All* i 34.
[99]   *Leg All* ii 86.
[100] *Decal* 13.

evidence of the truth' — in the form of water and manna from the rock — that the law came from God and not from man. Thus, in depriving men of water and food, and then supplying them with manna for food, God intended to make the people believe his law.[101]

As in the OT, for Philo, the traditions were designed to cause commitment to God. His view of the gifts of manna and water is well summarised when he says: 'after experiencing strange events ... [the people] should have put their trust in him ...'.[102]

4.3.8   The traditions in other Jewish writings

In Josephus the wilderness motif remained largely undeveloped, although its deprivations were regarded as a testing of the Israelites in their loyalty to Moses.[103] Otherwise, the wilderness was the place where messianic movements began.[104]

In other Jewish writings including wisdom literature and the apocalyptic and eschatological material, the WT do not figure prominently. When they do, they are normally used as examples of how God judges those who have disobeyed.

Wisdom literature linked the wilderness with God's gift of wisdom.[105] The book of Wisdom showed God revealing, through Wisdom, his care for his people. There is no mention of grumbling, rather a 'virtuous' people called on God when thirsty (Wisdom 10:15-11:4). Even when the people sinned God was slow to anger (15:1-3). But there is little development of the theme. The contrast between Egyptians and Israelites is exemplified in God giving his people 'angel's food to eat and providing bread from heaven' (16:20).

Sirach 15:1 identifies the law with wisdom. Fear of the Lord leads to God's gift of 'the bread of understanding' and the 'water of wisdom' is given as drink (v 3).

Baruch 1:17-22 describes the cursing of the Israelites ever since 'our fathers' came from Egypt because everyone walked 'in the imagination of his own heart to serve strange gods'.

In 4 Ezra the readers are reminded of God's revelation to 'our fathers in the wilderness' (9:29-37; 14:27-36). The Israelites transgressed the law 'even as you also after them have transgressed it'. Thus, says the

[101] *Decal* 15-17.

[102] *Mos i* 196. On manna in Philo see Borgen, *Bread*.

[103] Josephus, *Ants* 3:13-38; esp 3:14-15.

[104] Cf *De bello Judaico* 2:258-260. On the basis of certain OT texts, Rabbinic thought developed the idea of flight to the desert before the eschaton — an idea presaged by the Qumran community. See Kittel, "Ἔρημος" 659. Cf Hos 2:14; 12:9.

[105] For a full examination of wisdom as 'nourisher' or food, and thus of its links with manna, see Sandelin, *Nourisher*.

writer, (14:34) 'If you, then, will rule over your own understanding and discipline your heart, you shall be kept alive.'

The use of the traditions is too infrequent to determine a consistent function. Generally, however, the uses we have found emphasise the gift of law and wisdom in the desert and warn of the danger of turning from either. However, the need properly to 'understand' what went on in the wilderness (in order to learn from it) is similar to what is required in the canonical texts. The paradox of the wilderness continues: it is both the place where God remembered his covenant and blessed Israel (with law and/or wisdom) and also the place where God cursed Israel for her disobedience.

The stress on obedience to the law is not unlike that found at Qumran, but is somewhat removed from the way the traditions developed in the prophets with their emphasis on the Spirit and the need for a heart commitment to God himself.

4.3.9   The traditions in John 6:25-65

The text of 1 Corinthians 10 is probably the earliest use of the traditions in the NT, and therefore a discussion of other NT texts may be anachronistic for our purposes. The use of the traditions in the Gospels has been adequately dealt with by many others[106] and adds little to our understanding of Paul's application of the themes. There is further treatment of these themes in Heb 3:7ff and in Acts 7.

John 6, however, needs mentioning because it is supposed that 'the parallel to 1 Corinthians 10:3 is quite apparent'.[107] In this text, John emphasised 'signs'. These were visible, wondrous events, 'But they [were] ineffective in bringing about the full Christian faith if they [were] perceived only externally or sought for as sensations (cf 4:48).'[108] They had an inner meaning that was to be grasped by faith.[109] Where faith was lacking, the truth about Christ was not revealed[110] and the signs remained uninterpreted miracles. Signs were closely linked to the revelation of salvation in the person of Christ and it was this idea that lay behind John's use of the wilderness motif in ch 6.

After feeding the five thousand (6:1-14) the crowd came to Jesus, who perceived that they came not because they saw signs[111] but because they

---

106   See Mauser, *Wilderness* 75ff; Bonnard, "Désert"; Chavasse, "Christ and Moses"; Glasson, *Moses*.

107   Mauser, *Wilderness* 76.

108   Schnackenburg, *John* I 519.

109   Cf 3:11, 12; 6:26, 27.

110   6:36-40.

111   Barrett, *John* 289: had the Jews seen the feeding as a 'sign' they would have recognised Jesus for who he is.

had eaten their fill (v 26). Jesus encouraged them to look for food 'which endures to eternal life', this meant that they had to 'believe' on him (vv 27-29). The people then asked for a sign, giving the wilderness as an example where 'Our fathers ate the manna ... bread from heaven' (v 31).[112] Jesus argued that the Father, not Moses, gave the bread — a bread that gives life to the world (vv 32-33). When Jesus revealed that he was that bread, the Jews 'murmured' against him — recalling the response of the Israelites under Moses. The fathers had died in the wilderness even though they ate manna (vv 47-49), but there is a greater bread in which to believe and that leads to life (v 58). The source of such provision is the Spirit (v 63).[113]

There are parallels here with 1 Corinthians 10 but also with the traditions examined so far. The need to understand something deeper than simply that at the level of food is common with the other traditions, as is the 'murmuring', the lack of belief, and the fact that the Spirit provided the bread. But, more importantly, the paraenetic function is somewhat similar. Although in John 6 the main function of the discussion of the manna was to teach about commitment to and belief in Jesus, this seems to be a new application of the traditional call to a renewed commitment to and belief in God. But there are a number of differences as well, especially in the discussion of 'flesh' and 'blood'. In 1 Corinthians 10 Paul seems to have more in common with the other Jewish traditions than with John 6.

4.3.10 Summary

There is an interesting level of conformity among the WT examined, while a marked development in interpretation is also displayed. Both these points have been largely ignored by scholars but will prove helpful in the exegetical sections which follow. Some points can be made now and others addressed later.

1)   There were from the earliest times WT retold in terms of what 'our fathers' experienced.[114] Although it is unlikely that Paul used 'without modification, an existing Exodus midrash',[115] this provides one reason for believing the traditions were handed down in a reasonably stable form.[116]

---

112 Quoting Ps 77:24 (LXX).
113 Cf Barrett, *John* 304.
114 Num 20:15; Neh 9:9, 16, 32, 34; Ps 78:5; 106:6, 7; 1QS1:25; 4QDib Ham 2:8. Sometimes 'your/their fathers' appears: Deut 8:3, 16, 18; Ps 95:9; Ezek 20:4, 18, 27, 30.
115 A possibility suggested by Barrett 220.
116 Cf 1 Cor 10:1.

2)   The WT became an example *par excellence* of God's 'covenant' dealings with his people. That is, certain features linked to covenant treaties, or renewal ceremonies, are found in the traditions. For example, a) law was given and obedience required; b) no other gods could be served; c) the dual covenant sanctions of blessing and curse were manifest;[117] d) God himself remained faithful and therefore could be trusted for the future.

3)   God's faithfulness was repeatedly mentioned,[118] often being reflected in the epithet 'rock'.[119]

4)   Some authors showed a certain ambivalence to the traditions themselves. On the one hand they demonstrated God's gracious gifts to his community while, on the other, they depicted the outcome of disobedience. The question of 'which side are you on?' remained implicit through much of the material[120] and became explicit in the description of the wilderness as a place of 'testing' for the people.

5)   In Exodus and Numbers the apparent reason for disobedience was centred on the Israelites' 'craving' for conditions left behind in Egypt.[121] In other documents, where God's blessing and gifts were stressed,[122] the sin of 'presumptuousness' was prominent. Having 'grown fat' they 'forgot' God, became arrogant, and turned to other gods.[123]

6)   In a number of writings, especially in Deuteronomy, the Israelites' lack of 'understanding' of God's work was regarded as a major factor in their downfall. It was assumed that there was more 'behind' the gifts God supplied than the meeting of immediate physical needs. Lessons

---

[117]   Cf Ex 20:24; 32:33-35; Num 10:29; 11:33-34; 25:10-13; Deut 8:18-20; 11:26; 29:9, 20; 30:1; 32:19, 39; Neh 9:23, 27-28; Ps (all LXX) 76:2-16; 77:58-59; 105:40, 45-46; Hos 2:13-23; Ezek 20:8b-9, 36ff; Is 50:2; 43:18-21; 4Q Dib Ham 4-5; 1QS2; *Leg All* ii 84-85; Bar 1:17-22: Wis 16:18-20 etc.

[118]   E.g., cf Ex 32:13-14; Deut 7:9-11; 8:18; Neh 9:17, 31-32; Ps (LXX) 77:35; 95:7; 105:7, 45; Hos 2:19; Ezek 20:14-17; 4Q Dib Ham 5; etc.

[119]   Apart from refs mentioned above also cf Deut 32:4, 15;; 95:1; Is 44:8; 4Q Dib Ham 5; etc.

[120]   Cf Ex 20:20; 32:26; Num 25:10-13; Deut 8:2; 29:25; 32:15-16, 46-47; Neh 9:35-38; Ps 77:8; 95:7; 105:19b, 28b; Ezek 20:30, 39; Is 45:5. Also cf Hos 2:1-4, 13. Esp note the functions of the traditions in initiation to the community at Qumran: 4QDib Ham 6; CD3; 1QS2:17; 8:13ff. Also cf Josephus, *Ants* 3:13-38.

[121]   Cf Ex 16:2-3; Num 11:4.

[122]   Cf Deut 4:35-39; 7:9-11; 8:11-13; 32:10ff; Neh 9:9ff; Ezek 20:10-12; Is 48:20-21; 43:18ff; 4QDib Ham 2-3; 4 Ez 9:29-37; Philo, *Mos* i 176-180; Wis 10:15ff.

[123]   Cf Deut 32:15-18; Neh 9:16-17; Ezek 20:16; 4Q Dib Ham 4-5; 1QS2:12-17.

were to be learned about relying entirely on God for everything.[124] They were to respond with a heart and faith commitment to the gracious God.[125]

7)   As this last point developed so did the association of God's Spirit with his blessings for his people.[126] The Spirit also brought that understanding that had been missing.[127]

8)   In the prophets the idea of a second entry into the wilderness developed. There a purification would take place,[128] and God's Spirit would be poured out on his people and an eternal covenant made.[129]

This broad over-view of the WT has shown that, although differing in application in different contexts, the broad paraenetic purposes remained largely constant. People were to 'understand' the function of God's gifts in his community. Proper understanding would lead to praise of God and 'heart' commitment. This, in turn, would lead to covenant blessings. Becoming 'arrogant', 'filled' and 'fat' on God's gifts and beginning to 'crave' for other things could lead to judgment of the sort experienced by the Israelites in the wilderness.[130]

On returning to 1 Corinthians 10, it becomes evident that Paul's message, though now for those in the 'last days', was still essentially the same: there was a danger of arrogance in the light of God's gifts, and there was a failure to understand. Judgment was a real possibility.

4.4   Israel's spiritual food and drink (Verses 3 - 4a)

Interpreting these verses largely depends upon our understanding of πνευματικός. Nowhere in the WT was the word πνευματικός used. It does not appear in the LXX and is found only rarely in the NT outside Paul.

---

124   Cf Deut 8:3; 29:2-4; Neh 9:17; Ps 77:2; 94:10; 105:7; Ezek 20:11-12; Is 44:18-20; 4Q Dib Ham 5; Bar 1:17-18; 4 Ez 14:34. Cf Hos 2:8.

125   Cf Ex 14:31; 19:9; Deut 1:32-33; 4:39; 7:9; 8:2; 32:46; Neh 9:38; Ps (LXX) 77:18; 94:8, 10; 105:12; Ezek 20:16; Is 44:18-22; 47:10; 4Q Dib Ham 2:12-14; 1QS1:1; CD 3; Philo, *Decal* 14-17; 4 Ez 14:34.

126   Neh 9:20; Is 44:3; 4Q Dib Ham 5. See also next note.

127   Cf Neh 9:20; Is 63:10-12; 1QS4; 8:16-17; Wis 9:17.

128   Cf Ezek 20:36-38. This is little more than the belief that where the first wilderness generation had failed the second would succeed. It was basic to the beliefs of the Qumran community (1QS1:1ff).

129   Cf Is 44:3; 54:10; 55:3; 61:8; 1QS2:1ff.; CD3:12ff.

130   These two aspects of the WT ('positive' and 'negative') are well drawn out by Barth "Wüstentradition". We are not fully convinced with his conclusion that the WT *always* contain the negative element (23).

Tò αὐτό accentuates the *unity* of the experience of all (πάντες) who were in the wilderness. Each had the *same* gifts.[131] But what did Paul mean by describing the gifts of food, drink, and rock as πνευματικός? The context here does not help much. The adjective is derived from the noun πνεῦμα but this need not indicate its meaning.[132] The noun πνεῦμα is not mentioned in this immediate context.

Some believe the word refers to the *origin* of the food and drink.[133] Certainly the divine origin of these gifts was mentioned in all the traditions examined. This has led to πνευματικός being translated 'supernatural'.[134] But does the question of origin exhaust Paul's meaning? Käsemann has argued controversially that Paul 'undoubtedly' means 'food and drink which convey πνεῦμα'.[135] For him these verses can only be understood as 'Pauline utterances on Baptism ... and the Lord's Supper'. In fact, Käsemann, like so many, reads back the content of the words μετέχω and κοινωνία of vv 16-17 into vv 3-4. He says, 'the gift takes on the character of the Giver and through the gift we become partakers of the Giver himself'.[136] Further, he reads the Eucharist in terms of the influence of mystery cults, where to partake of the meal was to partake of the deity. Christians have a unity in a common participation in the same 'heavenly substance' — the πνεῦμα.[137]

Dunn has argued, against a 'sacramental' understanding, that here 'πνευματικός is better understood in the sense "allegorical"' [sic].[138] Πνευματικῶς means this in Revelation 11:8, but there it is an adverb.[139] However, Paul was not suggesting that the Israelite manna was a 'figure' for something else[140] nor, as we shall see, did he wish to make an allegory.

---

131   Bengel 639; Barrett 221-222. This does not mean that the Israelites had the same "sacraments" as the Christians. *Contra* Senft 129.

132   Cf Revelation 11:8.

133   Cf ἐξ οὐρανοῦ, Nehemiah 9:15.

134   So *RSV*; *NEB*; Lietzmann 46; Allo 230; *inter al.*

135   Käsemann, *Essays* 113. Cf Hanson, *Jesus* 18, 'conveying the real presence of Christ'; Davidson, *Typology* 246.

136   Käsemann, *Essays* 113.

137   Ibid 115. Cf Ruef 90. For criticism of this: Conzelmann 166 n 22; Dunn, "Spirit" 706. Selwyn, *Peter* 281-285 says of 1 Cor 10:3-4: '"acramental" is the best translation of πνευματικός'.

138   Dunn, *Unity* 165.

139   Caird, *Revelation* 138, translates πνευματικῶς as 'figurative'.

140   Cf Amsler, "Typologie" 118; 124ff.

Others suggest that πνευματικός refers to things that come from the Spirit bringing a sustenance from God for the recipient's spirit.[141] This understanding also depends on these verses referring, at least typologically, to the Lord's Supper.[142]

In the section which follows, we examine the use of the word πνευματικός in some detail to see whether further light can be shed on the matter.[143]

4.4.1 Πνευματικός

In 1 Corinthians πνευματικός appears as both noun and adjective. It is possible that πνευματικός was part of Corinthian religious vocabulary — one which Paul sought to redefine. This cannot be proved, but its wide use in this letter (as compared with other NT writings), together with its use following περὶ δέ in 12:1, could point to this.

In 2:13 πνευματικοῖς may be masculine or neuter. This text was examined above[144] when looking at the meaning of ἀνακρίνω. The argument is fairly clear: 'if the Corinthians do not understand, they show themselves to be "psychical"'.[145] Judgment and discernment are important in this passage, for it is clear that Paul regarded some people as 'spiritual' and some as not.[146] This was probably what the 'strong' were doing.[147] It seems that the problem of spirituality centred on 'understanding' or 'discerning' things in a particular way. The πνευματικά needing to be understood were the 'gifts of God to us' (v 12). The Spirit was given 'so that we may understand' (ἵνα εἰδῶμεν) these gifts. The ψυχικός (v 14) was one who did not have the understanding to judge (ἀνακρίνω) 'the things of the Spirit'. Thus the word 'spiritual' is applied by Paul both to the things needing to be discerned and to the people involved in this judgment.

Understanding, wisdom, discernment and judging were at the heart of what it was for someone to be 'spiritual'. Words such as ἔγνωκεν (v 11), εἰδῶμεν (v 12), συγκρίνοντες (v 13), μωρία, γνῶναι, ἀνακρίνεται (v 14), ἀνακρίνει, ἀνακρίνεται (v 15), ἔγνω (v 16) make this evident.

---

141 Cf Calvin 203-204; Barrett 222; Bandstra, "Interpretation" 10: 'vehicles of the saving work of God in Christ'.

142 For positions of different scholars see Davidson, *Typology* 224-230.

143 The word πνευματικός appears 26 times in the NT: only twice is this non-Pauline (1 Pt 2:5, 5). It occurs 15 times in 1 Cor. The adverb appears twice: 1 Cor 2:14; Rev 11:8.

144 p 73.

145 Conzelmann 67.

146 On ψυχικός and σαρκικός pp 74-75 above.

147 Cf Dunn, "Spirit" 707.

The goal of this discernment is also evident in the context: it is to be able to say with Paul, 'we have the mind of Christ' (v 16). The 'spiritual' man was one who judged the gifts of God (v 13), discerning, as suggested earlier, their true function in the community. This was to build people up to understand more of the revelation of Christ. For Paul, no doubt, such a person would see Christ as 'wisdom' (1:30) and as 'Lord of glory' (2:8).

All of this must bear on any definition of πνευματικός drawn from 2:10-16. As we suggested earlier, it was people with a 'fleshly' understanding who were jealous and quarrelsome.

This is clearer in 3:1. (Πνευματικοῖς is dative masculine plural.) Paul could address the Corinthians only as 'fleshly' (σαρκικοί). They were 'infants in Christ', unable to discern things as they should. Their problem was not simply their quarrelling but, as the rhetorical question of v 16 shows, it was that they were not recognising the presence of the Spirit of God. The problem arose from their own supposed 'wisdom' (v 18) and conceit (v 21).

In 9:11, the neuter plural πνευματικά is used. Paul almost certainly had the argument of ch 2 in mind, where the imagery of planting seed (2:6) and of watering occurred. Πνευματικά refers to the content of what was sown, that is the proclaimed 'gospel' (vv 12, 14 etc). The structure of vv 11-15 makes this clear and also demonstrates that σαρκικά is not an opposite to πνευματικά but something of a different order.

Verses 11-12	*Verses 14-15*
(εἰ ἡμεῖς ὑμῖν)	(ὁ κύριος διέταξεν τοῖς)
τὰ πνευματικά	τὸ εὐαγγέλιον
ἐσπείραμεν	καταγγέλλουσιν
(μέγα εἰ ἡμεῖς)	
ὑμῶν τὰ σαρκικά	ἐκ τοῦ εὐαγγελίου
θερίσομεν	ζῆν

Conclusion:	
οὐκ ἐχρησάμεθα	Ἐγὼ δὲ οὐ κέχρημαι
τῇ ἐξουσίᾳ ταύτῃ	οὐδενὶ τούτων

Πνευματικά is virtually a short-hand for the 'gospel'. Sowing 'spiritual things' ought to bring 'material benefits' (living by the gospel) but, as noted in some detail earlier, Paul relinquished those for the sake of the gospel (i.e., in this argument, for the sake of τὰ πνευματικά).

In 12:1, as in 2:13, πνευματικῶν may be neuter or masculine. Many argue that the context talks of 'gifts' and therefore neuter is the best translation.[148] However, the *immediate* context refers to persons (v 2 —

---

148   *AV*; *RSV*; *JB*; *NEB*; Calvin 226; Robertson 259; Lias 136; *inter al.*

the people he addresses; v 3 — οὐδείς; v 6 — πᾶσιν; v 7 — ἑκάστῳ) and on this ground we prefer the translation 'Now concerning spiritual people'.[149]

On this reading, Paul was demonstrating how one 'spiritual' person could be distinguished from another. Again two concepts, attached to the word elsewhere, are present here. The Corinthians must not be 'uninformed' (v 1) and must 'understand' (γνωρίζω — v 3). The content of this understanding concerned the Holy Spirit and his witness to Jesus as Lord.

In 14:1, most to be desired of the πνευματικά is the gift of prophecy for it reveals God's mysteries in an intelligible manner, unlike 'tongues' (14:2-5) which does not speak μυστήρια (14:2) openly and thus does not edify the body of Christ.

When Paul returned to the question of the 'spiritual man' in 14:37, the issue of discerning and understanding was again central. A 'spiritual' man would know (ἐπιγινώσκω) that what Paul had been writing was a command of the Lord.

Finally, the adjective πνευματικός appears four times in 15:44-46 in antithesis to ψυχικός. Paul apparently did not see the antithesis in terms of Greek 'substance', but formed his contrast between a 'natural' and a 'spiritual' body. This resurrection body was 'spiritual' in that it derived from the πνεῦμα ζωοποιοῦν (15:45). Also it found its existence in the second man (v 47). 'Spiritual' was again at the heart of an antithesis centred on Christ. The basis on which Paul could contemplate a 'spiritual body' was that Christ himself, the second man,[150] had become a 'life-giving Spirit'. Christ stood in exemplary contrast to the first man (v 45).

Πνευματικός occurs occasionally elsewhere. In Romans 7[151] Paul called the law 'spiritual'. In a complex argument, he contended that the law had not been understood in the way God intended. The law was given by God and through it God revealed his will.[152] But the new life of the Spirit (7:6) was needed if the function of the law was to be understood. Paul contrasted the νόμος πνευματικός with himself as σαρκικός. His 'fleshly' nature was one which did not 'know' (γινώσκω — v 15) things properly. While the exceedingly difficult exegetical problems of this text cannot be addressed here, it does seem that, in talking of the law as 'spiritual', Paul was describing that which was

---

149 With Lake 202; Bruce 116.

150 In 15:47 glosses appear in some texts explaining second man as both κύριος and, in p[46], πνευματικός. The latter shows the influence of v 46.

151 For detailed discussion of this passage: Cranfield, *Romans*, I 330-370.

152 Rom 2:18ff.

given by God through the Spirit to reveal God's purposes (always for Paul, in Christ).

In Colossians 1:9 readers are exhorted to 'be filled with the knowledge of [God's] will in all wisdom and spiritual insight' (καὶ συνέσει πνευματικῇ). This 'spiritual insight' is possibly to be linked to the πνεῦμα (v 8). The Christocentric nature of this insight is expounded in vv 10-19. This focus on Christ is also found in Colossians 3:16 and Ephesians 5:19 ('spiritual songs'). In the latter text the songs seem to arise from being 'filled with the Spirit'. Both contexts stress the need to understand the 'wisdom' and 'will of the Lord'.[153]

In Ephesians 1:3 Christ is actually the *source* of all 'spiritual blessing'. The Spirit is not mentioned. The focus is on God's plans for 'us in Christ' (vv 4-14). It is this 'wisdom and insight' (v 9) which is the content of the spiritual blessing ἐν τοῖς ἐπουρανίοις ἐν Χριστῷ (v 3).[154]

In 1 Peter 2:5[155] the adjective πνευματικός is used twice. A 'spiritual house' and 'spiritual sacrifices' are mentioned. The work of the Holy Spirit is not specified. If the adjectives in 2:5 recall their etymology then perhaps the words themselves imply the helping Spirit. However, the connotation of the adjectives is reasonably clear. The house and offering point towards God through Christ (εὐπροσδέκτους τῷ θεῷ διὰ Ἰησοῦ Χριστοῦ). Christ is the focal point as both the cornerstone and the one who makes the sacrifices acceptable.

4.4.2   Summary

It is evident that πνευματικός/ά could be used in a variety of ways in the NT. It could mean 'figurative' in Revelation, or describe a non 'natural' body in 1 Corinthians 15, or people enlightened by the Spirit in ch 2, and it could describe gifts from God that needed evaluation and discernment (14:1). Nevertheless, an examination of the contexts in which the word was used indicates an underlying continuity of connotation. 'Spiritual things' discerned by a 'spiritual person' were expected to reveal the mysteries of God (2:7ff). Thus it is not surprising that πνευματικά have been seen to include verbal and revelatory gifts like gospel proclamation, prophecy, and interpretation (cf 12:13; 9:11; 14:1)[156] For Paul, in that the mysteries of God were revealed in the

---

153   Cf Eph 5:17; Col 3:16b.

154   Eph 6:12 is unique: 'the spiritual things of evil'. Perhaps the word, normally applied to things relating to Christ, served to emphasise the danger. Only the Spirit can protect a person from these.

155   A passage probably indebted to Paul (Dunn, "Spirit" 706).

156   There is no need to suggest πνευματικά actually *denotes* these gifts (Ellis, *Prophecy* 24-27).

Gospel of Christ, it is also understandable that πνευματικός came regularly to focus on Christ himself. To fail to see God's plans in *Christ* being revealed in 'spiritual things' was precisely *not* to be 'spiritual'.[157] Πνευματικά discerned by a spiritual person reveal the mysteries of God.[158]

The etymology clearly remained important. Several passages have revealed the Spirit to be the source of things spiritual. The Spirit also gave the understanding with which properly to evaluate those things.

Having explored the meanings of πνευματικός elsewhere, we can return to 1 Corinthians 10:3-4a. Πνευματικὸν βρῶμα / πόμα is unlikely to mean 'figurative' or even 'allegorical'.[159] Paul's point was that all *did* eat and drink but ... some 'were destroyed'. There is no *direct* suggestion that the Spirit was the source of the food and drink, but there is a strong Christological connection in v 4c: 'the rock was Christ'. We shall examine this in detail later but, for the moment, it raises the possibility that Paul, when talking of the 'spiritual rock', had in mind something from God that needed proper evaluation — which he gave it. This seems likely given that we have seen elsewhere how a proper understanding of something 'spiritual' normally pointed to Christ.[160]

However, more may be said about the meaning of πνευματικός here, given the use of the WT as we analysed them above. In order to do this, those findings must be combined with our general observations about the meaning of the word πνευματικός in other contexts.

Firstly, the traditions consistently regarded the manna and water as 'gifts' from God. A few linked the work of the Spirit with the gifts. Since Paul was recalling those traditions, the word πνευματικός probably connoted the *gift*-nature of the food and drink and possibly their *source*, the Spirit.[161]

Secondly, we noted that 'discernment' or 'understanding' was required of a 'spiritual person', but also that 'spiritual things' needed to be understood. These ideas were also present in the WT, in which the

[157] The adjective has similar connotations to the noun πνεῦμα. Schweizer's summary is revealing, 'For Paul ... the Spirit reveals to the believer God's saving work in Christ and makes possible his understanding and responsible acceptance thereof' (Schweizer, "Πνεῦμα" 436). This Christ-centredness of the revelation given by the Spirit is rarely emphasised. It is evident in John 14:25; 15:26; 16:13-14.

[158] Esp 2:7ff.

[159] Clearly we agree with Dunn, *Baptism* 124-125, that this passage is not about 'sacramentalism'. However, the WT are functioning as more than 'an allegory of *Christian* experience'.

[160] 4.4.1 above.

[161] Cf 2 Cor 8:14-15 where the OT quotation about manna is used as an example of God's grace given to the Corinthians.

Israelites failed to 'understand', and where the gifts of manna and water needed to be 'understood' or else judgment would follow.

Thus, we suggest that in 10:3-4a the adjective πνευματικός was functioning, if not as a technical term, at least with recognisable and broad connotations. A πνευματικὸν βρῶμα would have summarised aspects of the earlier traditions: the food was a *gift* of God and needed properly to be *understood*; it may have indicated the Spirit as the specific source. The new Pauline element was that, when properly discerned, the gifts pointed to *Christ*.

Could one adjective have conveyed this much information? In light of our work so far the answer must be a cautious affirmative.[162] Paul's argument in 2:6-3:3 makes this likely, and if the word 'spiritual' was important among the Corinthians, they might readily have understood most of this. This would be more likely if 2:6-16 was a 'pre-formed piece' which they knew beforehand and which Paul had 'employed and adapted to its present context'.[163]

It is also possible that the combination of this adjective with 'food' and 'drink' specifically conveyed the idea that Paul was thinking of a *revelatory* gift. Given the way manna and water were used in the WT for 'the word of God',[164] and the way the πνευματικά in 1 Corinthians are linked frequently with revelatory gifts, we believe this may indeed have been the case.[165] It is not necessary to propose that Paul was drawing on wisdom traditions[166] to suggest that, in the light of what we have seen, both he and the Corinthians may have used the manna traditions to describe God's *gifts* to his people, specifically the *verbal* revelatory gifts. In other words, gifts of σοφία, γνῶσις, or προφητεία may have been particularly easily associated with the manna/rock traditions.[167]

To conclude, the Corinthians may have regarded themselves as 'spiritual' because they had the gifts of the Spirit — especially γνῶσις. If so, then they would have seen themselves as people who possessed revelation given by the Spirit. We suggest that not only did they probably understand the word 'spiritual' in more or less the way Paul used it, but that his use of it in 10:3-4a would have made them think of

---

162   Davidson, *Typology* 247, admits that the word is 'a catchword for a whole complex of concepts'.

163   Ellis, "Traditions" 490, although Ellis does not suggest the Corinthians knew it.

164   E.g., Deut 8:3 etc. Also cf Wis 16:25-26, where obedience to God's 'gift' which 'nourishes' is obedience to his 'word', which preserves 'those who have faith'.

165   Sandelin, *Nourisher* 169; cf 108-111 etc. Cf 4.3.7 above and Bandstra's position: 4.5.1 below.

166   See further possible links with wisdom traditions in sects 4.5.1-2.

167   Cf Sandelin, *Nourisher* 169.

specific 'spiritual gifts' — *not the sacraments*, but γνῶσις, wisdom, tongues, prophecy, etc, for these have been the gifts already mentioned, or shortly to be mentioned, in this epistle.[168] Additionally, reference to the 'food' (manna) may have made them think especially of verbal and revelatory gifts, thus further clarifying the link with γνῶσις.

4.5   God's judgment (Verses 4b - 5)

The Christological emphasis commonly associated with the word πνευματικός is to be found in the clause: ἡ πέτρα δὲ ἦν ὁ Χριστός (v 4c). On the basis of the work so far we suggest that a 'spiritual rock' meant that it was one given by God and which needed properly to be 'understood'. But two problems arise: i) What did Paul mean by a *'following* rock' (ἀκολουθούσης)? ii) Given Paul's understanding that the 'rock was Christ', in what sense was this true?

We will argue that Paul's use of 'rock' was based upon the epithet for God frequently employed in the WT. However, firstly we shall review the rabbinic traditions to which many commentators suggest Paul alluded.[169] In doing this, we must bear in mind that some of this material is decidedly anachronistic thus a healthy scepticism about such 'parallels' should be maintained.[170]

4.5.1   The following rock

The problem of the ἀκολουθούσα πέτρα has been examined by many.[171] In Hebrew two words for 'rock' are used: in Exodus 17:6, צוּר, and in Numbers 20, סֶלַע. In the LXX both λίθος and πέτρα can be used to translate either Hebrew word. But in neither text is there any indication that the rock moved with the wandering Israelites.

The Rabbinic sources cited for the origin of the phrase 'following rock' are various. Most of these so-called sources appear to go back to a Targumic interpretation of Numbers 21:16ff. In *Neofiti* I on Numbers 21:16ff[172] the names of the places past which the Israelites travelled

---

168   Cf 1:4-7; 2:12-14; 12:4-11; 13:1-2: 14:1-5 etc.

169   Cf Weiss 251; Senft 129; Héring 87; Wolff II 42; *inter al.* Also next footnote.

170   See the warnings of Neusner, "Scripture" 269ff; "Method" 89-111; "Use" 215-225; Sandmel, "Parallelomania" 1-13.   Macho, *Neophyti I* "Introduction", suggests a date as early as second century AD for *Neophyti.* Cf McNamara *Targum* 186ff. *Num Rab* in its final composition may be as late as the tenth century AD, although it draws on earlier texts.

171   Cf Hanson, *Jesus* 22-23; Ellis, *Use* 66-70; Cullmann, "Πέτρα" 97; Conzelmann 166; Davidson, *Typology* 233-247; S-B 3:406-408. Also note additional detail in Glasson, *Moses* 58-59.

172   The Diez Macho edition has been used.

were interpreted literally: Beer — 'well', Mattanah — 'gift', Nahaliel — 'torrent', Bamoth — 'high places'. The resulting interpretation was that the well (Beer) was a gift, which 'gift' became a torrent that went with them up to the high places and down to the valleys. Another Targum adds that the well went around the entire camp of Israel and gave a drink to each person at his tent door.[173]

However, while this may explain the idea of a source of water 'following' the Israelites, there is no link here between 'well' and 'rock'. To bridge that gap other sources are examined. Frequently, *Numbers Rabba* on 21:17 is cited: 'How was the well constructed? It was rock-shaped like a kind of bee-hive and wherever they journeyed it rolled along ... When the standards halted ... that same rock would settle ...'[174] The writer also wrote of the well having been 'given' as evidenced in the text 'he opened the rock'.

The idea of water following the Israelites was present in earlier traditions. *Sifre* on Numbers 11:21 reads 'did not a brook follow them in the wilderness and provide them with fat fish?'[175] In the *Tosefta Sukka* 3:11ff we read, 'So the well which was with Israel in the wilderness, was like a rock ... travelling with them ... and it made mighty streams'.[176]

In the first century, Philo appears to have known two separate traditions concerning streams from the rock[177] and streams from a well,[178] while Pseudo-Philo speaks of 'a well of water following them brought he forth for them'.[179]

A comparison of these traditions with 1 Corinthians 10:4 shows that the main tradition is based on Numbers 21 and refers to a well and streams, *not* to the rock.[180] Pseudo-Philo and *Neofiti* knew of the following *well* tradition giving early evidence for that. However, when Philo used the *rock* tradition he was much nearer to the Biblical text concerning the wilderness rock than to any elaborate 'following well' tradition.[181] As Driver noted,[182] even in the much later text of *Numbers*

173   Diez Macho IV 582 n 2 (*Pseudo Jonathan*). Cf also *Tg Yer* Num 21.

174   *Num Rab* I 5.

175   Probably edited in fourth century but representing traditions of Tannaitic rabbis; from *Midrash Sifre on Numbers* (trans Levertoff) 77.

176   This is believed to draw on early collections of *beraithot*. c 250 AD? This text also mentions the well going up the mountains and down valleys.

177   *Leg All* ii 86; *Det* 116.

178   *Som* ii 271; *Ebr* 112.

179   *Bib Ants* 10:7.

180   Ellis, *Prophecy* 211.

181   Cf *Det* 116 with Ps 78:15-16 or with Deut 32:13. Philo's comments seem to build on the poetic hyperbole found in the OT surrounding descriptions of water flowing from the *rock*.

182   Driver, "Notes" 17.

Rabba where the well was rock-shaped, the commentary was based on a text about the well and not the rock of Exodus 17 or Numbers 20.

In 1 Corinthians 10, Paul's reference is clearly to the *rock* as source of that water. Thus, if Paul knew these traditions, he was applying them in quite a new way. We shall suggest that, whether he knew them or not, they were not his concern at this point.

Bandstra, who argues Paul did not use midrashic traditions, regards the γάρ of v 4b as giving 'the reason why' the food and drink may be called 'spiritual', even though only the drink and rock are mentioned.[183] He believes Philo shows how the rock might be the source of *both* food and drink. Philo identified the rock[184] and well[185] independently with the wisdom of God. Philo also said that Moses used a synonym for 'rock' and called it 'manna'. This 'rock-manna' was then identified as the 'divine word'. Deuteronomy 32:13 influenced this interpretation. Israel took 'honey' and 'oil' from the rock — both properties are ascribed to manna in Exodus 16:31 and Numbers 11:8. Bandstra concludes: 'Thus for Philo the Rock, identified as divine wisdom, was Israel's source of both food and drink'.[186] Paul, Bandstra argues, worked with a similar understanding of Deuteronomy 32 and 'on his own might well have constructed his idea of the "spiritual Rock which followed them"'.[187]

Others see similarities with Philo based on his equation of the rock with pre-existent wisdom[188] even if, as Barrett says, it 'does not mean that he [Paul] wished to say about Christ all that Hellenistic Judaism said about wisdom'.[189] But we return to this shortly.

While Bandstra's argument is intriguing, Paul gives no indication that honey and oil should cause *him* to link the manna and the rock in this way. Even if Bandstra's suggestion is accepted, there is still the problem that Philo did not mention a '*following*' rock.

In our examination of the WT we noted that their *function* was to remind Israelites of God's faithfulness in giving gifts to his people, but also to warn them against becoming arrogant and 'fat' on those gifts. In the descriptions of God's generosity, considerable hyperbole was used. For example, 'he cleft rocks in the wilderness, and gave them drink abundantly as from the deep. He made streams come out of the rock, and

---

183 Bandstra, "Interpretation" 12.
184 *Leg All* ii 86.
185 *Ebr* 112.
186 Bandstra, "Interpretation" 13.
187 Ibid 14.
188 *Leg All* ii 86. Cf Conzelmann 167; Hammerton-Kelly, *Pre-existence* 131-132.
189 Barrett 223.

caused waters to flow down like rivers'.[190] The Hebrew plural צֻרִים at least opens up the possibility that later generations would understand that *throughout* the wanderings rocks had been 'cleft' to provide water.

In 10:3-4 Paul, too, was emphasising God's graciousness to *all* Israelites. It therefore seems possible that such texts provided him with the figure of a 'following rock'.[191] Certainly, the word 'following' conveys to the reader the *continuous* nature of God's care for his people.[192]

4.5.2   The rock was Christ

Whatever background caused Paul to talk of a 'following rock', our second question is not yet answered: 'In what sense was Christ present in the rock?'

Knox turns to the equation of the rock with wisdom in Philo and the exegesis of the Dispersion, and concludes that 10:4c 'was simply the equation of Jesus with the Wisdom of God, for which the water from the rock was a standing type ...'.[193] Bourke[194] says the equation is more likely to be based on the books of Wisdom and Sirach[195] than on Philo. Wisdom was the food and drink but also the one who gave the gifts.[196] Therefore, as the rock was the source of drink and the rock was wisdom, so the rock was Christ because Christ is wisdom (1 Corinthians 1:30).[197]

Such equations do not remain unchallenged. Fee makes three points against these positions. i) In 1:24 and 30 Christ is not the personified wisdom of other hellenistic literature. Paul's statements concerning wisdom are 'soteriological'. 'Christ is the "wisdom of God" precisely because he is "the power of God for the salvation of everyone who believes"'.[198] ii) 'Only the *fact* that [wisdom traditions] interpret the rock is in common'. Philo's interpretation was 'pure allegory'. iii) Paul was not saying 'that Christ is now the rock, but that in the rock he was somehow himself actually present in Israel'.[199] Even Bourke also admits that there is no '*Grundlage* in the Book of Wisdom' for the move

---

[190]   Ps 78:15-16 (LXX — Ps 77 where the singular πέτρα is used). Cf Ps 105:41 (LXX: 104:41); 114:8 (LXX: 113); Is 48:21.

[191]   Cf Ellis, *Prophecy* 212. Cullmann, "Πέτρα" 97.

[192]   Loc cit.

[193]   Knox, *Gentiles* 123, 87-88.

[194]   Bourke, "Eucharist" 376-377.

[195]   Cf Wis 11:4; Sir 15:3.

[196]   Cf Sir 24:19-21.

[197]   Also see Robertson 201-202. Cf McKelvey, *Temple*, who suggests links between 10:4 and Jewish ideas of the temple.

[198]   Fee 77, 86-87, 448-449.

[199]   Ibid 449, n 37.

from the natural to the spiritual level of the water miracle.[200] Feuillet also says that only Philo can be appealed to for the equation of rock with wisdom. That Paul had read Philo is only 'une possibilité qu'on ne saurait excluire'.[201]

A more direct answer to our question arises from the earlier analysis of the WT and the point made above, in agreement with Cullmann, that ἀκολουθοῦσα teaches about God's *continual* supply of the water. We noted that in three of the traditions (Deuteronomy 32, and Psalms (Hebrew) 78 and 95) 'rock' was an epithet used for God. It referred to his covenant faithfulness to his people.[202]

It is possible that Paul could simply have had in mind God, the Rock — in a similar manner to the way in which he applied the OT κύριος texts to Christ. The evidence for this is circumstantial but, we believe, is greater than commentators have recognised.[203]

Firstly, Deuteronomy 32 is used by Paul in this context (10:20, 22), and was probably used in 8:4-6.[204] Thus the ideas of that passage may have been in his mind in v 4.

Secondly, in these three traditions where God is called 'rock', the function of the stories was to rehearse i) the faithfulness of God in providing gifts to his people and ii), the sin of the people so that lessons might be learned. 10:1-14 seems to function in the same way. The past faithfulness of God was held out as hope for the present (v 13); it was this that the epithet 'rock' so aptly described. But the Israelites sinned and 'tested' God (Psalm 78:18, 41). They 'scoffed' at the rock and 'stirred him to jealousy' (Deuteronomy 32:15-16). In 10:9 the one who was 'tested' was Christ,[205] and in 10:22 it was the 'Lord' who might be provoked to jealousy — perhaps also referring to Christ.[206]

---

[200] Bourke, "Eucharist" 376

[201] Feuillet, *Sagesse* 106. Bourke, "Eucharist" 377: Paul and Philo were independent interpreters of sapiential traditions.

[202] This point can be demonstrated in most texts where either סֶלַע or צוּר apply to God. God faithfully provides in time of need, and brings judgment on sin. Cf Deut 32 (צוּר is used four times); 1 Sam 2:2-3; 2 Sam 22:47; 23:3; Ps 31:2-4; 62:2, 6-8; 71:3; 89:26; Is 17:10; 30:29; 44:8. For a similar use of the epithet also see 1QH9:2; 11:15.

[203] Several commentators suggest that v 4c may be based on the God = Rock equation. Cf Bruce 91; Godet II 57-58; Davidson, *Typology* 243; Van Roon, "Relation" 229; Fee 449.

[204] Above sect 2.2.

[205] We read 'Christ', with Nestle[26], rather than 'Lord'. See detailed arguments in Osburn "Text", also Metzger, *Commentary* 560.

[206] Barrett 238; Fee 474 n 57; *inter al.* 'Paul's reference to Christ here is analogous to that in ver. 4' (Metzger, *Commentary* 560).

Thirdly, the move from rock to Christ would be particularly straightforward if these three WT were in mind, or even if Paul only drew on Deuteronomy 32. The 'rock' is qualified in each instance by phrases Paul could have applied to Christ. For example, in Deuteronomy 32:15 and Ps 95:1, 'the rock *of his salvation*' (cf Phil 3:20); in Deuteronomy 32:18, 'the rock that begot you' (cf 1 Corinthians 8:6 — 'Christ, through whom we exist'); in Psalm 78:35, 'God was their rock ... their redeemer' (cf 1 Corinthians 1:30).

As mentioned in 4.1 above, the coming of Christ affected the whole of Paul's understanding of God's redemptive purposes among his people throughout history. Paul saw Christ as the fulfilment of God's faithfulness and the embodiment of his grace (1:4). 'In Christ Jesus' the Corinthians received every spiritual gift (1:4-7). In line with OT teaching, Paul regarded the manna and water as gifts from the faithful God who was called 'rock'. But Paul had a new 'spiritual' understanding of this. Christ was the source of the water: water which was 'spiritual' in that it pointed back to Christ. To ask questions about the *manner* in which this was true misses Paul's point and is a question perhaps more prompted by anachronistic sacramental discussions than by v 4c. Paul was direct. The rock *was* Christ. Detailed analysis of how Christ was there is not addressed. For Paul the fact is that he *was* — and that is God's revelation to him.

It is thus meaningless to ask whether the Israelites should have seen Christ in the wilderness, for that understanding is precisely what is new to Paul. It is not that 'Paul's readers should see the rock then as an equivalent to Christ now',[207] but rather that they should look at Scripture and see a directly parallel example to their own situation. The covenant Lord, 'tested' and 'provoked to jealousy' in Paul's day, was the same covenant Lord who was tested in the wilderness. He was the faithful supplier of needs and hence the rock of Deuteronomy 32 or Psalm 78. Once this was accepted Paul could move to application. But first Paul had to make the main point that he wished to draw from these traditions.

4.5.3   They were destroyed

Paul continued to use the WT in the way they had so often been used. Having pointed to the gifts that *all* the Israelites received, Paul showed that most were destroyed.[208] The specific sins are addressed in vv 6-14.

Ἀλλά (v 5) distinguishes between what might have been expected and what actually happened to the recipients of the gifts. The verb εὐδοκέω denoted God's purposive decision.[209] In its negative form it

---

[207]   *Contra* Dunn, *Christology* 184.
[208]   Esp cf (LXX) Ps 79:29-31.
[209]   Schrenk, "Εὐδοκέω" 740-741.

means 'rejected'.[210] Perhaps there is an implicit contrast with 1:21 where God was pleased (εὐδοκέω) to save διὰ τῆς μωρίας τοῦ κηρύγματος. This seems to accord well with the WT recounted elsewhere where, depending on the people's response to God's gifts, either blessing or judgment would be experienced. The dual sanctions of the covenant still had to be understood in Paul's day. The Israelites felt they were secure ... 'nevertheless ... they were scattered over the desert', that is, they were judicially dealt with by God.[211]

4.5.4   Summary

The first five verses, an 'implicit midrash' on various OT texts, set the basis for Paul's application which was to follow. Paul showed that all the Israelites were blessed by God, being separated out into a nation under Moses. They all received the same gifts given by God, who faithfully continued to give them food and drink.[212] The use of the word 'rock' probably comes from the epithet for God, so frequently found in the WT. God was continually present with and faithful to his people — a point which will be addressed again in v 13.

However, the Israelites' security did not lie in those 'spiritual' gifts of manna or water for, even having received them, they were judged by God. With Paul's understanding of events still more than this could be said — even *Christ's* supplying of needs did not guarantee protection for the majority of members.

If our understanding of the argument thus far is correct, then this scenario provided by the WT gave Paul a perfect example for the Corinthian church. They thought that the gifts they had received from God marked them out as people 'known by God'. Paul showed that these gifts provided no more security than gifts had provided for Israelites in the wilderness.

4.6   Lessons from the past (Verses 6 - 14)

Paul made two specific applications of the WT as τύποι (τυπικῶς, vv 6, 11).[213] The first was a matter of principle. People who thought they 'stood' needed to take heed lest they fell. This was at the root of the Corinthian problem. Many thought they were 'standing', but were in fact falling. The second application concerned the particular evidence of the

---

[210] Senft 129.

[211] Καταστρώννυμι is used in Num 14:16 when Moses interceded to stop God 'slaughtering' the Israelites.

[212] Note the imperfect: ἔπινον (vv 3-4).

[213] See sect 4.1. Note the broad definition of 'type' in that discussion. Here, Paul was talking of 'potential' judgment rather than real. It was his hope that the 'types' would have *no* fulfilment.

breaching of covenant 'standing': idolatry (v 14). This problem had been addressed in ch 8 and required further attention. We shall examine vv 6-14 in three sections. In the first we shall look at the particular sins of the Israelites and their possible parallels at Corinth (vv 6-10). In the second, Paul's general application of principle will be discussed (v 12) and in the third we shall look at Paul's comment on God's faithfulness and the application of the message to the subject of idolatry (vv 13-14).

4.6.1   Καθώς τινες αὐτῶν

It was to 'judgment typology'[214] that Paul moved after presenting God's grace in vv 1-4. The WT had presented God's covenant dealings in terms of both blessings *and* curse or judgment. Ταῦτα δὲ ... (v 6), therefore, looks back to vv 1-4 and forward to the examples of judgment.[215]

Κἀκεῖνοι ἐπεθύμησαν refers generally to the Israelites' sin in the wilderness.[216] 'Craving' may have become a prominent description of general sin in the light of the decalogue: οὐκ ἐπιθυμήσεις.[217]

The sin of 'craving evil' is set out in four examples which were prominent in the WT: idolatry, immorality, testing Christ,[218] and grumbling. This fact, together with the rhetorical pattern in vv 7-10[219] may indicate that Paul was simply listing sins rather than describing specific Corinthian sins.[220]

Certainly the traditions were well suited for Paul's attack on idolatry.[221] Paul probably had in mind the idolatry mentioned in 8:10 — eating at a table in an idol's temple.[222] Apart from the links between this chapter and ch 8, in vv 14-22 Paul discusses cultic meals and in v 7 quotes from Exodus 32 about an idolatrous meal.[223] The original issue of εἰδωλόθυτα (8:1) is still of great concern.

[214] Ellis, *Prophecy* 168.

[215] Bengel 639.

[216] Meyer 286; Godet II 61. Cf Num 11:4; esp 11:34: Deut 9:22; Ps 77:29 (LXX); 105:14 (LXX).

[217] Exod 20:17.

[218] See above p 146-148. In the OT, of course, God was 'tested'.

[219] Willis 147 mentions 'an A-B-B-A pattern between imperative and subjunctive'. Each sin is followed by καθώς τινες αὐτῶν.

[220] Cf Willis 147; Barrett 226.

[221] Cf Deut 32:16-17, 21, 37-38; also Ps 77 (LXX v 58); Ps 105 (LXX vv 28, 36-37); Ezek 20:8, 16, 18, 24 etc; 4QDib Ham 2-7; 1 Baruch 1:22 etc.

[222] Fee 454.

[223] Fee (loc cit) argues that the choice of Exod 32:6a would have better suited a general discussion of idolatry. Instead v 6b was chosen by Paul as 'specifically identifying the idolatry as a matter of cultic meals in the idol's presence'. Cf Malan, "Use" 152-153.

Whether the other three examples in vv 8-10 addressed specific sins in Corinth is not so clear. Perhaps they were chosen for the sake of the warning involved in the attached punishment. However, the text of Exodus 32:6 used in 10:7b may imply Corinthian involvement in πορνεία. The word παίζειν[224] referred to the cultic use of dance and games, translating the Hebrew צָחַק which also may have had an erotic sense of cultic licentiousness.[225] The Corinthian idolatrous rites may have involved sexual sin. On the other hand, the traditions regularly linked idolatry with immorality as is the case in both Exodus 32 and Numbers 25 which Paul cited in vv 7-8. Since instances of πορνεία had already been addressed in this letter,[226] perhaps the application of this material was meant to be wider.

'Testing' God was also prominent in the WT and frequently linked to 'craving'.[227] Paul, as one 'on whom the end of the ages has come' (v 11), could talk of *Christ* being 'tested' instead of 'God'.[228] This change may have been facilitated by the LXX of Numbers 21 where the people were sinning against the κύριος, but it was also in accordance with Paul's understanding of Scripture seen in v 4c.[229]

Verse 10 mentions 'grumbling'. This sin is nowhere directly linked to a 'Destroyer'.[230] A substantive use of ὀλοθρεύω appears in Exodus 12:23 and Wisdom 18:25 but neither offers the form Paul chooses. However, in the accounts of the WT in Psalm 105:23-25 (LXX) the verb ἐξολεθρεύω appears twice in close connection with the verb γογγύζω. There the same form is found as in 1 Corinthians 10:10 (ἐγόγγυσαν). This may therefore be Paul's source.[231]

Whether or not these three examples were directly paralleled by behaviour in the Corinthian community, Paul's repetition of καθώς or καθάπερ (v 10) τινὲς αὐτῶν[232] drew attention to the judgment of community members. The use of ἀπόλλυμι in vv 9 and 10 recalled the warning of destruction in 8:11, but also portrayed the result of the 'sin against Christ' in 8:12.

Even without the specific application Paul made in v 12, the combination of words associated with judgment[233] and the force of the

---

224 A NT *hapax legomenon*.
225 Bertram, "Παίζω" 628-630.
226 5:1-2; 10-11; 6:9, 13, 18.
227 Ex 17:2; Deut 6:16; Ps (LXX) 77:18; 94:8-9; 105:14; etc.
228 n 205 above.
229 Above sect 4.5.2. Cf Cerfaux, "Kyrios" 182.
230 Ὀλοθρευτής is a *hapax legomenon* in the NT.
231 Cf Schneider, "Ὀλοθρεύω" 170; Lightfoot, *Horae* IV 225-226.
232 Τινες αὐτῶν contrasts with the πάντες of vv 1-4.
233 οὐκ ... εὐδόκησεν; κατεστρώθησαν (v 5); καὶ ἔπεσαν (v 8); ἀπώλλυντο (v 9); ἀπώλοντο ὑπὸ τοῦ ὀλοθρευτοῦ (v 10).

message of vv 5-10 indicate that Paul faced people who thought they were safe from such judgment. The fact that even people who had received God's spiritual gifts could sin in a way which would lead to their destruction had been firmly established.

4.6.2   Lest he fall

The word Ὥστε shows the centrality of v 12 to Paul's argument. He had already talked of the arrogance and self-confidence of the 'strong',[234] and now summed this up in the phrase ὁ δοκῶν ἑστάναι .... The broad principle that he drew from 'these things' was one which had been made in many of the WT. Israelites, blessed by God, felt secure, grew fat and still became arrogant and sinned in a way that led to destruction.

The use of the verb ἵστημι probably indicates that Paul was still thinking in 'covenant' categories and of 'standing' before the Lord who judged his people.[235] The verb ἵστημι invariably carried some theological weight when employed by Paul. Apart from where it meant 'established' or 'stands secure',[236] it normally referred to 'standing before God'. People stood before God by faith[237] and only the Lord could enable that standing. Judgment concerning a person's 'standing' was therefore God's alone.[238] Once 'justified by faith' a person 'stood in grace'.[239]

This concept of 'standing' is similar to that found in the OT where ἵστημι was sometimes used to translate both the words עָמַד and כּוּן. God's covenant stood firm,[240] and God could make the psalmist's feet 'stand secure' if he trusted the Lord.[241] The one who could 'stand' in God's holy place had a 'pure heart',[242] but this standing was achieved by God's grace. Jeremiah 7:8-15 shows that those who sought after other gods could not 'stand' (v 10) before God.

The Qumran documents employ עָמַד and כּוּן similarly.[243] The manner in which man might 'stand secure' before God was examined in 1QS 11:4-16. The rock (סֶלַע) of man's steps is the truth of God (11:4-5). This is the source of righteousness, therefore man cannot make his

---

[234]   This problem of arrogance underlies Paul's polemic in 1:26-2:5. It is clear in 3:1-4, 18-21; 4:6-8; 8:1-3.

[235]   *Contra* Conzelmann 168 n 43.

[236]   Rom 3:31; cf 2 Cor 13:1.

[237]   Rom 11:20; 2 Cor 1:24.

[238]   Rom 14:4.

[239]   Rom 5:2.

[240]   LXX: Ps 104:10.

[241]   LXX: Ps 30:8.

[242]   LXX: Ps 23:3-4. Cf Sir 40:12.

[243]   For further details see Grundmann, "Ἵστημι" 645-648.

own steps 'stand secure' כּוּן — v 11). Only God can do this (עָמַד —
v 12). The section ends with a prayer for a heart of knowledge and the
right to stand before God for ever (כּוּן — v 16).[244]

If this is what Paul meant by ἵστημι in v 12, then he clearly believed
the 'strong' 'thought' (δοκέω) that they had complete covenant security,
being able to 'stand' before God (cf 8:8). Paul saw this as a false
security, and taught a fuller understanding of what membership of the
covenant community implied.

The alternative to 'standing' was 'falling' (πίπτω). The danger was
acute for the 'strong', for 'falling meant the loss of salvation', just as
'stumbling' might mean 'destruction' for the weak (8:8, 11).[245] Perhaps
Paul is ironical in using πίπτω here. The 'strong' had been warned of the
danger of causing the weak to 'stumble', now it is *they* who will 'fall'.

Thus, v 12 reveals the heart of Paul's concern for the Corinthians.
They were indeed part of the new covenant community, 'known by God'
(8:3), because God had called them into the κοινωνία τοῦ υἱοῦ αὐτοῦ
(1:9). The call and grace of God were fundamental to membership. But
'knowledge' and others of God's gifts were no guarantee or marker of
that security, any more than manna had been to the Israelites.

This suggested link between 10:12 and 8:3 receives support not just
from the progression of Paul's discussion, for which we have argued
throughout, but also from the fact that ὁ δοκῶν ... (10:12) was probably
the same class of person intended by the phrase εἴ τις δοκεῖ ... (8:2).[246]
Paul sought to demonstrate that security was only shown externally in a
response of love and obedience to God. Ultimately all was dependent on
the faithful God who 'keeps', to the end (1:9; 10:13), those he knows,
those who love him.[247] .

4.6.3   Πιστὸς δὲ ὁ θεός

Some encounter problems with v 13. Godet is typical,

> This verse is undoubtedly one of the most difficult of the whole Epistle, at
> least as to the logical connection joining it to what precedes and to what
> follows.[248]

But the problem is less significant when it is remembered that the
message of God's covenant faithfulness, even to a rebellious people, was

---

[244] Cf also 1QH4:21-22.
[245] Roetzel, *Judgment* 172. *Contra* Michaelis "Πίπτω" 165. Cf 1 Cor 6:9-
10; Rom 11:22; Gal 5:4.
[246] Cf 3:18.
[247] 8:3 cf Deuteronomy 7:9 below.
[248] Godet II 68.

common to most of the WT. We have noted the epithet 'rock' in that connection and now we read πιστὸς θεός.

The description of God as πιστὸς θεός appears only twice in the LXX and both occurrences were examined above. Deuteronomy 7:9 says, ὅυτος θεός, θεὸς πιστός, ὁ φυλάσσων διαθήκην καὶ ἔλεος τοῖς ἀγαπῶσιν αὐτὸν .... In Deuteronomy 32:4b (possibly the basis for this whole section) we read, θεὸς πιστός, ... δίκαιος καὶ ὅσιος κύριος. Interestingly in the Massoretic text אֵל אֱמוּנָה (v 4b) is in parallel poetic construction with הַצּוּר. The covenant context of the phrase is important.[249] Even as the Israelites were being warned of judgment, the faithfulness of God in forgiving his people was stressed. God brought them out of Egypt and brought people through 'testing' because he was faithful to his promises.

In God's faithfulness lay the possibility of being 'established' (βεβαιόω) until the judgment day and being found 'blameless',[250] (ἀνέγκλητος — 1:8). This was surely an integral part of Paul's understanding of the lessons to be learned from the wilderness.

Thus we suggest that v 13 is not difficult to locate logically in Paul's argument once it is realised that he was using the traditions *as they had normally been used in Jewish history*. The function of the verse is the same as the function of the stress on God's covenant faithfulness in those traditions. There God 'tested' (πειράζω) his people, so that they would learn to rely on him (cf Deuteronomy 8:2). When they failed this test they were guilty of 'tempting' or 'proving' God.[251] But the writers recognised that the human situation was hopeless if the one who first chose the Israelites did not remain faithful to them. This was what Paul had acknowledged in 1:8-9, but it needed repeating if these traditions were truly to function as warnings against arrogance and false security.

Various understandings of the word ἀνθρώπινος have been suggested.[252] It probably meant 'commonly experienced by men'. Perhaps it referred to the general sin of 'desiring evil' (v 6), or the specific sin of idolatry (vv 7, 14). However, we feel it more probably referred to the sin of self-pride seen in a person who believed he 'stood' when he did not. For community members, however, God faithfully provided the 'way out' of this sin (ἔκβασις — 10:13).[253]

---

249   Cf Is 49:7: πιστός ἐστιν ὁ ἅγιος Ἰσραήλ. Note the covenant context (v 8).

250   1 Thess 5:23-24; cf 2 Thess 3:3.

251   (ἐκ)πειράζω — Ps (LXX) 77:18 and 1 Corinthians 10:9.

252   Cf Murphy-O'Connor 96: the 'common lot of humanity'; similarly Barrett 229; Ellicott 182, 'commensurate with man's powers'; Conzelmann 169; Bengel 640, a temptation that '*oponitur tentatio daemoniaca*'.

253   Robertson 209, noting the article with ἔκβασις, says: 'there is no πειρασμός without its proper ἔκβασις. Conzelmann 169 regards the ἔκβασις

Verse 13 is neither simply an 'encouragement',[254] nor a further warning.[255] It serves both those ends[256] but also functions as a reminder of God's covenant faithfulness to his people even when they were being tempted to break that covenant. It is perhaps significant that God's faithfulness helps them 'bear up under' (ὑποφέρω) the temptation, that is, it prevents the 'falling' (indirectly confirming our understanding of ἵστημι).[257]

4.6.4 Summary

The sin of idolatry was uppermost in Paul's thoughts in this section. This is confirmed, as we shall see below, in v 14.

Paul was confronting people who believed they were secure before God. Verse 12 is, therefore, a summary of Paul's message. The grounds on which the Israelites felt secure (God's blessings and gifts) were the grounds on which the Corinthians felt secure. Paul warned against this attitude.

True grounds for security lie in the faithful God. If, instead of relying on a false sense of security, the Corinthians were to do his will, then they would be secure, and the ἔκβασις would be theirs.

4.7 Provoking the Lord to jealousy (Verses 14 - 22)

This much discussed section contains one of the few references in the NT to the Christian communion meal. While something of Paul's view of this meal may be gleaned from these verses, this was not the focus of his argument. We shall see that it was the problem with idols and idolatry that gave rise to the mention of the Christian meal,[258] rather than the other way around, and that this becomes especially evident in the application Paul made in vv 20b-22. In this section, we shall examine the meaning of the word κοινωνία — something Paul believed to be present in both the meals he mentioned in vv 16-20. We shall see that the so-called 'covenantal' ideas, present in the first section of this chapter, are still prominent and shall suggest that Ἰσραὴλ κατὰ σάρκα is likely to refer not just to historical Israel but to *sinful* Israel. In terms of the structure of Paul's argument we shall contend that there are not three meals discussed here (Christian, Israelite and pagan) but one: the

---

as 'the *one* eschatological act of salvation'. Weiss 255, says it means 'conclusion'.

[254] Robertson 208-209; Meyer 292; Allo 235.

[255] Chrysostom 324; Bengel 641; Olshausen 161.

[256] Calvin 214.

[257] Cf use of ὑποφέρω in Micah 7:9; Amos 7:10.

[258] Barrett 231; Willis 166; Meeks, "Midrash" 71. *Contra* Conzelmann 170: 'Here the emphasis is on the sacrament'.

Israelite — briefly illustrated by the Christian meal. The problem for the Corinthians was the problem for the Israelites: joining an idolatrous sacrificial meal led to a breach of the covenant relationship with God. He was provoked to jealousy.

4.7.1   Shun idols

Brash self-confidence in their position of security before God had led Christians to attend idol temples and to join in eating idol meat (ch 8). Verse 14 is a straightforward command to flee idolatry in idol temples. That this verse follows directly from the preceding argument is evident from the word Διόπερ.[259] This is used only here and in 8:13. In both places it introduces an unambiguous consequence of the preceding discussion.[260]

This further discussion of the implications of idolatry is now addressed in vv 15-22. Verse 14, therefore, forms a bridge between vv 1-13 and the following verses dealing with meals.

Excursus

The debate about the background to the meals discussed in these verses is extensive and cannot be fully examined here as it is not wholly relevant to our thesis. However, a brief review of scholarly opinion in this area is in order.

Led by Heitmüller, Eichorn, Loisy and others, many commentators sought to explain Paul's sacramental thought against a hellenistic-mystery background.[261]

However, this approach of the *religionsgeschichtliche Schule* was attacked by MacGregor, who was more eclectic. He looked at both hellenistic pagan cults and Jewish meals: the problems he saw with 'mystery' parallels included i) anachronism, ii) the fact that meals did not appear to be central to the cults anyway, and iii) that crude theophagy was probably not evident in the mysteries.[262]

---

[259] *Contra* Conzelmann 170, who does not discern a 'strict connection of thought' here.

[260] Also see the textual variant in 14:13. If original, its function there would be identical to that found in 10:14.

[261] Heitmüller, *Taufe*. Cf Harris, *Origins*. Loisy, "Mystery" 54, argues: Christians 'do not only commemorate this [the death of Jesus]; we may say they go over it again (la réitèrent) for themselves, as the votaries of Osiris or of Attis renewed for themselves the death of their god'. For contrary arguments see Wagner, *Mysteries* part 2; Käsemann, *Essays* 108-109.

[262] MacGregor, *Origins* 27-28. 'Whatever may be said of its evolution the origin of the Eucharist can hardly be sought in Paganism' (23-24). In fact, MacGregor argues for a background in the Sabbath *kiddush* rite — a position treated with scorn by Jeremias, *Eucharistic* 26ff. Cf Gavin *Antecedents*.

This more open approach, still indebted to pagan cult parallels but also aware of Jewish influences on Paul, was espoused by Lietzmann whose conclusions were later followed, at least in part, by many including Marxsen.[263] Lietzmann's commentary on 1 Corinthians contained a significant excursus on 'Kultmahle' in which he adduced numerous apparent parallels between the cult meals and the Lord's Supper.[264] Later he summarised his conclusions that the Lord's Supper was a typical hellenistic 'Gedächtnismahl' meal.[265] However, when he discussed the relationship between the sacramental aspects of the Supper and the 'agape' of 1 Corinthians 11, he found that we have 'genau das Abbild einer judischen Festmahlzeit im engeren Kreis der Genossen (הבודרה [sic])'.[266]

According to Lietzmann, the Corinthians had apparently moved away from Paul's Hellenistic sacramentalism, based on analogy with cult-meals, to a purer, earlier form of table fellowship based on the typically Jewish meal (*Haburah*). This meal had nothing to do with the redemptive aspects of Jesus' death. Such a meal, said Paul, involved a 'lack of discernment' and led to judgment (11:27ff).[267]

In a recent work Klauck examines the possible 'meal' backgrounds and concludes that virtually all the cult meals had at least some parallel with Paul's 'original synthesis': 'Lassen sich so für einzelne Punkte Analogien unterschiedlichen Grades beibringen, bleibt das Ganze doch eine unableitbare kreative Synthese eigener Art, Ausdruck des Glaubens an die *Präsenz im Herrenmahl*'.[268] Klauck also says, 'Gewisse Parallelen gibt es nur in der hellenistischen Theophagie, nicht im biblischen Denken'![269]

Jeremias denied there was evidence of a *haburah* meal on a regular daily or weekly basis.[270] Instead, he listed a number of aspects of the Lord's Supper found in *Paul's* accounts which he believed indicated that the meal was derived from the *Passover* meal.[271]

263 Marxsen, *Supper* esp 26ff.

264 Lietzmann 50-51, 57-58.

265 Lietzmann, *Messe* 228.

266 Ibid 228. The case for a *kiddush* meal had earlier been argued by Box, "Antecedents" 360-365.

267 Ibid 249-255; esp 254.

268 Klauck, *Herrenmahl* 374.

269 Op cit. Perhaps Klauck pays too little attention to the question of anachronism. Also some of the 'parallels' found are based on inadequate exegesis of 1 Cor 10. His lack of reference to Wagner's work (*Mysteries*) is surprising.

270 Jeremias, *Eucharistic* 29-31. See also Ridderbos, *Paul* 24.

271 Jeremias, *Eucharistic* 46; also "Body". Cf Gray, *Sacrifice* 340-342.

Others have also discussed the link that Paul made between the 'new covenant' and 'blood' in the Christian meal (11:25; cf 10:16) in terms of the Passover. They have suggested the Passover was a form of 'covenant meal'. Segal, for example, tentatively endorses the views of Trumbull in arguing that, in the confirmation of the covenant, a meal was eaten and that the blood ritual at the Passover had much in common with a covenant meal.[272]

The relationship of covenant to Passover is important since NT traditions concerning the Last Supper do retain a reference to 'covenant blood'.[273] Most commentators believe the reference is to the covenant meal of Exodus 24:8.[274] But Jeremias, following Dalman,[275] has argued that even the expression 'blood of the covenant' has its interpretation in the thought of the Passover. He highlights rabbinic material in which, he says, covenant blood is linked with redemption from Egypt.[276]

Leonard has also shown possible links between the covenant concept and the Passover. Building on the work of Baltzer, Leonard applied Baltzer's 'definite schema'[277] to the Mishnaic account of the Passover.[278] These findings he then applied to the Lord's Supper narratives in Luke. The covenantal implications of the Passover liturgy were drawn out and certainly elements of Baltzer's schema are in evidence. The historical outline of God's dealings with his people and the blessings and curses are a dominant motif, although the 'obligations' are less clear in Leonard's analysis. However, Leonard has demonstrated that certain categories of meal are probably correctly described as 'covenantal' as they reflect aspects of various treaty patterns in biblical, Hittite or Assyrian texts.

Given the tendency to link the Exodus, the Red Sea, and the wanderings in Sinai, it should be no surprise that the Passover would recall God's 'covenant' dealings with his people. However, the very fact that the phrases concerning 'covenant blood' in the Last Supper can be attributed to different OT sources is indicative of the pervasive nature of

---

272   Trumbull, *Blood Covenant* 230-238, also *Threshold Covenant* 203-214, both quoted in Segal, *Passover* 105-106. He does not endorse the point that a 'Threshold' Covenant existed (Ibid 185).

273   Mk 14:24; Mt 26:28; Lk 22:20; 1 Cor 11:25. Cf Barth, *Abendmahl*.

274   So Taylor, *Sacrifice* 139; Conzelmann 199 n 73; Allo 280; Ruef 119; Barrett 269.

275   Dalman, *Jesus-Jeshua* 167. Cf Barrett 269 who sees Exod 24:8 explained in Paschal terms.

276   Cf Jeremias, *Eucharistic* 225.

277   Baltzer, *Covenant* 10. Cf Mendenhall, two articles in *BA* 17.

278   Leonard, *Supper* 26ff.

the covenant concept.[279] So while Leonard has shown that in the
Passover festival the 'covenant' God is worshipped in a form to be
expected of a people in such a covenant, we remain unconvinced that the
Passover meal was specifically a 'covenant' meal.[280]

One of the very few clear examples of a 'covenant' meal in the OT is
to be found in Exodus 24:11 where, following God's covenant with
Israel, Moses took the blood of burnt-offerings and threw it over the
people. After this (vv 9-11) Moses and Aaron and the elders 'beheld
God, and ate and drank'. Just a few other meals were associated with
specific covenants or treaties: Isaac and Abimelech, Jacob and Laban,
Israel and Moab, Joshua and the Gibeonites.[281] Some believe Paul
probably had in mind these 'covenant meals' (especially Exodus 24)
rather than pagan or other Jewish meals. This is further examined below.

4.7.2   Κοινωνία

In vv 15-22, it is the interpretation of the word κοινωνία that has
caused some of the strongest debate. But it is also this word which helps
us understand Paul's teaching on these meals. Paul applied the term
κοινωνία to that which was created by or occurred in eating the
Christian meal (v 16) and the Israelite meal (vv 18-20).[282] The word's
use in Greek literature has been exhaustively examined.[283] It could
indicate both a variety of levels of intimacy in which people shared
things with each other and a variety of different relationships, including
relationships formed at sacrificial meals.[284]

Campbell argued that the 'primary idea' expressed by κοινωνός and
its cognates is not that of association with other people 'but that of
participation in something in which others also participate'.[285] When he
comes to 1 Corinthians 10:14ff he therefore says,

[279] Dodd, *Scriptures* 45 argues Mt 26:28 reflects dependence on Jer 31:31.
Manson, *Messiah* 142, sees the covenant references relating to the Isaianic
servant passages. Héring 117, connects the references with Exod 24.

[280] As Conzelmann notes, τὸ ποτήριον τῆς εὐλογίας says nothing about
whether the meal was viewed as a Passover meal.

[281] Gen 26:28-30; 31:44, 51-54; Num 25:1-5; Josh 9:3-15. We believe the
golden calf meal probably falls into this category, Ex 32:6; 1 Cor 10:7. See
below.

[282] Verses 19-21 also concern an Israelite meal, see below.

[283] Cf works by Panikulam, Scott, Jourdan, Seesemann, McDermott. See
below. Also cf the unsatisfactory attempt by Sampley (*Partnership*) to link
κοινωνία with the Roman concept of *societas*. For criticisms see *New Docs* 3
19 *inter al.*

[284] For detail see Willis 168-174.

[285] Campbell "Koinonia" 353.

Now to those familiar with ordinary Greek usage as we have found it in non-biblical writers ... these phrases could naturally mean only "Participation (with others) in the blood of Christ" and "participation (with others) in the body of Christ." First, because when a genitive is used with κοινωνία it is, five times out of six, a genitive of the thing shared; and second, because αἷμα and σῶμα denote *things*, in which one can participate, but with which one cannot properly have fellowship.[286]

Scott had reached similar conclusions earlier[287] but emphasised the result of the κοινωνία: a 'society' or 'people of God'.[288] Jourdan said that the word implied 'communal "sharing together"' but stressed more powerfully the 'spiritual and holy graces ... [which came] within the compass of that extraordinary word of multiple import'.[289]

Seesemann distinguished three meanings of the word: i) 'Mitteilsamkeit' (generosity), ii) 'Teilnahme' and 'Anteilhaben' (participation), and iii) 'Gemeinschaft' (Community).[290] Interestingly, with the exception of Galatians 2:9, he did not classify a Pauline text under iii) as Scott, Jourdan and others have done. Indeed he concluded 'Nirgends ist uns κοινωνία bei Paulus als "Gemeinschaft" im Sinn von Societas = Genossenschaft begegnet'.[291]

However, Panikulam pointed out that the three categories 'do share common elements'.[292] Continuing Seesemann's stress on the religious aspect of κοινωνία in Paul, he said,

Paul employs the term for the religious fellowship of the believer in Christ and Christian blessings and for the mutual fellowship of the believers ... .
    1. the primary stress in Pauline koinonia is on a Christocentric life;
    2. Paul never uses koinonia for the individual sharing of someone in Christ'.[293]

A survey of the use of Κοινωνία in the NT indicates that it was at the heart of the Gospel and of God's electing purpose (1:9).[294] In Acts 2:42 it is part of the description of believers who 'devoted themselves to ... κοινωνία, and to breaking of bread'. When the Gospel was evident in Paul's life a 'right hand of κοινωνία' was extended to him.[295] Paul gave thanks for κοινωνία in the Gospel.[296] In 1 John 1:3 κοινωνία was a

286   Ibid 375.
287   Scott, "Communion" 122-123.
288   Ibid 121-122.
289   Jourdan, "Koinonia" 120; 124.
290   Seesemann, *Koinonia* 24.
291   Ibid 99.
292   Panikulam, *KNT* 3.
293   Ibid 5.
294   Currie, *Koinonia* 14.
295   Gal 2:9.
296   Phil 1:5.

result of hearing the gospel proclamation. Then in 1 Corinthians 9:23 Paul was a συγκοινωνός in the Gospel.[297]   As we consider the word in ch 10, two points must be remembered: i) the Supper was the point of comparison. The theology of the Supper was what Paul assumed was known. ii) Paul's *purpose* was to demonstrate the nature of idol feasts from that which was known — the Supper.

In v 16 Paul spoke of a κοινωνία τοῦ αἵματος τοῦ Χριστοῦ and τοῦ σώματος τοῦ Χριστοῦ. The debate about these phrases resolves itself into basically two different views which are not necessarily mutually exclusive. The first stresses that κοινωνία relates to a 'vertical' fellowship with or 'participation' in Christ and the second that it relates to a 'horizontal' fellowship with other Christians.

From an early date the vertical has been stressed. Irenaeus said that the fellowship created in the communion was with Christ crucified, the sin-bearer.[298] Chrysostom likewise stated: 'For, as that body is united to Christ, even so, through this bread, we are also united to him'.[299]

Emphasis on the *vertical* relationship is dominant among those taking a strongly sacramental approach to this passage. Paul's reference in v 20 to 'participating' in/with demons may make this position plausible. But that, in turn, often depends on a 'sacramental' view of pagan cult meals in which it is said that the people involved drank and ate in the belief that they were thereby absorbing the deity. Recently Willis has challenged this view of the cults, saying there is little evidence of such 'sacramentalism'.[300] In the light of his work, it does appear unlikely that κοινωνούς τῶν δαιμωνίων could mean that demons were being absorbed or ingested by eating in the sacrificial cultus. Willis also dismisses the 'communal interpretation' that those who ate at such meals were 'partners along with the demons in the sacrifice'.[301] On the basis of his examination of pagan cult meals he opts for a 'social interpretation' or 'alliance' interpretation.[302] That is, he takes a position somewhat similar to Campbell (above) that the issue is partaking in a meal with others with whom a relationship is thus created — what we have termed a 'horizontal' fellowship or communion.

Scott also sees this κοινωνία in 'horizontal' terms. He builds his argument on the view that the Supper in ch 10 was a Passover Meal and that a 'haburah' ('group of comrades or a society') met to partake of the

---

297   Cf Philem 6.

298   Irenaeus, *Against Heresies* (18:2, 3) *ANF I* 446.

299   Quoted in Panikulam, *KNT* 23 n 31.

300   Willis 1-64 examines pagan meals. He applies his results to 1 Cor 10:14-20 on pp 182-212.

301   Ibid 190.

302   Ibid 20 for his definition of 'social'; 211.

paschal lamb.[303] The emphasis in the Pauline passages is therefore on the fellowship formed at the sacrificial meal.[304]

While unity is indeed a prominent motif of this passage, that alone does not do justice to v 16 and the specific mention of the cup and the body of Christ. To deny that Paul primarily had in mind the relationship between those who were eating and their God (or demons) seems completely to ignore Paul's summary of the problem in v 22. Surely by 'provoking to jealousy' he meant that something was taking *God's* place — specifically *demons* (v 21).[305]

Paul's use of the genitive with κοινωνία simply exacerbates the problem.[306] An indication of its meaning is supplied in 1:9. There Paul outlined how the Corinthians shared together in the 'enrichment' in Christ (v 5), the spiritual gifts (v 7), and the benefits accruing to those in Christ Jesus. This resulted from the preaching of 'Christ crucified' (vv 17, 18, 23). This was the κοινωνία 'of' God's Son. 9:23 also refers to sharing in the product of the Gospel (συγκοινωνός + genitive). Indeed many of Paul's references to κοινωνία and its cognates refer to the good things (and difficult things) that come from an acceptance of the Gospel message or to a partnership in the spread of that message.[307] The negative side of κοινωνία must be interpreted in the light of the positive κοινωνία of Christ.[308]

If κοινωνία refers to sharing in the results of the Gospel message[309] then a κοινωνία in the blood and body of Christ may mean a sharing in the results of Christ's sacrificial death. In this epistle these specifically have to do with the formation of a 'new Covenant' (11:25) and the forming of a unified community.[310]

[303]   Above pp 156-158.

[304]   Scott, "Fellowship" 567; "Communion" 121, 130.

[305]   Cf Käsemann, *Essays* 124: κοινωνία 'conveys the sense of falling into a sphere of domination'.

[306]   In effect Scott distinguishes between the genitives of v 16a and v 16b. The latter means the fellowship of Christ's body = church. The former is a genitive of origin of the Fellowship which is sealed in Christ's blood. Scott, "Communion" 122 ff.

[307]   In 2 Cor 1:7 Paul and the Corinthians are κοινωνοί in 'suffering' (genitive) and 'comfort' (gen), but it is Christ's suffering and comfort (1:5) and is directly related to the Gospel of salvation (v 6). In Phil 3:10 the 'κοινωνία of his sufferings' relates to Christ's death. Generally elsewhere κοινωνία is to be found in benefits, good things, or the work arising from the Christian faith (Gal 6:6; 2 Cor 8:23; Phil 1:5). Even 'κοινωνία of the Spirit' may reflect specifically the benefit of being in Christ: Phil 2:1; 2 Cor 13:14.

[308]   1 Cor 10:18, 20.

[309]   Barrett 232: sharing 'in the benefits secured' by Christ's death.

[310]   11:33-34; 1:9; 12:12ff. The notion of bread and body comes from v 16. Translation is difficult. The *AV* has 'For we, being many, are one bread and one

As Willis has shown, this may indicate that Paul regarded the Supper as a 'covenant' meal in 10:16-19. Following Currie, he points to the 'formal parallelism between 10:16 and 11:24':

ποτήριον = κοινωνία τοῦ αἵματος (1 Cor 10:16)
         = ἡ καινὴ διαθήκη ἐν τῷ ἐμῷ αἵmati (1 Cor 11:25)
ἄρτος = κοινωνία τοῦ σώματος (1 Cor 10:16)
      = τὸ σῶμα τὸ ὑπὲρ ὑμῶν (1 Cor 11:24)

The parallelism shows that the terms κοινωνία τοῦ αἵματος and ἡ καινὴ διαθήκη ἐν τῷ ἐμῷ αἵματι are equivalent.[311]

The general 'covenantal' terminology that we noted in vv 1-14 probably further supports the view that Paul had this concept in mind as he spoke of κοινωνία at a meal.[312]

Paul's use of the word 'cup' may also support our view that κοινωνία relates to sharing in the covenantal blessings/judgments of the sacrifice of Christ. Further, we shall argue that vv 18-22 are a direct continuation of the argument from vv 1-14 and that Paul was still drawing lessons from *Israel's* covenant disobedience.

In the LXX ποτήριον translates the Hebrew כוֹס often used metaphorically 'for that which is portioned out, and of which one is to partake'.[313] Although there is a 'cup of salvation' and a cup supplying God's faithful people,[314] it is the 'cup of wrath' and of judgment which predominates in the word's metaphorical use.[315]

The possibility of a Passover background in these verses was mentioned earlier. The 'cup' metaphor is also important in the Passover: 'the four cups correspond to the four cups of punishment which God will someday cause the nations of the world to drink ... and corresponding to them God will some day cause Israel to drink four cups of consolations'.[316]

---

body'. But it is difficult to make 'one bread' the predicate of ἐσμεν. (Lenski 411.) This has the unfortunate effect of making the κοινωνία of v 16 dependent on the fact that 'we are one bread and one body'. The dependence is rather the other way. 'Because there is one bread we, the many, are one body, for we all partake of the one bread'. (So Barrett 233.) Οἱ πολλοί refers to all who partake. (Cf πάντες, v 17b. Also cf v 33.)

311   Willis 206.

312   Currie, *Koinonia* 42ff also suggests the word has 'covenant' connotations as Paul used it to convey 'part of the meaning of *hesed*'.

313   Jacobs, "Cup" 836.

314   Ps 16:5; 23:5; 116:13. Also cf Philo, *Som* ii 246 ff.

315   Ps 75:8; 11:6; Jer 49:12; Lam 4:21; Is 51:17, 22; Jer 25:15, cf v 17, 28; Ezek 23:33; Hab 2:16. Cf Philo, *Quod Deus* 77; 1 QpHab 11:14; *inter al.* Cf Cranfield, "Cup" 137-138.

316   *jPes*, 10:37c, 5 quoted by Goppelt, "Ποτήριον" 150-151; Cohn-Sherbok "Note"; cf Howard, "Passover".

In the Gospels the cup-sayings ascribed to Jesus may also point to his death and ultimately to judgment.[317] In Mark 10:38[318] the reference to 'the cup that I drink' is paralleled by the reference to his 'baptism'. In mind is Christ's death on the cross. This inclusion of the idea of 'judgment' in the use of the 'cup' metaphor may well be substantiated by the redactor's use of the cup-saying in Mark 14:36.[319] Goppelt has suggested that 'cup' in these texts refers to 'horror ... at the judgment which delivers up the Holy One to the power of sin'.[320]

In 1 Corinthians 10:16 the cup brings blessing, because it represents the 'new covenant'.[321] For Paul, the covenant was made in the 'blood of Christ' (11:25). The significance of the cup lay in the proclamation of Christ's death (11:26) as the inauguration of that covenant. In 10:16 the main emphasis is on the blessings and benefits received in the cup through Christ's death. In 11:25ff, however, as Moule has shown,[322] 'judgment' is a pervasive theme. To eat or drink in an 'undiscerning' manner is to incur 'judgment' (11:27ff) because it is an 'outrage against the death of the Lord.[323]

Taking the cup, then, seems to have involved an acknowledgement and proclamation of the covenant made through the death of Christ. The concept of 'covenant blood' probably draws on the covenant treaty of Exodus 24:8 where the shedding of the sacrificial blood confirmed the covenant.

If Paul was using the word 'cup' figuratively for the covenant made through the blood of Christ, it is a further indication of the meaning of κοινωνία. 'Participation' in the cup involved accepting the covenant and its benefits which arose on the basis of its inauguration through the death of Christ.[324] What the Corinthians had not realised through arrogance and complacency was the fact that the cup also committed them to covenant judgment when they sinned.[325]

The fact that the cup was uniquely placed *before* the bread in v 16 (also in v 21) may draw attention to the *blood* which, as we have seen, was equivalent to the 'new covenant'. The bread and κοινωνία τοῦ σώματος τοῦ Χριστοῦ also affirm covenant allegiance brought about through the death of Christ. But, lest we be too quick to assume that this

[317] Cranfield, op cit., also his *Mark* 337; but cf Nineham, *Mark* 284.
[318] Cf Mat 20:22.
[319] Lk 22:42; Mat 26:39, 42.
[320] Mk 14:41; par Mat 26:45, cf Lk 22:53. Ibid 153.
[321] Note that the place of ἐστιν in 11:25 separates 'new covenant' from 'blood'. 'In my blood' describes how it 'is' the new covenant.
[322] Moule, "Judgment" 470ff.
[323] Ibid 471.
[324] Fee 473. Cf Sigal "Note".
[325] 10:21-22; 11:27-32.

refers exclusively to a 'vertical' relationship, Paul uniquely explained the phrase in v 17. Marshall is surely correct in saying of that verse: 'Here Paul must be using 'body' in a non-technical sense to refer ... to the church'.[326]

Thus it seems that the Christian meal was being used by Paul to illustrate that such religious meals involved people in a *covenant allegiance*. In one sense, therefore, κοινωνία was a 'vertical' relationship because the basis of the covenantal relationship with God was recalled in drinking the cup (Christ's self-sacrifice). But there was also a 'horizontal' significance, for Paul could not have talked of the 'new covenant' without thinking of its benefits.[327] These benefits are more prominent in 1:9 and 9:23, but 10:17 shows that one particular blessing was the unity of those involved. 'They are a cultic community'.[328]

4.7.3   Ἰσραήλ κατὰ σάρκα

In v 18, Paul resumed his discussion of the example of Israel. He argued that Israel κατὰ σάρκα was allied to demons and shared in what accrued from that allegiance. Probably he still had in mind the golden calf incident (v 7). In other words, he considered this a *negative* example, an example of how dangerous participation in a pagan meal could be. There are a number of reasons for us taking this position.

i)   Although Paul could use σάρξ simply to refer to 'historical flesh and blood',[329] the phrase κατὰ σάρκα in this context places emphasis on the *sin* of Israel. Israel had just been used by Paul in a negative comparison with the church (vv 1-14). This expression seems to continue that comparison. Lessons must be learned. It was being used, we suggest, in a similar way to that found in Romans 8:5a and it contrasted strongly with 'the church of God' in 1 Corinthians 10:32.[330]

ii)   This interpretation makes sense of v 19.[331] Thinking of the unity of the Israelites in an allegiance to a false god, Paul asked whether this meant (v 19) that the Israelites' idols were anything? His answer reached

---

[326] Marshall, *Supper* 121; cf Bonnard "L'Église" 271; *contra* Schmithals *Gnosticism* 246 n 173; Wedderburn "Body". Further on Paul's use of σῶμα see Bultmann, *Theology* I 192ff; Stacey, *Man*; Robinson, *Body*; Gundry, ΣΩΜΑ — with a discussion of this in Ziesler "ΣΩΜΑ". On the possibly different meaning of σῶμα in vv 16b and 17 see Best, *Body* esp 87ff.

[327] Fee 468.

[328] Willis 187.

[329] Rom 4:1; 9:5; 11:14; cf 2 Cor 5:16.

[330] Note the negative estimation of the 'wise κατὰ σάρκα' of 1:26.

[331] Some commentators refer to an unnatural jump between 10:18 and vv 19-20. Cf Weiss 259-260; Conzelmann 172-173; Lenski 414.

the heart of the problem of κοινωνία: No. It was the action of joining together to bring offerings to other gods/demons that caused the problem ... and thus his argument proceeds.

iii) Although the usual reading of v 18 (that the κοινωνία was formed by an offering to *Yahweh*) is bolstered by Gressmann's suggestion that τοῦ θυσιαστηρίου is a metonym for Yahweh,[332] there is no evidence that θυσιαστήριον could mean this.[333]

iv) There is complete continuity of argument with vv 1-14 if Paul was still taking *sinful* erring Israel as his example through to v 22.

v) His quotations from Deuteronomy 32 in vv 20 and 22 referred, in their original context, to *sinful* Israel.[334]

Against this stands the introduction of τὰ ἔθνη as a subject for θύουσιν in v 20. However, the textual evidence for including τὰ ἔθνη is not conclusive. It is largely Alexandrian (p[46vid], ℵ, A, C, P, Ψ, 33, 81 etc). The words are omitted by B, D, F, G, Ambst, and were considered to be an 'ancient gloss' by Tischendorf.[335] The harder reading omits the subject and is probably the one to be accepted. This, together with our other reasons for regarding *Israel* as the subject, confirms us in the view that τὰ ἔθνη is a gloss.

Secondly, we have suggested that Deuteronomy 32 may have been in mind throughout chs 8-10, but it was now to the forefront of Paul's thought, as he quoted from it. In Deuteronomy 32:17 ἔθυσαν δαιμονίοις καὶ οὐ θεῷ clearly has the *Israelites* as the subject. There the writer warned of the arrogant 'fat' Israelites who sacrificed to 'demons' and 'not to God'. This was a natural text to use if Israel is still seen as a negative example. Further, it should be noted that the *progression* in Paul's argument from the benefits brought by the 'rock' (Christ — v 4) to the danger of taking those benefits for granted accurately parallels the experience of *Israel* (not τὰ ἔθνη) in Deuteronomy 32.

Thirdly, Robertson, who accepts τὰ ἔθνη as the subject, correctly notes that according to his understanding οὐ θεῷ 'introduces a thought that is quite superfluous: there was no need to declare that sacrifices to

---

332 Gressmann, "Κοινωνία" 224. Cf Bengel 641, and Olshausen 165.

333 For the *one* passage in Philo that just might give grounds for this (*Spec Leg* i 221) see the argument by Campbell, "Koinonia" 377, who concludes: 'Here it is perfectly clear that βωμός is *not* a substitute for the divine name. Κοινωνὸν τοῦ βωμοῦ is exactly parallel to ὁμοτράπεζον ... and if βωμός is a substitute for anything else it is for the offerings made upon it'. Cf Aalen, "Abendmahl" 137.

334 See v 20 below.

335 Tischendorf, *Testamentum* 518, also Zuntz *Text* 102; Metzger, *Commentary* 560-561.

idols are not offered to God'.[336] He therefore wishes to translate οὐ θεῷ as 'to a no-god'. However, there is no redundancy once it is recognised that the LXX is being quoted and that the subject of the verb θύω is the same there and in Paul. The Israelites were sacrificing to demons and 'not to God'. Indeed there is some indication that in the golden calf incident the Israelites felt they were making 'God' for themselves and were still involved in *his* worship.[337] The interpretative problem arose simply because no one would ever have suggested that *Gentiles* sacrificed to God — self-evidently they did not.

Finally, the use of the word δαίμων also furthers our argument. Demons were the object of worship in Deuteronomy 32:17 and Baruch 4:7.[338] In both places the same clause was used and it was unfaithful *Israel* who worshipped demons. In Psalm 105:36-7 (LXX) Israel is also said to have served images which became a σκάνδαλον to them and to have sacrificed its sons and daughters to *demons*. In Is 65:11 Israel forsook the Lord and set 'a table for a demon'.[339] Other uses of 'demons' are rare, although more common in later literature.[340] The rarity of the word in the LXX and its use in connection with *Israel's* worship of idols is a further indication that Israel is the subject of θύω in v 20. 1 Timothy 4:1 shows that it was quite possible to conceive of the man of faith following after 'demons'.

Thus, in spite of the lack of support from commentators, it seems there is good reason to believe that in 1 Corinthians 10:18-22 Paul continued to use Israel as a *negative* example, mentioning just two meals: the Israelite meal and, by way of illustration only, the Christian meal.

The nature of the 'participation' in the Israelite meal can therefore be read in the light of vv 7-10. Idolatry was taking place and they were putting the Lord to the 'test'. We have already seen that 'testing' the Lord was a theme that recurred in the WT. It involved breaching covenant stipulations. To worship other gods meant relinquishing one covenantal allegiance for the sake of another.[341] The Corinthians should have deduced this from their own communion meal which recalled the covenant-forming sacrifice.

The truth of the analogy from Israel κατὰ σάρκα ought to have been obvious in the light of the *Christian* practice. This is the point of vv 16-17 which are to be seen as a brief confirmatory illustration of the main argument of vv 1-22. The introduction in v 15 to vv 16-17 also seems to confirm that they are illustrative. The Corinthians did have something by

---

336   Robertson 216.
337   See Moberly, *Mountain* esp 46-48.
338   Bar 4:7 may rely on Deut 32. Cf Is 65:3.
339   Cf 1 Cor 10:21. On links between this passage and 8:5 see above 2.2.
340   Cf Tobit chs 3 and 6; Bar 4:35.
341   E.g., Ps 78:10, 37.

which to 'judge' or 'assess' (κρίνω — v 15) the truth of what Paul was saying. In the slight digression of vv 16-17 he reminded them of this.[342] ὡς φρονίμοις λέγω is probably somewhat ironic.[343]

In terms of the *type* of κοινωνία established there is no suggestion in any of the texts that the Israelites had been involved in theophagy or that they had achieved union with the demons through some sort of 'sacramentalism'.[344] Rather they were celebrating in the meal the sacrifices made (e.g., burnt and peace offerings — Exodus 32:6), and eating, drinking and 'playing' before their created god, just as they had done 'before Yahweh' only a short time earlier. This was a complete betrayal of Yahweh. The people were to be destroyed and a new 'great nation' to be formed.[345]

The opening question of v 19 need not be seen as a change in the argument once it is accepted that v 18 refers to Israel worshipping *idols*.[346] Had v 18 referred to the Israelite worship of Yahweh, then v 19 would seem like a sudden interruption.[347] Participation in idol sacrifices (θυσία — v 18) *does* achieve a κοινωνία of the sacrifice. It is therefore the logical question to ask whether this participation is achieved because the idol is at the sacrifice or because the special food eaten in celebration causes the κοινωνία. Paul's answer to both these questions is 'no'.

The answer to the problem of *how* Israel participated in heathen sacrifices lay not in the specific nature of the food, nor in the existence of the idol at the meal. Rather 'participation' lay in taking part in alien worship. Willis has phrased it thus: 'Just as one shows his master by whom he serves (Rom 6:16ff.), so also one shows allegiance by the worship in which he participates'.[348] Verse 20 takes up the question of v

---

[342]   Cf 11:13 where κρίνω also introduces an illustration as an aid to the main argument.

[343]   So Weiss 256 but *contra* Robertson 211; Allo 237. Κρίνω may also be ironic in the light of passages such as 2:14-16. Above sect 3.2.1.

[344]   Willis 188.

[345]   Exod 32:10.

[346]   Most commentators accept ἢ ὅτι εἴδωλόν τί ἐστιν as correct. (See Barrett 236; Godet II 86; Allo 243ff; Meyer 304; Conzelmann 173 n 36.) p[46] ℵ* A C* Ψ and others omit the clause possibly as a result of homoioteleuton. (Metzger, *Commentary* 560.) However, the problem here is the apparent introduction of the 'different' problem of εἰδωλόθυτον. (Conzelmann 173n 34.) Weiss (261) has argued that these words, if genuine, show the verse belongs to an earlier letter although he doubts their authenticity in view of the following θύουσιν after εἰδωλόθυτον. However, there need be no conflict between these questions and the next verse. Omission because of homoioteleuton remains a plausible suggestion.

[347]   See above n 331.

[348]   Willis 192.

19: 'No, rather (I imply) that the things they sacrifice they sacrifice to demons and do not sacrifice to God'.

4.7.4   The Lord or demons

If 'Israel κατὰ σάρκα' is the subject of v 20, the ensuing quotations from Deuteronomy 32 are readily comprehensible. Deuteronomy 32 offers one of the clearest descriptions in the OT of the rebellion of God's covenant people in turning to worship other gods ('demons'), in spite of God's faithfulness to them:

> they have dealt corruptly with him [the Rock, the θεός πιστός — LXX] ... you waxed fat, you grew thick, you became sleek; then he forsook God who made him and scoffed at the Rock of his salvation. They stirred him to jealousy with strange gods; with abominable practices they provoked him to anger. They sacrificed to demons which were no gods, [and not to God — LXX] to gods they had never known ... You were unmindful of the Rock that begot you.[349]

Seen in their original context, these quotations provide Paul with an excellent summary of his whole argument in chs 8-10. The Israelites became 'unmindful of the Rock' (v 18), because they presumed upon God's gifts and became arrogant. This resulted in worship of other lords and gods in the nature of demons. Such was Paul's message for the Corinthians who, he believed, had gone the same way as Israel κατὰ σάρκα and become involved in showing allegiance to other lords.

This is further expounded in v 21. Paul maintained the order of cup first, as in v 16, for he was counting on the parallel between the two situations being evident to the Corinthians. The whole logic of vv 19-20 (food offered to idols ... which is sacrificed to demons) shows that Paul was concerned with the *worship* of idols/demons rather than simply eating εἰδωλόθυτον.

The emphasis on *allegiance* and *lordship* is to be seen in a number of ways.

i)   The reference to the '*cup* of demons' probably referred to the 'benefits' accruing from the sacrifice. With the Christian 'cup', Paul had stressed the covenant identification of those who participated as one body. The direct comparison between the one cup and the other suggests that Paul had in mind a similar 'covenantal' identification of the people in allegiance to demons.

ii)   The use in vv 21-22 of 'Lord' no doubt refers to Christ. But it is mildly surprising that Paul did not use 'Christ' as he did in vv 4, 9,[350] 16. We suggest Paul deliberately wished to stress the issue of *lordship*. He was still answering the questions of v 19. The truth of worship was to

---

349   Deut 32:4ff; 15-18.
350   As above n 205

be found in the 'lord' for whom it was intended. This also pointed away from the specific issue of idol-meat to the deeper issue of worshipping the one true Lord.[351]

iii) The antithesis τραπέζης κυρίου ... τραπέζης δαιμονίων probably was derived by analogy from ποτήριον κυρίου ... ποτήριον δαιμονίων.[352] Again the emphasis was not on the food so much as on the object of the worship.

iv) The contrast Paul built up was not between foods at the respective feasts but between the Lord and demons. This strong contrast is frequently overlooked: (v 20) ... demons ... God ... demons ... (v 21) Lord ... demons ... Lord ... demons ... (v 22) Lord.

In using the phrase 'table of the Lord' Paul may have been thinking of the 'sitting down to eat and drink' of v 7. But there is also a possible linguistic dependence on Malachi 1:7, 12. There the prophet referred to the altar on which sacrifices were made to God.[353]

Paul has subsumed the full content of worship under the phrases, 'cup of the Lord', 'table of the Lord'.[354] In other words, his thought was far wider than a specific act of sacrifice. It was centred on the commitment to and identification with the one to whom the worship was offered.

The phrase 'table of demons' was probably being applied broadly as well. Here Isaiah 65:11 is enlightening: ἑτοιμάζοντες τῷ δαίμονι τράπεζαν. It is the 'characteristic quality' of the table that is clear. The context suggests 'table' was not synonymous with the altar but used as a metonym for the total worship of the demon.[355]

---

351   Thus, Meyer 305 is correct in saying that κοινωνούς (v 20) points back to the κοινωνοί of v 18. It indicates the idol sacrifices of the Israelites.

352   Cf Goppelt, "Τράπεζα" 214.

353   Cf Ezek 44:16; *T Judah* 21:5; *T Levi* 8:16. Goppelt "Τράπεζα" 214 accepts a biblical background here. *Contra* Conzelmann 174 n 47, but see next note.

354   Conzelmann 174 n 43 is wrong in saying that τράπεζα κυρίου is 'the table of shewbread' (This cannot be the case in Mal 1 or in Ezek 44:16 — my table.) Usually that table is the τράπεζα τῆς προθέσεως (e.g., Exod 39:17; 1 Chron 28:16). Admittedly in 1 Clem 43:2 this becomes the τράπεζα τοῦ θεοῦ, but this probably shows the influence of pagan religions. (Cf Dittenberger, *Sylloge* III No 1106, 99. Further refs in Goppelt "Τράπεζα" 214 n 42.)

355   *Contra* Allo 245. Even if the phrase τραπέζα δαιμονίων comes from a pagan source, Paul's argument remains the same. Many scholars have pointed to possible pagan understandings of a τράπεζα in a cult meal. Usually these arguments have been used to promote a particular 'sacramental' understanding of the passage, but there is no reason why this should be so. The common use of the word τράπεζα among pagans dining at cult meals in the Corinth of Paul's day would serve to make Paul's imperative the more clearly understandable to his readers. For detailed discussions on this subject see *inter al*, Lietzmann 50-

Paul's message to the Corinthians was that they could not be κοινωνοί in two different ways at the same time. If the Corinthians were wise enough to understand the broader implications of the *worship* involved in idol-feats and in the Lord's Supper then the incompatibility should have been obvious.

A reference to Deuteronomy 32:21 brings Paul's argument to a climax. The use of παραζηλόω is not found in secular Greek and occurs only four times in the NT. It is no doubt derived from ζῆλος (zeal) for maintaining God's honour. Paul reminds the Corinthians of the wrathful zeal of God for his own honour. This zeal becomes operative against all worship that is not intended for him. In Ezekiel the zeal was likened to marital jealousy[356] — a 'jealousy' that brought wrath and judgment.

Paul used παραζηλόω on four occasions. In Romans 10:19 and here in 1 Corinthians 10:22, Deuteronomy 32:21 was his source. Paul's concern was that the Lord would be angry with them as he had been with the idolaters in Deuteronomy 32.[357]

Paul concluded by challenging the 'strong'[358] with heavy irony: 'Are we stronger than he?'

4.7.5   Summary

We have suggested that in vv 15-22 Paul took up the specific problem of idolatry. The issue he confronted was the involvement of the Corinthians in idolatrous *worship* centred on cultic meals, which almost certainly took place in temples — continuing the line of thought from 8:10.

Many have discussed this section at great length in an attempt to learn more about Paul's view of the religious processes involved in the Lord's Supper. No doubt this is a valid exercise in itself but it is one which we have deliberately avoided, being more concerned to examine the function of vv 16-17 in the larger context. We have argued that the Lord's Supper provided an illustration from normal Christian practice about the nature of worship in cultic meals. Paul was particularly interested in drawing the Corinthians' attention to the 'covenant' background of the Supper. This was seen in the emphasis he laid on the 'cup' and the resulting community (v 17), but also in what has seemed a

---

51; Gill, "Trapezomata"; Willis 15-17; *New Docs* 2 36. Also cf comments on *PYale* 85.

356   Ezek 16:38; 23:25. Cf 2 Cor 11:2.

357   Idolatry frequently causes the Lord's jealousy: 1 Kg 14:22; Ps 78:58; Deut 29:20; etc.

358   Wendland 74, 'Diese drohend ernste und zugleich spöttische Frage ist an die "Starken" in Korinth gerichtet'; also Héring 97.

probable explanation of the nature of the κοινωνία involved, given the context as a whole (of vv 1-14 and 18-22).

Our exegesis of vv 18-22 has allowed us to interpret the verses consistently with the rest of Paul's argument. Paul was still using the example of sinful Israel from the WT. Israel κατὰ σάρκα is the subject of v 20 and the gloss, τὰ ἔθνη, is unnecessary. This has enabled us to see that Paul used the quotations from Deuteronomy 32 from *their* context. That it was the Israelites who were judged for being fat, arrogant, and worshipping demons was crucial to Paul's teaching in this section. The quotations emphasised the issue of commitment to a lord through worship. Paul's appeal to Scriptures has also suggested that Paul saw Israel as a negative example throughout vv 5-22. There was no change in his analogy. This was how those who had thought that they were standing fell — through κοινωνία with demons.

4.8   Other problems with food (Verses 23 - 30)

Thus far in chs 8-10 it has been argued that Paul was concerned with the Corinthian belief that they were secure enough before God to be able to eat meat ἐν εἰδωλείῳ. Now the matter of meat ἐν μακέλλῳ is addressed.

4.8.1   Μηδεὶς τὸ ἑαυτοῦ ζητείτω

Although the word 'love' is not used here (cf 8:3) the idea is certainly present.[359] The word οἰκοδομέω (v 23b) makes this clear.[360] Again Paul was contrasting 'rights' with Christian behaviour.

Πάντα ἔξεστιν also appears in 6:12[361] where it is normally considered to be a quotation from the Corinthians. Paul may have been drawing his readers back to the debate about ἐξουσία by quoting them again, although here his qualification that 'not all things build up' concerned building *others* up rather than oneself (6:12).[362]

It is commonly held that Paul agreed with this 'slogan' despite his qualification of it, but this is to misunderstand the force of his argument.[363] The οὐ δύνασθε of v 21 has already demonstrated that such a slogan could never have been accepted as an absolute.[364] The qualifications, even in vv 23-24, were strong enough for the slogan to be

359   Conzelmann 176 n 9.
360   See 8:1c.
361   On ἐξουσία and ἔξεστιν see sect 2.4.1 and 3.4.1 above.
362   Weiss 262.
363   Willis 224 n 1; Fee 251-252.
364   Senft 136, sees the slogan as evidence that the subject is now entirely irreconcilable with vv 21ff.

rendered effectively worthless. However, the assumption has had a forceful impact on the interpretation of this section of text, for it is often believed that Paul was speaking to the 'strong' about the attitude of *the weak* towards eating meat.[365]

The word οἰκοδομέω[366] here explains συμφέρω.[367] The building up was church centred and was to be tested by examining the type of building achieved. The slogan 'all things are lawful' did not stand up to Paul's examination. When something did not build up then it was not to be used. Effectively this meant that an ἐξουσία that has failed the test is no longer an ἐξουσία. This was the message of ch 9.

Verse 24 states the positive side of the message. The examples given here showed that a person should seek the good of another rather than of himself. Verse 33 summarises this. Once again, the heart of Paul's message was that Christians had to be 'marked' by love — a point that becomes evident in 13:5 where we read ἡ ἀγάπη ... οὐ ζητεῖ τὰ ἑαυτῆς.[368]

4.8.2   Market meat

The first practical example Paul addressed concerned food sold ἐν μακέλλῳ (v 25).[369] This could be eaten μηδὲν ἀνακρίνοντες διὰ τὴν συνείδησιν. But what do ἀνακρίνω and συνείδησις mean? Was Paul now beginning to address the weak who worried about such things?

Two things may be said initially. Firstly, this food sold ἐν μακέλλῳ had to do with the resale of food that had been offered as sacrifices in the temples. The word ἱερόθυτον in v 28 probably refers to such food sold in the market. There is some evidence that most of the meat was first slaughtered in temples for sacrifice and then sold in the market.[370]

---

365   Weiss 263-264; Lietzmann 52; Meyer 307 *inter al.*

366   Sect 2.1.5.

367   Like οἰκοδομέω, συμφέρω may draw on popular philosophy. Cf Willis 226-227.

368   Ch 14 should also be seen as a commentary on the problem of self-seeking people enthusing about themselves and their spiritual gifts. In 14:1 Paul again set the gifts of the Spirit alongside love. Love should be the aim (14:1a). There he faced the problem with 'tongues' which 'built up oneself' (ὁ λαλῶν γλώσσῃ ἑαυτὸν οἰκοδομεῖ — 14:4).

369   On the *macellum* in Corinth see Cadbury, "Macellum"; Barrett, *Essays* 47-48.

370   See sect 2.1.1 on Εἰδωλόθυτα. Cf Barrett, loc cit. Recent work on the sale of sacrificial meat in the market is enlightening. Willis points to occasions when 'members of cults were permitted to take portions of sacrificial meat home' (p 64). However, apart from the reference to Herondas, *Mimiambi* 4:1-95, the evidence Willis cites is mostly derived from statements forbidding such action (cf Pausanius 2.27:1).

Secondly, part of this sentence is repeated in v 27, thus it seems reasonable to assume that an adequate interpretation of v 25 will aid interpretation of v 27.

Most commentators assume that 'conscience' means 'moral conscience' and that the 'weak' converted *Jews* would have had the greatest problem with eating such meat.[371] Barrett sees the statements in vv 25 and 27 as Paul's hedging of his views 'by reference to the conscience, not of the eater, or potential eater, but of his weak Christian brother'.[372] Certainly a possible parallel to 'examining' food lay in Jewish food laws where meat was examined carefully to discern its origin before being eaten.[373] However, this background does, we believe, remain unproven in the light of our comments on the 'weak' person in 8:7.

Others have suggested that Paul now actually *addresses* these weak Christians.[374] However, it is improbable that Paul should have suddenly, and for the first time in the whole discussion since 8:1, changed his direction and encouraged the weak to eat certain food. It is even less likely, given that, in the following verses (vv 28-33), Paul reverted to addressing the 'strong', for it was they who were likely to give 'offence' (ἀπρόσκοποι — v 32) to others (cf 8:9). Also it was probably only they (in v 29) who would have been concerned with someone else limiting their 'freedom'.

Some who believe the weak were addressed in v 25 suggest that ἀνακρίνοντες διὰ τὴν συνείδησιν means that the weak should not

The selling of cult meat can, in fact, be more clearly established than this. Cf *Thorikos Test. no 50*, line 23 (probably a fourth century BC inscription): Ἀθηνᾶι οἶν πρατόν: '(sacrifice) for Athena, a sheep which may be sold'. (Cf the Dunst edition: *ZPE* 25 (1977) 243-245. This line, does not appear to be the same in Vanderpool's edition: *Thorikos and the Laurion in Archaic and Classical Times* in spite of comments and summary in *New Docs* 2, 36. (Ref. there *incorrectly* refers to *ZPE* 27. Dunst 263, points to prices mentioned for the sales on lines 28-30 and 55-56.) Priests were apparently allowed to sell off their portion. In other contexts these μάγειροι are called 'cooks and/or butchers'. (Willis 64 n 239.)

371   Although cf Fee 481-482: The problem was Jewish-styled investigations into the origin of the food, but Paul was more concerned to show that such questions lay 'outside the concerns of conscience altogether' than to deal with the weak. Theissen, *Setting* 121-143 offers a variation on a theme of the weak being Jewish. They may have continued to have been influenced by pagan or Jewish traditions but these traditions were effective 'only because they undergirded a class specific attitude' (138).

372   Barrett, *Essays* 46.

373   Although in its current form anachronistic for our purposes, *Abod Zar* 2:3 gives an impression of what may have been involved.

374   Maurer, "Συνείδησις" 915.

raise questions about the origin of meat lest they upset their consciences.[375]

If the 'strong' were being addressed then διὰ τὴν συνείδησιν is usually understood differently. For example, Fee believes that Paul 'is contending that "conscience" is not involved at all, so an investigation is irrelevant'.[376] This latter interpretation sounds reasonable, fitting in with Paul's continuing address to the 'strong', and yet it still does not help define the word 'conscience'. In most commentaries, whichever interpretation is accepted of the whole clause, it is generally assumed that 'conscience' means 'moral conscience'. Maurer is an exception in emphasising a 'self-awareness which condemns'.[377] Possibly Paul was telling the 'strong' that although their 'conscience' should be exercised about eating meat ἐν εἰδωλείῳ, they should not worry about eating ἐν μακέλλῳ. The problem with this is that the 'strong' clearly were *not* concerned, so why should Paul mention it? Also, why did Paul justify his position in v 26 to a group who already ate this meat?

We argued earlier that in 8:10-12 the word συνείδησις probably did not mean 'moral conscience'[378] but rather 'self-awareness'. Although our conclusion was tentative, we interpreted 'having a weak conscience' as describing a person who lacked self-awareness or self-consciousness[379] of community status and therefore lacked security. With this understanding of the word it was clear why the 'strong' should have wished to 'build up' the weak to eat idol meat, for that helped demonstrate γνῶσις and community security.[380]

Interpreting συνείδησις as self-awareness/consciousness does, we suggest, make coherent sense also of 10:25. The 'strong' saw eating ἱερόθυτον as *evidence* of γνῶσις. It needed to be *seen*. Paul had denied that meat could be eaten ἐν εἰδωλείῳ but no worship was involved with meat bought ἐν μακέλλῳ and the food itself was not 'anything' (cf 10:19). Thus, this meat could be eaten *but not for the reasons proposed by the 'strong'*. They were to eat 'not at all (μηδέν) evaluating for the sake of (δία) self-awareness'. This was *why* the 'strong' ate idol meat. They were thoroughly 'conscious' of their actions, seeing them as an outworking of their γνῶσις. To them Paul said, 'Eat, but it has nothing to do with your self-awareness in the community'.

---

[375]   Loc cit.

[376]   Fee 482 following Conzelmann 176; Horsley, "Consciousness" 587; Von Soden "Sakrament" 14.

[377]   *Idem.*

[378]   Sect 2.3.2.

[379]   Cf Horsley, "Consciousness" 585-587: 'the weak "consciousness" of some of the Corinthians was merely less secure in its *gnosis*'; Maurer, op cit.

[380]   Above 2.3.2 esp pp 43-45.

This interpretation allows a straightforward, grammatically correct translation of the whole clause μηδὲν ἀνακρίνοντες διὰ τὴν συνείδησιν and leaves no problem with v 26. The γάρ of v 26 follows quite naturally: it indicates *Paul's* reason for eating. Paul ate because 'the earth is the Lord's'.[381]

It is a consequence of this interpretation that even here Paul was not agreeing with the 'strong'. No doubt they would have eaten this food but Paul urged them to eat on *an entirely different basis* that had nothing at all to do with self-consciousness. This meat could be eaten, not to 'show standing before God' or to build up the self-consciousness of the weak, but because there was nothing wrong with the meat and it was not being eaten as part of an idolatrous rite.

It is likely that if the 'strong' were being told not to make an issue of market-place meat[382] the weak were indeed worried by it. Whether this was because many were converted Jews or 'until now accustomed to idols' (8:7) matters little at this point if our reconstruction is correct. The 'strong' were doing this 'for themselves' (τὸ ἑαυτοῦ — v 24). It was they who were self-indulgently eating this food while drawing attention to its origins. In doing so they were probably flaunting their γνῶσις in the way they had been when eating meat ἐν εἰδωλείῳ. For Paul, the difference between the situation in 10:25 and 8:10 was simple. To eat ἐν εἰδωλείῳ was sinful idolatry, to eat food bought ἐν μακέλλῳ was to enjoy God's creation. In terms of 10:31-32 the one caused offence and the other brought glory to God.

4.8.3   An invitation to dinner

If a person is invited out to dinner[383] by unbelievers (ἄπιστοι — v 27) then, says Paul again, 'Eat ... not at all evaluating (the action) for the sake of self-awareness'. This clause means the same as in v 25.

Verse 28 offers a further but hypothetical qualification of the situation in this unbeliever's house. But to whom did the τις (the μηνύσας) refer? Was it the pagan host[384] or another pagan guest,[385] or another believer either present at the meal[386] or, if absent, who knew about the

---

381   Lohse "1 Cor 10" discusses the use of Ps 24:1.

382   That is by saying, 'Look at us — we eat this meat'.

383   The nature of this dinner invitation is not clear. Was it to a home, a 'restaurant' possibly associated with a temple, or was it to a 'post-sacrificial meal at a pagan temple'? (Willis 235-240.) The latter is unlikely in view of ch 8. Most see this as a home invitation: Barrett 241; Robertson 221; Fee 483; *inter al.*

384   Bultmann, *Theology* I 219; cf Senft 138.

385   Lias 103. Osburn, "Συνείδησις" 178; Lietzmann 53.

386   Meyer 311; Robertson 221; Weiss 265; Allo 248; Barrett 242; *inter al.* In this case the informant is normally assumed to have been a *weak* Christian.

invitation?[387] Alternatively, Willis has proposed that 'Paul has moved from specific cases (10:25, 27) to general admonitions', thus 'the search for the "someone" (τις) who objects ... becomes fruitless and unnecessary'.[388]

The fact that Paul used the word ἱερόθυτον rather than εἰδωλόθυτον has caused some to think that the τις must be a pagan individual, otherwise the rather more derogatory Jewish?/Christian[389] word would have been employed.[390] Yet it is difficult to imagine how such a statement would have benefited a *pagan* (v 28b) or how a pagan's 'self-awareness' might have been affected by a Christian's eating (v 29a).[391] Ingeniously Fee suggests the pagan spoke to the Christian from a 'sense of moral obligation to the Christian' — assuming Christians would not eat such food. The Christian, not wanting to offend the pagan's expectations of Christians and 'precisely because it is *not* a matter of Christian moral consciousness', decided not to eat.[392]

However, this view assumes a 'noble' motivation on the part of a pagan which is rather untypical of Paul's illustrative material. Also, v 29b becomes virtually unintelligible. Fee remarks that v 29b represents a 'final word'[393] on freedom and is a 'sudden burst of rhetoric' etc. While such is possible, we believe there is a more satisfactory explanation.

Many believe this exegetical problem is best solved by suggesting that the 'informant' is another *Christian* present at the meal,[394] who was drawing attention to the moral problem that needed to be confronted. However, there are problems with this. Firstly, if the Christian were 'strong', why would he bother mentioning the food? Secondly, if, as most suggest, the Christian were weak, why had he accepted the invitation in the first place? We believe that neither question has been addressed satisfactorily.

It does seem likely that τις refers to another *Christian* commenting on the food to the 'strong' brother present at the meal.[395] A 'weak' Christian is unlikely to have been at the meal and, even if he were, if he was not going to eat the meat, how would his conscience or

[387] Godet II 97; Murphy-O'Connor 101, says it was a 'weak Christian'.
[388] Willis 243.
[389] 2.1.1 above.
[390] Fee 484; cf Barrett 241. Meyer 311 says that ἱερόθυτον is 'a more honourable expression, because the words are spoken at table *in the presence of heathen* ... a delicate touch ...'. See 'Additional Note' below.
[391] Barrett 242. Although cf Von Soden, "Sakrament" 14.
[392] Fee 485.
[393] Ibid 486. This is the position of the *RSV* where vv 28-29a are in brackets.
[394] See nn 386-387 above.
[395] ῾Υμῖν (v 28a) refers to the one to whom the 'strong' person was speaking: probably another Christian who was prepared to attend such a meal.

consciousness have been hurt? A 'strong' Christian would have had no moral qualms about eating, so why would he have raised the subject?

Although the text gives limited information, we suggest it was indeed a 'strong' Christian who would have been likely to raise the issue as a matter of self-awareness, just as we suggested for the situation in v 25.

If our analysis of the position of the 'strong' has been correct, then it is other 'strong' Christians who might say, 'This is meat offered to idols'. They would then have consciously applied their γνῶσις to the situation and used it as an excuse to demonstrate their self-awareness as secure people. In *this* situation Paul would not eat, for he would not lend support to or 'build up' (cf 8:10) a false self-consciousness of this sort.

This understanding of vv 28-29a avoids the difficulties of i) explaining why a *weak* Christian would have accepted an invitation from an unbeliever, and ii) of explaining why 'not eating' would help a *pagan's* 'conscience'. It also explains why the 'strong' might raise the matter in the first place. Finally, it does justice to the γάρ of v 29b.

Verse 29b may be translated, 'For why should my freedom be judged by another consciousness/self-awareness (ὑπὸ ἄλλης συνειδήσεως)?' Throughout chs 8-9 Paul was concerned that the 'strong' should not judge people on the basis of their ἐξουσία. Paul had insisted on his 'freedom', whether or not he exercised his 'rights'. Here in 10:29b he was simply making the same point. Given the situation of v 28a, Paul would *not* eat simply to make a point for the sake of *another person's* understanding of self-awareness. Paul's 'liberty' could never be 'judged' in this way.

For the sake of clarity we may paraphrase vv 28-29 thus:

> If, at a meal with an unbeliever, a 'strong' Christian draws attention to the fact that you are eating idol meat and that, therefore, this is a good occasion to exhibit your 'freedom', then you should decline to eat. You do not want further to encourage this 'strong' Christian in *his* false understanding of self-awareness. Anyway, why should another (and false) type of self-awareness be allowed to decide whether or not one is 'free'?[396].

Verse 30 poses problems whichever way the previous verses have been interpreted. In the example of eating most recently addressed, Paul's command was 'Do not eat it', but in v 30 it seems that he was talking not only of eating but of someone 'reviling' him *for* eating!

---

[396] Cf Bultmann's similar paraphrase: 'No other person has the right to force his judgment upon me: "for why is my freedom decided by any other conscience [than my own]?"'. (*Theology* I 219.)

We agree with Bultmann [397] and Barrett[398] that Paul was continuing to defend a position of *not* eating. The use of the first person singular in vv 29b-30 was probably simply 'representative' of a class of people supposedly adopting Paul's position on freedom[399] and who understood that when they ate food they did so 'by grace' (χάριτι)[400] and because 'the earth is the Lord's' (v 26). This position was not to be 'reviled' (βλασφημέω).

The 'strong' were not allowed to sit in judgment on anyone's freedom. Why should a person be reviled for eating (or not eating) food when that food is given 'by grace' for 'the earth is the Lord's'? This interpretation makes sense of v 30 and shows a continuation of argument from v 23.

It is possible that 4:7 was still in Paul's mind.[401] The problem was similar. The 'strong' no longer regarded even the food they ate as a gift for which to give thanks, but rather saw it as an excuse to boast about themselves and their self-awareness as secure and safe people: 'What have you that you did not receive? ... why do you boast as if it were not a gift?' Paul's basis for eating was that God had given it.

4.9   Paul's summary (10:31 - 11:1)

These verses form a *general* summary. Οὖν establishes the link between vv 30 and 31 — a link that is also with the whole previous argument of chs 8-10. The broad nature of this conclusion is emphasised with the triple use of εἴτε and the extension of the discussion of ἱερόθυτον to include εἴτε τι ποιεῖτε.

The command πάντα εἰς δόξαν θεοῦ ποιεῖτε is at the heart of what Paul has said. Chapters 8-10 have primarily concerned people's self-glorifying actions which brought sin and harm. Thus, as vv 32-33 make clear, bringing 'glory to God' is at least partly to be defined in terms of seeking τὸ τοῦ ἑτέρου (v 24) rather than τὸ ἐμαυτοῦ σύμφορον (v 33).

However, doing things to the 'glory of God' is more than living in a way which no longer offends people. Willis points to an interesting parallel between this passage and Philippians 2 to help explain what the phrase means. There Paul also encouraged concern for others (μὴ τὰ ἑαυτῶν ἕκαστος σκοποῦντες, ἀλλὰ καὶ τὰ ἑτέρων — v 4) as he had

---

[397] Bultmann (loc cit) paraphrases: 'I am free to eat anything that I can eat with thanksgiving (i.e. with a "good conscience"; v. 30); but I do not surrender my freedom either, if I decline out of consideration for another's conscience'.

[398] Barrett 243-244: 'Paul is still justifying abstention by the strong ... '

[399] Robertson, *Grammar* 678.

[400] Calvin 224. This takes the dative as instrumental of means rather than of manner (*contra* Fee 487: 'If I partake with gratitude').

[401] Also cf 11:1 with 4:16.

done in 1 Corinthians 10:24. He also urged the imitation of Christ in both passages,[402] and talked of bringing 'glory to God'.[403]

Willis argues that this last parallel is limited as the verse in the hymn 'clearly refers to the conversion of people to Christ'.[404] Whether or not this is the case,[405] the main emphasis was on the exaltation of Christ as 'Lord' and the acknowledgement by all of that fact.[406] 'Whenever and by whomever the confession is made that "Jesus is Lord" ... [God] is glorified'.[407]

This surely was Paul's meaning in 1 Corinthians 10. To bring 'glory to God' was to exalt Christ. It was not to 'provoke the Lord to jealousy' (10:22) or have κοινωνία with demons (10:20). It was to run in a way which would prevent disqualification (9:24-27), not 'putting Christ to the test' (10:9). It was to acknowledge 'one God ... and one Lord, Jesus Christ' (8:6), and that 'the earth is the Lord's' (10:26).

The use of ἀπρόσκοπος (v 32) also makes this evident. Paul deliberately drew attention again to the 'stumbling' theme of these chapters.[408] He commanded, 'Give no offence — no cause for stumbling — to anyone'. As noted earlier, people's salvation or destruction was at stake.[409] Paul again made this point by reference to his own exemplary work in 10:33 ... ἵνα σωθῶσιν (cf 9:22c).

11:1 concludes Paul's discussion of the issue of idol meat. He had discussed his own behaviour after each main section above, in 8:13, in ch 9 and in ch 10:29b-30. The particular contrast implied here between himself and those to whom he was speaking was that they *did* give offence (v 32) and were not trying 'to please all men' (v 33). This had been Paul's concern throughout these chapters.

Paul's appeal to his own imitation of Christ must be understood in the light of his argument in the epistle as a whole. Chapter 4, where Paul also encouraged imitation of himself (v 16), is instructive. There he saw his weakness (v 10), suffering and persecution as part of his 'ways in Christ' (v 17). At the heart of Paul's ministry was a theology of 'Christ crucified' (1:23). It was in stark contrast to the arrogance of the 'strong'. This basic difference in approach between Paul and the Corinthians had

---

402   Phil 2:5; 1 Cor 11:1.

403   Phil 2:11.

404   Willis 253.

405   It seems doubtful. See comments in Martin, *Philippians* 101-102; Hawthorne, *Philippians* 92-95.

406   It is curious that although Willis demonstrated Paul's 'covenantal' concerns earlier in this chapter he does not draw attention to the 'Lordship' theme here.

407   Hawthorne, *Philippians* 94.

408   2.4 and esp 2.4.2 above.

409   2.4.2-2.4.3 above.

been argued carefully in the first four chapters, it needed no further development as a succinct summary of Paul's position.

4.10   Conclusions

1 Corinthians 10:1-14 has often been studied with a view to discovering more about Paul's use of the OT. This study has normally been influenced by a predisposition that here Paul was primarily concerned with 'sacraments'. Theological questions concerning the way in which Christ was or is present in the sacrament have been addressed to the text. Thus questions about whether Christ's presence in the wilderness was 'realistic' or not have dominated discussions.

Help in interpreting the passage is rarely sought from an examination of other uses of the WT except to note possible 'verbal' parallels with Paul's writing. Then the comparison frequently serves only to suggest that Paul was relying on this or that text for his own work.

We have deliberately taken a broad over-view of those WT. This has revealed that each *functions* in a very similar manner. It is not just the content of the traditions that is similar, but their paraenetic purposes.

We discovered that at the broadest level these traditions were recounted with a primary intention of calling people to recognise God as a gracious God who gave gifts to his people. Secondly, they were intended as reminders that the Israelites, who received such gifts, became arrogant, presumptuous and 'craved' other things. Notably, they turned to other gods and so were judged. Thus the dual covenant sanctions of 'blessing' and 'curse' figure prominently throughout the traditions. But this 'covenant' emphasis also meant that, thirdly, the traditions consistently referred to God's faithfulness to his people even when they had sinned. Verbal parallels between those traditions are very limited, but at the *functional* level these similarities are evident. In other words, the traditions expressed ideas and concerns that were at the heart of the identity of the Israelite community.

Paul alluded to various different texts but his account of the WT *functioned* similarly to most.

i)   He accentuated the graciousness of God who gave gifts of food and water to all the people in the covenant community under Moses (10:1-14).

ii)   He reminded the Corinthians that in spite of this (ἀλλά — v 5) the people 'craved' evil and so were judged. Paul listed a number of the sins found in several of the traditions, but stressed idolatry (especially vv 7, 14 and possibly v 8).

iii)   Paul reminded the Corinthians that their God was faithful (v 13).

An examination of the word πνευματικός showed that it did not mean 'figurative' or 'allegorical' or 'sacramental'. Nor did it simply indicate the origin of the food. For Paul the word, although being used in different ways, seemed to incorporate two factors also evident in the discussion of the gifts of manna and water in the WT, a) the giver of 'spiritual things' was God (or his Spirit), b) 'spiritual things' required an enlightened understanding which itself was given by God or his Spirit. Thus it was possible to talk of 'spiritual things' (given by the Spirit and needing to be properly 'understood') and to talk of 'spiritual people' (who, with the Spirit's help, could 'understand' the gifts).

Thus we can paraphrase the meaning of 'spiritual food' as 'food *given by God that had a deeper significance that had to be understood.*' This was how also the food and drink were treated in the LXX and other Jewish WT even though the word 'spiritual' was not used. Those gifts from God, or his Spirit, needed to be 'known' or 'understood'.

At just this point of understanding Paul differed from the earlier traditions. For him the 'understanding' of spiritual things was *Christ*-centred. This became clear in two ways: i) in the immediate context the 'spiritual rock' was *Christ*, ii) elsewhere when Paul used the word 'spiritual' it focussed on understanding more about Christ.

Paul saw Christ as the covenant Lord, the one who continually and faithfully supplied his people. Christ could therefore be called the 'rock'. Such 'spiritual' understanding allowed Paul to say that the 'rock was Christ' and to indicate that *Christ* was 'tested' in the wilderness.

To discuss whether Christ's presence in the wilderness was 'realistic' is unhelpfully to import anachronistic sacramental terminology. For Paul, Christ was present *then* and that is why 'these things' were so important for 'our instruction'. But there was no question of the Israelites having been expected to see or acknowledge Christ in the wilderness for that, after all, was precisely the revelation now available to those 'upon whom the end of the ages has come'.

Paul was not primarily concerned in 10:1-14 with 'sacraments'. His concern is expressed in categories which emphasize the incompatibility of different 'lordships'.[410] Idolatry, arising out of an over-confidence in God's gifts, was wrong on this basis.

The links with chs 8 and 9 are firmly established. Spiritual gifts received in the wilderness no more authenticated 'standing' in the covenant community of the OT than did spiritual gifts such as γνῶσις in the Corinthian community. A person's security in the covenant community lay in God's call and continuing faithfulness to his people. A response of love (8:3) and obedience (9:24-27) will mark out the one who 'stands'. The temptation to be 'puffed-up' and arrogant, like the Israelites, was serious enough. It was even leading the Corinthians to the

---

[410] Cf Sander's emphasis on 'lordship' and 'participatory union' when discussing this passage (*PPJ* 455-456; 503; 512).

same sort of sin, idolatry and possibly immorality. It could lead to sin against Christ (8:12), destruction (8:11; 10:9, 10), the possibility of disqualification (9:27), and to 'stumbling' and 'falling' (8:8, 13; 10:12 cf 9:13 and 10:32).

This passage was both a warning and an encouragement, but fundamentally it taught lessons about the nature of the covenant community overseen by the God who brought it into being, gave gifts to its members and both blessed and judged it. Total allegiance was required of its members, so idolatry was especially wrong for it involved another allegiance.

While it is likely that vv 16-18 provide some instruction about Paul's attitude to the Lord's Supper, we have seen that there was no significant change in subject between vv 1-13 and vv 14-22. Paul was using Israel κατὰ σάρκα as a *negative* example. In the first thirteen verses he talked of the identity of the people under Moses and God, of God's gifts to them, and of the fact that, in spite of this, the Israelites were punished. In the next nine verses Paul showed *why* the Corinthian eating in idol temples was wrong, and thus why it was so necessary to 'flee idolatry' for fear of the penalties mentioned in vv 1-13.

The reference to the Lord's Supper was an illustration. Just as eating and drinking in the Supper demonstrated the community's covenant allegiance to the Lord, so eating in a temple showed similar allegiance to demons. Verses 1-22 must be taken as a whole argument about the danger of presumptuous behaviour by those who 'think they stand'.

Verses 22-30 address a related but different topic. While Paul would not eat εἰδωλόθυτον served ἐν εἰδωλείῳ, he would eat ἱερόθυτον bought ἐν μακέλλῳ.[411] In these complex verses, we have cautiously suggested that Paul continued to argue against the 'strong'. The 'strong' ate to show their 'standing' and to draw attention to the fact that the meat had been offered to idols, in order to show their self-awareness as marked out and secure people. For Paul, this was an illegitimate motivation for eating, so he offered his alternative. People should not be 'judged' or 'evaluated' by their eating or not eating. Paul would not be party to confirming them in their wrong understanding of 'conscience' — understood as self-awareness or self-consciousness.

Additional Note
The use of the word ἱερόθυτον

One further suggestion may be made in the light of our interpretation of this section (vv 23-30). Paul was still addressing the 'strong' about their eating habits. We have argued that Paul would *never* have eaten

411   See Additional Note below.

εἰδωλόθυτα served ἐν εἰδωλείῳ. Now he used the word ἱερόθυτον and was prepared to eat, provided no one else's self-awareness was affected in doing so. We suggest that this change of words had nothing to do with the sensibilities of the pagans, but rather was Paul's way of distinguishing the issues the more clearly between idolatry and eating other meat that may have had its origins in sacrificial rites. Thus it is possible that εἰδωλόθυτα was virtually a Christian technical term for that which was eaten ἐν εἰδωλείῳ, in other words, specifically food eaten as part of worship to idols or demons.

If this were correct, then it would go at least a certain distance to answering one of the more intractable problems of this section of 1 Corinthians: Why did Paul not refer to (nor perhaps even obey) the Council of Jerusalem decree in Acts 15:29?[412] If εἰδωλόθυτα in Acts *also* referred specifically to meat linked with participation in the worship of idols, then Paul followed the Council's injunction *completely*, on our understanding of 1 Corinthians 8-10. This would mean that ἱερόθυτον as used in 1 Corinthians 10 was not an issue addressed by the Council, so Paul was at liberty to take a liberal attitude to this sort of meat.

There is some slight indication in Acts 15 itself that *worship in temples* was in mind there as well. The debate in Acts had not discussed meat generally. It is, for example, strange that, if the issue primarily concerned not giving offence to *kosher* sensibilities, pork meat was not mentioned. James' judgment in vv 19-20 centred on the requirement that Gentiles abstain from ἀλισγήματα. In spite of the textual problems of 15:20, 29 and 21:25[413] there is no great textual problem with ἀλισγημάτων τῶν εἰδώλων in 15:20 nor with what appears to be an *interpretation* of that in 15:29, where ἀλισγήματα is replaced by εἰδωλόθυτα. This *might* suggest that the meat problem was specifically (even then) one of pollution with *idols*.

Of course there are problems with this, especially in that the phrases that require abstention from 'what is strangled' and 'from blood' seem to point to a more general understanding of meat than simply that eaten 'in temples'. However, if even these terms are defined by ἀλισγήματα then perhaps there is scope to examine more closely the type of sacrificial processes used in the temples of the first century. Were particular forms of strangulation used? Was drinking blood or some eating of coagulated blood involved in the sacrifices? If there was, then it is possible that the problem with idol meat was not *that* it had been sacrificed but where and why it was being eaten. This is the distinction that we believe Paul made. Was it a distinction inherent in the word εἰδωλόθυτα, that is, did the word denote meat offered to an εἴδωλον ἐν εἰδωλείῳ?

---

412   Cf Geyser, "Decree".
413   See Metzger, *Commentary* 429-434.

Such a suggestion is for now a mere possibility. However, we note that Harnack suggests something rather similar.[414] He says that εἰδωλόθυτον referred not so much to sacrificed *meat* but 'to Idolatry generally'. He goes on to say of Acts 15:20, 'Participation in the idolatrous feasts is especially emphasised, simply because this was the crassest form, of idolatry'. Perhaps our suggestion here may stimulate some further thinking along these lines, if only to discount it in the end.

[414] Harnack, *Acts* 257.

5. Conclusions.

Each chapter has ended with a series of conclusions drawn from the exegesis of the passage concerned. Our purpose here is not to repeat those points but to draw the work together by showing that an hypothesis that began to emerge towards the beginning of the exegesis of ch 8 has been refined and confirmed in the subsequent exegesis of chs 9 and 10.

This hypothesis has emerged in a context which we have deliberately kept as free as possible from reliance upon a particular disposition to any religious 'background'. We have not formulated a view about whether the audience was predominantly from a Jewish or pagan background, or whether it was being influenced by pagan-gnosticism or Jewish-gnosticism. Rather we have sought to understand the dynamics of the *religious* problem that Paul believed he was facing. We have done this through an examination of his perspective on and response to this Christian community.

5.1 An Hypothesis

Our hypothesis for the situation Paul was confronting in 1 Corinthians 8-10 may be stated simply:

In the Corinthian church the gift of the Spirit called γνῶσις was regarded by the 'strong' as an authenticator of their secure status in the covenant community.

The value of such a marker was in its visibility, thus, in this case, in order to *demonstrate* that they possessed such a gift the 'strong' ate idol meat in an idol's temple.[1]

---

[1]   Although in chs 8-10 Paul's particular concern was with the gift of γνῶσις, elsewhere other gifts of the Spirit were addressed. Notably *verbal* gifts of tongues and prophecy were mentioned earlier, and Paul's polemic against the Corinthian approach to 'wisdom' in chs 1-4 was probably directed against a

This hypothesis has been derived from examining Paul's message to the Corinthians. Paul proposed that love marked out the one 'known by God' (8:3). This he contrasted with γνῶσις. It has been suggested, therefore, that the Corinthians were allowing γνῶσις to *function* in the way Paul believed ἀγάπη should function. This function of ἀγάπη was not developed by Paul in response to the Corinthian situation, but was already enshrined in the Gospel tradition and the summary of the law.

Chapter 8 made it clear that γνῶσις was linked to the subject of εἰδωλόθυτα because it was being offered as the reason for eating ἐν εἰδωλείῳ. Paul's response to this issue was formulated on three levels:

i)   he challenged the fundamental assumption concerning the *function* of γνῶσις;

ii) he challenged the specific content of their so-called knowledge that had led them into demon worship;

iii) he proposed a different theological basis by which to justify eating idol meat in various *non*-temple situations.

We shall now briefly review those levels of response.

i)   Paul's challenge to the assumption that γνῶσις could function as an authenticator or marker of membership in the Christian community proceeded in four steps.

a)   He pointed to the danger of becoming 'puffed up' with knowledge and contrasted it with love which 'built up' and which was the true marker of those known by God. The lack of 'building up' was demonstrated in the way weaker Christians were being led towards 'destruction'.

b)   Paul showed that 'building up' others to the view of the 'strong' caused the 'strong' themselves to sin (8:12) thus denying the very security which they believed was demonstrated in the practice of their γνῶσις.

c)   The practice of γνῶσις in the eating of idol meat could never show a person's 'standing' before God (8:8). By way of illustration Paul proffered his own apostleship. This, he argued, was not authenticated by the exercise of any ἐξουσία but by obedience to the divine commission.

d)   In ch 10 Paul drew upon the experiences of the Israelites in the wilderness to show beyond doubt that receiving spiritual gifts did not guarantee security of status in the covenant community.

ii) Paul's challenge to the *content* of their so-called 'knowledge' is also to be found through all three chapters and is interwoven with his attack on the *function* of γνῶσις. The γνῶσις of the 'strong' had led them to eat εἰδωλόθυτα. Paul showed that their knowledge that 'an idol has no existence' was at best incomplete, for demons *did* exist. This

wisdom which had its origins in some supposed manifestation of a gift of the Spirit (cf 2:6-16. See Davis, *Wisdom*, 98).

argument began in 8:4-6 and was continued in 10:14-22. In both passages Paul was probably drawing on Deuteronomy 32. He would not accept the position of those whose 'knowledge' was leading them towards κοινωνία with demons. Paul further showed that their γνῶσις was deficient in two other ways:

a)   it led to the *exclusion* from the community of some Christians rather than the authentication of their real status as 'brothers' (8:9-13);

b)   it led to the 'strong' having a false sense of security (8:8, 12b; 9:24-27; 10:12 etc).

iii) Finally Paul briefly examined the more general question of sacrificial meat available outside the temples. This meat could indeed be eaten, but it was not to be eaten for purposes of building up a person's self-awareness and consciousness of Christian status and security. Rather, it could be eaten on the basis that the earth was the Lord's. Thus, again, any 'boasting' would be in God's graciousness rather than in the flaunting of a particular ἐξουσία for the sake of status.

We believe that this reconstruction makes sense of the whole argument in chs 8-10. There is no need to ascribe different parts of these chapters to different letters, since Paul was dealing throughout 8:1-10:22 with εἰδωλόθυτα. The change of subject matter, in 10:23-30, to ἱερόθυτον bought ἐν μάκελλῳ is explained naturally. Paul did not want his readers to assume that all sacrificial meat in all circumstances was to be avoided. Then, in his general summary of these chapters (10:31-11:1), Paul drew together aspects of each part of his argument. No 'stumbling' was to be caused. Self-aggrandizement was wrong. No one was to be excluded from the community and what *was* eaten was to be eaten for God's glory (and not with other purposes in mind).

This reconstruction, we suggest, also makes sense from the standpoint of the sociology of religion. The problem of regarding spiritual gifts as markers or *authenticators* of community membership could have arisen in a brief period of time and with a relatively minimal distortion of Paul's own teaching. Paul no doubt had taught that those who possessed the Spirit 'belonged' to God. That this formed part of his understanding of the definition of the people of God is stated clearly in Romans 8:9-11 and 14. The same is implied in 1 Corinthians 2:12-13 and 3:16. It would appear from the discussion of πνευματικά and χαρίσματα in this epistle and Romans 12:6[2] that Paul had also clearly taught that the people of God would receive gifts from the Spirit. In fact Paul probably taught that 'each one' would receive a gift from the Spirit.[3] It would require only a minor distortion of these two teachings to lead to the position we have suggested was held by the 'strong'. To move from

[2]   This Pauline understanding of 'gifts' is also clear in Eph 4:1-16.
[3]   1 Cor 12:7.

Paul's view that the Spirit was the guarantee of 'belonging', to the view that the gifts the Spirit gave were in fact that guarantee, is easily envisaged. It is especially easy to envisage that one or two of the more spectacular or revelatory gifts, such as γνῶσις, wisdom or prophecy, were most to be desired as being the clearest evidence of the indwelling Spirit and that possession of these gifts guaranteed that a person 'belonged'.

Paul's response to this in ch 12 was that people had *different* gifts. His response in chs 8-10, dealing with one such gift, was that the possession of γνῶσις was no such guarantee. His challenge to the *content* of their γνῶσις is probably an indication that some who were claiming this particular gift, to Paul's mind, did not really possess it.

Although it is beyond the purview of this dissertation to demonstrate this here, we believe that our hypothesis also makes satisfactory sense of the rest of the epistle. We have, throughout this dissertation, sought to demonstrate the way in which the argument of chs 8-10 develops points already made in the earlier chapters of the epistle. Especially we have noted how much groundwork is laid in chs 1-4. We have drawn attention to the gifts of the Spirit mentioned in the opening verses; to the centrality in Paul's theology of the 'word of the cross' (1:18) as opposed to the triumphalism of the 'strong'; to the importance of themes such as 'judgment' and 'discerning' and of what it is to be 'spiritual' (chs 2-4). We also noted the introduction of the 'stumbling' theme (1:23) and the contrast with the discussion of the 'foundation' (ch 3). Both of these were seen to be important for Paul's message in chs 8-10.

We also saw that Paul's concern for the weak, and his understanding that they too were part of the community because God had brought it into being, was at the heart of his discussion of community identity in the opening chapters, as in chs 8-10. The 'marker' of such people's status in the community was to be found in their response to this God: a response of obedience and love. That 'love for God' was introduced in 2:9 and developed in ch 8. This marker of love was seen in love for God (8:3) but also in love for the community, summarized in Paul's word οἰκοδομέω.

It is this concept of love, demonstrated towards God and his people, that also allows our reconstruction to make sense of chs 12-14. Chapter 13 distinguishes clearly between the gifts of the Spirit, such as knowledge and prophecy, and the marker of 'love' which does not ζητεῖ τὰ ἑαυτῆς and is not 'puffed up'. We have seen that this chapter may reasonably be regarded as a commentary on the argument so far in this epistle. In chs 12 and 14, Paul described the positive *function* of the gifts in building up the community. Not all have the same gift, but all have something from God with which to build up others.

Our hypothesis clearly does not require that every section of the epistle be explained in terms of this one underlying problem concerning the *function* of spiritual gifts as religious markers in Corinth. But we have seen that it makes sense of chs 1-4, 8-10 and 12-14, so it is worth indicating how it might make sense of the remainder, although to demonstrate this in any detail is not possible here.

Themes that have arisen in chs 8-10 are also prominent in chs 5-7. We have already paid some attention to the centrality in this epistle of 6:12: πάντα μοι ἔξεστιν ... οὐκ ἐγὼ ἐξουσιασθήσομαι ὑπό τινος. Once again it seems that the 'strong' were intent on flaunting certain actions that Paul considered wrong. As Thiselton has argued, Paul's censure of the Corinthians in ch 5 'relates not primarily to the [immoral] man in question, but to the fact that the community seemed pleased with the situation'.[4] Paul's response to the case of immorality is to turn again and criticise the Corinthian arrogance ('puffed up' — v 2) and boasting (v 6). Their actions, as in chs 8-10, seem to have been quite deliberately based, we suggest, on their 'knowledge' stated in their slogan of 6:12. Paul draws them back to the death of Christ, as he did in ch 8 — to the centre of the Gospel. Perhaps the talk of 'celebrating' (the Passover) in 5:8 implies that the Corinthians viewed their own action as a 'celebration' of their secure status in the community.

Chapter 6, like ch 10, shows the incompatibility of certain actions with commitment to the 'Lord' (cf 6:16-17). We have already mentioned the question of 'belonging' addressed in the latter part of the chapter. An abuse of the function of the gifts of the Spirit satisfactorily explains each issue in chs 5 and 6.

In ch 7 the issues can also be explained in terms of a received 'knowledge' perhaps seen in a statement like, 'It is well for a man not to touch a woman' (7:1). Such a view of ch 7 has been argued in particular by Hurd.[5] Paul's response deserves more consideration than it can be given here, but it is worth noting that it is again phrased in terms of 'calling'. The state in which a person is 'called' remains important. Status in the community is not demonstrated by the rigorous application of certain 'knowledgeable' statements. It is, as we have seen earlier, to be seen in terms of election and 'slavery' to the 'Lord' (vv 17-24). We may also note the use, even at this stage in the epistle, of Paul's argument that each person has his own χάρισμα from God (v 7).

Chapter 15 contains a number of exceedingly complex exegetical problems, and it may be that Paul here took up an altogether distinct issue. However, it is also possible that there were some links between the problem Paul faced over eschatology in ch 15 and the Corinthian

4   Thiselton, {"Realized"} 516.
5   Hurd 164ff.

view that their status in the community was secure. This chapter opens
with a creedal formula that emphasizes the grace of God which led to
their 'standing' (15:1c) in the community of the saved (15:2a). Paul
showed again the need to strive to remain in that status (εἰ κατέχετε —
v 2b) and once more pointed to his own example of 'working hard' (v
10b). It is possible that their apparent misunderstanding of the
resurrection was based on an inadequate eschatology in which the
authentication of present status had become much more significant than
consideration of the future hope.[6]

Even in the concluding remarks of ch 16 some of the ideas we have
noted in chs 8-10 are repeated again. For example, v 13 calls for
watchfulness for the future while 'standing in the faith'. The 'standing'
depends on the faith which is marked by the practice of 'love' (v 14).
Verses 22 and 24 again remind the community of the centrality of love
while linking it with the eschatological hope summarised in the liturgical
cry μαράνα θά.

Thus, we believe that our hypothesis concerning the religious situation
Paul faced at Corinth does make sense of chs 8-10, but also will help to
explain much of the rest of the epistle.

Finally, it is pertinent to this conclusion to list a few of the most
distinctive features of our exegesis, apart from the hypothesis to which it
has led:

1.   Most scholars believe that the Corinthians felt 'secure' primarily
because they took the 'sacraments'. Of course Paul never used this word
and its very use in this context seems anachronistic. However, our
exegesis has neither supported that view nor the view that Paul was
addressing the topic of sacraments in 10:1-14.

2.   Scholars have spent much time discussing the background that may
have given rise to the γνῶσις spoken of in 8:1-3 and 7. Murphy-
O'Connor and Fee have both suggested that this γνῶσις was the 'gift of
the Spirit' in 8:1-3 but, as far as we are aware, only the former has
maintained that this was true of 8:7 as well. We have argued that the
entire passage may be read as a discussion about the *function* of the gift
of the Spirit called γνῶσις. Whatever the background against which the
Corinthians understood what they called γνῶσις, it is its *function* which
is the better key to understanding the development of Paul's argument.
This does not exclude discussions about possible backgrounds nor, as we
have seen, does it preclude Paul's strong attack on the *content* of that
knowledge.

3.   We have argued that these chapters can be read throughout as
addressed by Paul in opposition to the prevailing opinion of the 'strong'.
This includes verses such as 8:8 and sections such as 10:23-30. While

---

[6]   This view relates closely to the work of Thiselton "Realized".

individual commentators mentioned in our text support certain different aspects of our argument, none, to our knowledge, supports this position throughout all three chapters.

4.   Some scholars have suggested that different sections of these chapters should be assigned to different letters. While there is nothing new in arguing that they do make coherent sense as they stand, our hypothesis does indicate a new way of seeing the development of a consistent argument through the chapters concerned.

Commentaries
(Method of Citation by Author Only)

Allo, E -B *Saint Paul Première Épître aux Corinthiens* (Paris, 1956 2nd ed).

Bachmann, P *Der Erste Brief des Paulus an die Korinther* (Leipzig, 1905).

Barrett, C K *A Commentary on the First Epistle to the Corinthians* (New York, 1968).

Bengel, J A *Gnomon Novi Testamenti* (Stuttgart, 1860).

Bruce, F F *1 and 2 Corinthians* in *New Century Bible* (London, 1971).

Calvin, J *The First Epistle of Paul the Apostle to the Corinthians* (1960, Edinburgh ET Fraser).

Chrysostom, St John *The Homilies of S John Chrysostom part 1: 1 Corinthians* (Oxford, 1839).

Clark, G H *1 Corinthians. A Contemporary Commentary* (New Jersey, 1975).

Conzelmann, H *1 Corinthians* (Philadelphia, 1975 ET Leitch).

Edwards, T C *A Commentary on the First Epistle to the Corinthians* (1903, London).

Ellicott, C J *St Paul's First Epistle to the Corinthians* (London, 1987).

Evans, E *The Epistles of Paul the Apostle to the Corinthians* (Oxford, 1930).

Fee, G D *The First Epistle to the Corinthians* in *NICNT* (Grand Rapids, 1987).

Godet, F *Commentary on St Paul's First Epistle to the Corinthians* (Edinburgh, 1898, 2 Vols).

Goudge, H L *The First Epistle to the Corinthians* (London, 1903).

Grosheide, F W *Commentary on the First Epistle to the Corinthians* in *NICNT* (Grand Rapids, 1953).

Heinrichi, G *Erste Brief an die Korinther* (Göttingen, 1988).

Héring, J *The First Epistle of Saint Paul to the Corinthians* (London, 1962).

Hurd, J C *The Origin of 1 Corinthians* (London, 1965).

Klauck, H-J *1. Korintherbrief* (Stuttgart, 1984).

Kümmel, W G *Handbuch zum N T. An die Korinther I, II. Erklärt von H Lietzmann* (Tübingen, 1949, 4th ed. This edition has notes added by Kümmel. These notes are cited by mention of Kümmel and page number).

Lake, K *The Earlier Epistles of St Paul. Their Motive and Origin* (London, 1911).

Lenski, R C *The Interpretation of St. Paul's First and Second Epistles to the Corinthians* (Minneapolis, 1937).

Lias, J J *The First Epistle to the Corinthians* in *Cambridge Greek Testament for Schools and Colleges* (Cambridge, 1897).

Lietzmann, H *Handbuch zum NT. An die Korinther I, II* (Tübingen, 1923).

Lightfoot, J B *Notes on Epistles of St Paul from Unpublished Commentaries* (London, 1895).

Luther, M *Commentary on 1 Corinthians 7* in *Luther's Works Vol 28* (St Louis, 1973) pp 9-56.

Mare, W H *1 Corinthians* in *The Expositor's Bible Commentary Vol 10* (Grand Rapids, 1976 ed Gaebelein).

Massie, J *Corinthians* (Edinburgh, No date).

Meyer, H A W *Critical and Exegetical Commentary on the New Testament* (Edinburgh, 1982).

Moffatt, J *The First Epistle of Paul to the Corinthians* (London, 1935).

Morris, L *The First Epistle of Paul to the Corinthians* in *TNTC* (Grand Rapids, 1980 12th printing).

Murphy-O'Connor, J *1 Corinthians* in *New Testament Message Vol 10* (Dublin, 1979).

Olshausen, H *Biblical Commentary on St Paul's First and Second Epistles to the Corinthians* (Edinburgh, 1863 trans Cox).

Orr, W F and Walther, J A *1 Corinthians* in *The Anchor Bible* (Garden City, 1976).

Parry, R St John *The First Epistle of Paul the Apostle to the Corinthians* (Cambridge, 1937 2nd ed).

Prior, D *The Message of 1 Corinthians* in *The Bible Speaks Today* (Leicester, 1985).

Robertson, A and Plummer, A *A Critical and Exegetical Commentary on the First Epistle of St Paul to the Corinthians* (Edinburgh, 1914 2nd ed).

Ruef, J *Paul's First Letter to Corinth* in *Pelican Commentaries* (London, 1977).

Schlatter, A *Die Korintherbriefe* (Stuttgart, 1950).

Senft, C *La Première Épître de Saint Paul aux Corinthiens* (Paris, 1979).

Thrall, M E *The First and Second Letters of St Paul to the Corinthians* (Cambridge, 1965).

Weiss, J *Der Erste Korintherbrief* (Göttingen, 1970 reprint).

Wendland, H D *Die Briefe an die Korinther* in *Das Neue Testament Deutsch, 7* (Göttingen, 1965).

Willis, W L *Idol Meat in Corinth. The Pauline Argument in 1 Corinthians 8 and 10* in *SBLDS 68* (Chico California, 1985).

Wolff, C *Der erste Brief des Paulus an die Korinther* (Berlin, 1982 2 Vols).

Selected Bibliography
(Method of citation by author and short title)

Aalen, S "Das Abendmahl als Opfermahl im neuen Testament", *NovT 6*, (1963), pp. 128-152.

Agrell, G *Work, Toil and Sustenance* (Lund, 1976).

Amsler, S "La Typologie de l'Ancien Testament chez saint Paul", *RThPh 37*, (1949) pp 113-128.

Angus, S *The Mystery Religions And Christianity* (London, 1928).

Arai, S "Die Gegner des Paulus im 1 Korintherbrief und das Problem der Gnosis", *NTS 19*, (1972/3) pp 430-437 ("Gegner").

Bailey, K E "The Structure of 1 Corinthians" *NovT 25*, (1983) pp 152-181.

Baltzer, K *The Covenant Formulary in OT, Jewish and Early Christian Writings* (Oxford, 1971 ET Green).

Bammel, E "Paul and Judaism", *The Modern Churchman 6*, (1962-3) pp 279-285.

Bandstra, A J "Interpretation in 1 Corinthians 10:1-11", *CTJ 6*, (1971) pp 5-21 ("Interpretation").

Banks, R *Paul's Idea of Community. The Early House Churches in their Historical Setting* (Grand Rapids, 1980) (*Community*).

Barclay, J M G "Mirror-Reading a Polemical Letter: Galatians as a Test Case", *JSNT 31*, (1987) pp 73-93.

Barr, A "Love in the Church in 1 Cor 13", *SJT 3*, (1950) pp 416-425.

Barr, J *The Semantics of Biblical Language* (Oxford, 1961).

— "Did Isaiah know about Hebrew 'root meanings'?", ET 75, (1963) pp 242.

Barrett, C K *From First Adam to Last: A Study in Pauline Theology* (London, 1962) (*First Adam*).

— *The Gospel According to St John An Introduction with commentary and notes on the Greek text* (London, 1978 2nd ed) (*John*).

— *Essays on Paul* (London, 1982).

Barth, C "Zur Bedeutung der Wüstentradition", in *Supplements to VT XV* (Leiden, 1966) pp 14-23.

Barth, M *Das Abendmahl Passamahl, Bundesmahl und Messiasmahl* in *Theologische Studien herausgegeben von Karl Barth, Heft 8* (Zurich, 1945).

Bauer, J "Uxores circumducere (1 Kor 9,5)", *BZ 3*, (1959) pp 94-102.

Baur, F C "Die Christus Partei in der Korinthischen Gemeinde", *TZTh 5*, (1831) pp 61-206.

— *Paul, the Apostle of Jesus Christ* (London, 1873-5, 2 Vols) (*Paul*).

— *The Church History of the First Three Centuries* (Edinburgh, 1878 3rd edition, 2 Vols).

Beekman, J and Callow, J *Translating the Word of God* (Grand Rapids, 1974).

Behm, J *Der Begriff DIATHEKE im Neuen Testament* (Leipzig, 1912).

Beker, J C *Paul the Apostle. The Triumph of God in Life and Thought* (Edinburgh, 1980).

Belleville, L L "Continuity or Discontinuity: A Fresh look at 1 Corinthians in the light of first-century epistolary forms and conventions", *EQ 59*, (1987) pp 15-37 ("Continuity").

Bender, W "Bemerkungen zur Ubersetzung von 1 Kor 1:30", *ZNTW 71*, (1980) pp 263-268.

Bertram, G "Παίζω", in *TDNT V* (Grand Rapids, 1967) pp 625-630.

Best, E *One Body in Christ* (London, 1955).

Betz, H D *Der Apostle Paulus und die sokratische Tradition* (Tübingen, 1972).

— *Galatians: A Commentary on Paul's Letter to the Churches in Galatia* in *Hermeneia Commentaries* (Philadelphia, 1979).

Bianchi, U ed *Le Origini dello Gnosticismo* in *Studies in the History of Religions* (Leiden, 1967).

Black, D A "A Note on 'The Weak' in 1 Cor 9,22", *Biblica 64*, (1983) pp 240-242.

Blevins, J L "Introduction to 1 Corinthians", *R Exp LXXX*, (1983) pp 315-324.

Bloch, R "Midrash", in *Dictionnaire de la Bible: Supplement V* (Paris, 1957) pp 1263-1281ff.

— "Methodological Note for the Study of Rabbinic Literature", in *Approaches to Ancient Judaism* (Missoula, 1978 ed Green) pp 50-75.

Bogle, M M "Τὰ τέλη τῶν αἰώνων 1 Corinthians 10:11 A Suggestion", *ET 67*, (1956) pp 246.

Bonnard, P "La signification du désert, selon le Nouveau Testament", in *Hommage et Reconnaissance Fests for Karl Barth* (Neuchatel, 1946 ed Allmen).

— "Introduction génerale à 1 Corinthiens", *Cahiers bibliques de Foi et Vie 3*, (1956) pp 561-567.

— "L'Église corps du Christ dans le Paulinisme", *RThPh 3*, (1958).

Borgen, P *Bread from Heaven. An Exegetical Study of the Concept of Manna in the Gospel of John and the Writings of Philo* in *SNT 10* (Leiden, 1965).

Bornkamm, G "Herrenmahl und Kirche bei Paulus", *ZThK 53*, (1956) pp 312-349.

— "Zum Verständnis des Gottesdienstes bei Paulus Die Erbauung der Gemeinde als Leib Christi", in *Das Ende des Gesetzes* (München, 1966) pp 113-123.

— "The Missionary Stance of Paul in 1 Corinthians 9 and in Acts", in *Studies in Luke-Acts. Essays Presented in Honor of Paul Schubert* (New York, 1966 eds Keck and Martyn) pp 194-207 ("Stance").

— *Paul* (London, 1971 ET).

Bosch, J S "Gloriarse" Según San Pablo. Sentido y teología de καυχάομαι in *AnBib 40* (Rome, 1970).

Bourke, M M "The Eucharist and Wisdom in First Corinthians", in *Studiorum Paulinorum Congressus Internationalis Catholicus, Vol I* (Rome, 1963) pp 367-381 ("Eucharist").

Bousset, W *Die Religion des Judentums im späthellenistischen Zeitalter* (Tübingen, 1966).

— *Kyrios Christos* (Nashville, 1979 ET).

Bouttier, M *En Christ* (Paris, 1962).

Box, G H "Antecedents of the Eucharist", *JTS 3,* (1902) pp 357-369.

Broneer, O "Paul and the Pagan Cults at Isthmia", *HTR 64,* (1971) pp 169-187.

Bruce, F F *The New Testament Development of Old Testament Themes* (Grand Rapids, 1977 US edition) (*Development*).

Brunt, J C "Love, Freedom, and Moral Responsibility: The Contribution of 1 Cor. 8-10 to an Understanding of Paul's Ethical Thinking", in *SBL Seminar Papers* (California, 1981) pp 19-33.

Buchanan, G W "The Use of Rabbinic Literature for New Testament Research", *BTB 7,* (1977) pp 110-122.

Büchsel, F "In Christus bei Paulus", *ZNW 42,* (1949) pp 141-158.

— "'Ἀνακρίνω", in *TDNT III* (Grand Rapids, 1965) pp 943-944.

Bultmann, R K *Theology of the New Testament* (London, 1952 ET, 2 Vols).

— "Γινώσκω", in *TDNT I* (Grand Rapids, 1964) pp 689-719.

— "Καυχάομαι", in *TDNT III* (Grand Rapids, 1965) pp 645-653.

— *The Old and New Man in the Letters of Paul* (Richmond, 1967 ET Crim).

Byrne, B *Sons of God — Seed of Abraham* in *AnBib* (Rome, 1979) (*Sons*).

Cadbury, H J "The Macellum of Corinth", *JBL 53,* (1934) pp 134-141.

— "Overconversion in Paul's Churches", in *The Joy of Study* (New York, 1951 ed Johnson) pp 43-50.

Caird, G B *The Apostolic Age* (London, 1955).

— "Everything to Everyone", *Interp 13,* (1959) pp 387-399.

— *A Commentary on the Revelation of St. John the Divine* (London, 1966).

— "The Development of the Doctrine of Christ in the New Testament", in *Christ for us Today* (London, pp 1968 ed Pittenger).

— "Review of Sander's PPJ", *JTS 29,* (1978) pp 538-543.

— *The Language and Imagery of the Bible* (London, 1980) (*Language*).

Campbell, J Y "KOINONIA and its Cognates in the New Testament", *JBL 51*, (1932) pp 352-380.

Campbell, W S "The Freedom and Faithfulness of God in Relation to Israel", *JSNT 13*, (1981) pp 27-45.

Carson, D "Pauline Inconsistency. Reflections on 1 Corinthians 9.19-23 and Galatians 2.11-14", *Churchman 100*, (1986) pp 6-45.

Casey, R P "Gnosis, Gnosticism and the New Testament", in *Background of the New Testament and its Eschatology* (Cambridge, 1956 eds Davies and Daube) pp 52-80 ("Gnosis").

Cerfaux, L *Le Christ dans la Théologie de saint Paul* (Paris, 1951) (*Le Christ*).

— "'Kyrios' dans les citations pauliniennes de l'Ancien Testament", in *Recueil L Cerfaux I* (Univ de Louvain, 1954) pp 173-188 ("Kyrios").

Chadwick, H "All Things to all Men", *NTS 1*, (1954) pp 261-275.

Charles, R H *The Apocrypha and Pseudepigrapha of the Old Testament in English* (Oxford, 1913) (*APOT*).

Charlesworth, J H *The Old Testament Pseudepigrapha* (New York, 1983-1985 2 Vols).

Chavasse, C "Jesus: Christ and Moses", *Theology 54*, (1951) pp 244-250; 289-296.

Clark, G H "Wisdom in 1 Corinthians", *JETS 15*, (1972) pp 197-205.

Clark, K W "The Israel of God", in *SNT 33* (Leiden, 1972).

Cohn-Sherbok, Rabbi D "A Jewish Note on ΤΟ ΠΟΤΗΡΙΟΝ ΤΗΣ ΕΥΛΟΓΙΑΣ", *NTS 27,* (1981) pp 704-709 ("Note").

Cole, A *The Body of Christ* (London, 1974).

Conzelmann, H *An Outline of the Theology of the N T* (New York, 1969) (*Outline*).

— "Current Problems in Pauline Research", in *New Testament Issues* (London, 1970 ed Batey) ("Problems").

Cooke, B "The Eucharist as Covenant Sacrifice", in *TS 21*(1960) pp 1-44.

Cooper, E J "Man's Basic Freedom and Freedom of Conscience in the Bible: Reflections on Rom 8-10", *ITQ 42*, (1975) pp 272-283.

Corsani, B "L'Unita della chiesa nella 1 Cor", in *Testament und Geschichte* (Leiden, 1972) pp 219-222.

Cottle, R E "All were Baptized", *JETS 17*, (1974) pp 75-80.

Coune, M "Le problème des idolothytes et l'éducation de la syneidesis", *RSR 51*, (1963) pp 508.

Craig, C T "Soma Christou", in *The Joy of Study* (New York, 1951 ed Johnson) pp 73-85.

Cranfield, C E B "The Cup Metaphor in Mark xiv.36 and Parallels", *ExT 59*, (1947-48) pp 137-138.
— *The Gospel According to Saint Mark* (Cambridge, 1959).
— *Romans* in *ICC* (Edinburgh, 1975, 1979 2 Vols).
Cullmann, O "Πέτρα", in *TDNT VI* (Grand Rapids, 1968) pp 95-99.
Currie, S D *Koinonia in Christian Literature to 200 AD* (Emory University, 1962 Unpublished DPhil dissertation).
Dahl, N A *Das Volk Gottes; eine Untersuchung zum Kirchenbewusstsein des Urchristentums* (Oslo, 1941) (*Volk*).
— "Paul and the Church at Corinth according to 1 Corinthians 1:10-4:21", in *Christian History and Interpretation: Studies Presented to John Knox* (Cambridge, 1967 ed Farmer) pp 313-336 ("Church").
— "The Messiahship of Jesus in Paul", in *The Crucified Messiah and Other Essays* (Minneapolis, 1974) pp 37-47 ("Messiahship").
Dalman, G *Jesus-Jeshua. Studies in the Gospels* (London, 1929 trans Levertoff).
Dana, H E and Mantey, J R *A Manual Grammar of the Greek New Testament* (New York, 1927).
Danby, H *The Mishnah* (London, 1933).
D'Angelo, M R *Moses in the Letter to the Hebrews* (Missoula, 1979) (*Moses*).
Daube, D *The New Testament and Rabbinic Judaism* (London, 1956).
— *The Exodus Pattern in the Bible* (London, 1963) (*Exodus*).
Dautzenberg, G "Der Verzicht auf das apostolische Unterhaltsrecht. Eine exegetische Untersuchung zu 1 Kor 9", *Biblica 50*, (1969) pp 212-232.
Davidson, R M *Typology in Scripture. A Study of Hermeneutical Τύπος Structures* (Michigan, 1981).
Davies, W D "Paul and the People of Israel", *NTS 24*, pp 4-39 *(PPI)*.
— *Paul and Rabbinic Judaism* (New York, 1967) *(PRJ)*.
Davis, J A *Wisdom and Spirit: An Investigation of 1 Corinthians 1:18-3:20 against the Background of Jewish Sapiential Tradition in the Greco-Roman Period* (New York, 1984).
Deidun, T J *New Covenant Morality in Paul* in *AnBib 89* (Rome, 1981).
Deissmann, A *Paul: A Study in Social and Religious History* (London, 1926 ET Wilson).
Delcor, M "The Courts of the Church of Corinth and the Courts of Qumran", in *Paul and Qumran* (London, 1968 ed Murphy-O'Connor) pp 69-84 ("Courts").
Delling, G "Καταργέω", in *TDNT I* (Grand Rapids, 1964) pp 452-454.
Démann, P "Moïse et la Loi dans la Pensée de saint Paul", in *Moïse L'Homme de L'Alliance. Cahiers Sioniens* (Paris, 1954) pp 189-242.
Detzler, W *Living Words in 1 Corinthians* (Welwyn, 1983).

Dibelius, M *Paul* (London, 1953 ed and completed by Kümmel).

Didier, G "Le Salaire du Désintéressement (1 Cor., ix, 14-27)", *RSR 43*, (1955) pp 228-251.

Dillistone, F W "How is the Church Christ's Body? A New Testament Study", *TToday 2*, (1945) pp 56-68.

Dodd, C H *According to the Scriptures* (London, 1952).

—   "Ἔννομος Χριστοῦ", in *More N T Studies* (Manchester, 1968).

Doughty, D J "The Presence and Future of Salvation in Corinth", *ZNW 66*, (1975) pp 61-90.

Dowdy, B A *The Meaning of Kauchasthai in the New Testament* (Vanderbilt University, 1955 unpublished PhD dissertation).

Drane, J W *Paul Libertine or Legalist? A Study in the Theology of the Major Pauline Epistles* (London, 1975) (*Paul*).

Driver, S R "Notes on Three Passages in St Paul's Epistles", *The Expositor*, (1889 3rd series) pp 15-23.

Dungan, D L *The Sayings of Jesus in the Churches of Paul* (Oxford, 1971).

Dunn, J D G *Baptism in the Holy Spirit* in *SBT 15* (London, 1970) (*Baptism*).

—   "Paul's Understanding of the Death of Jesus", in *Reconciliation and Hope Fests for L L Morris* (Exeter, 1974) pp 125-141.

—   *Jesus and the Spirit* (London, 1975) (*Spirit*).

—   "Spirit", in *NIDNTT III* (Exeter, 1978) pp 689-707.

—   *Christology in the Making* (London, 1980).

Dunst, G "Thorikos Testamentum No 50", *ZPE 27*, (1977) pp 243-264.

Dupont, J *Gnosis. La Connaissance Religieuse dans Les Épîtres de Saint Paul* (Louvain, 1949).

—   *SYN CHRISTO — L'Union avec le Christ suivant Saint Paul* (Paris, 1952) (*L'Union*).

—   "Réflexions de saint Paul à l'adresse d'une Église divisée", in *Paolo a Una Chiesa Divisa* (Roma, 1980) pp 222-228 ("Réflexions").

Dupont-Sommer, A Le Quatrième Livre des Machabées (Paris, 1939).

Eckstein H-J Der Begriff Syneidesis bei Paulus (Tübingen, 1983).

Ellingworth, P "Translating 1 Corinthians", *BiTr 31*, (1980) pp 234-238.

Ellis, E E *Paul's Use of the Old Testament* (Edinburgh, 1957) (*Use*).

—   "Christ and Spirit in 1 Corinthians", in *Christ and Spirit in the New Testament* (Cambridge, 1973 eds Lindars, Smalley) pp 269-277 ("Christ").

—   "'Wisdom' and 'Knowledge' in 1 Corinthians", *TynB 25*, (1974) pp 82-98 ("Wisdom").

—   "Christ Crucified", in *Reconciliation and Hope N T Essays in Atonement and Eschatology Presented to L L Morris* (Exeter, 1974 ed Banks) pp 63-74 ("Crucified").

— "'Spiritual' Gifts in the Pauline Community", *NTS 20,* (1974 now part of ch 2 in Ellis' *Prophecy*) pp 128-144 ("Gifts").

— "Exegetical Patterns in 1 Corinthians and Romans", in *Grace upon Grace Essays in Honour of C J Kuyper* (Grand Rapids, 1975 ed Cook) pp 137-142 ("Patterns").

— *Prophecy and Hermeneutic* (Tübingen, 1978) (*Prophecy*).

— "Traditions in 1 Corinthians", *NTS 32,* (1986) pp 481-502 ("Traditions").

Ellul, J "Le rôle médiateur de l'idéologie", in *Demythisation et idéologie* (Paris, 1973 ed Castelli).

Engberg-Pederson, T "The Gospel and Social Practice According to 1 Corinthians", *NTS 33,* (1987) pp 557-584.

Etheridge, J W *The Targums of Onkelos and Jonathan Ben Uzziel on the Pentateuch with the fragments of the Jerusalem Targum from the Chaldee* (New York, 1968).

Fahy, T "St Paul's "Boasting" and "Weakness"", *ITQ 31,* (1964) pp 214-217.

Faw, C E "On the Writing of First Thessalonians", *JBL 71,* (1952) pp 217-225.

Fee, G "II Corinthians vi.14-vii.1 and Food Offered to Idols", *NTS 23,* (1977) pp 140-161 ("Food").

— "Εἰδωλόθυτα Once Again: An Interpretation of 1 Corinthians 8-10", *Bib 61,* (1980) pp 172-197.

Fensham, F C "The Covenant as Giving Expression to the Relationship between Old and New Testament", *TynB 22,* (1971) pp 82-94 ("Covenant").

— "Father and Son Terminology for Treaty and Covenant", in *Near Eastern Studies in Honor of William Foxwell Albright* (Baltimore, 1971 ed Goedicke) pp 121-135 ("Father and Son").

Ferguson, E "The Church at Corinth Outside the New Testament", *RestQuart 3,* (1959) pp 169-182.

Feuillet, A *Le Christ Sagesse de Dieu* (Paris, 1966) (*Sagesse*).

— "L'éxplication 'typologique' des événements au désert en 1 Cor10, 1-4", *StudMReg 8,* (1968) pp 115-135.

Fishman, I *The Passover Haggadah* (London, 1970 5th ed).

Fitzer, G "Σφραγίς", in *TDNT VII* (Grand Rapids, 1971) pp 939-953.

Flusser, D "The Last Supper and the Essenes", *Immanuel 2,* (1973) pp 23-27.

Foerster, W "Ἐξουσία", in *TDNT II* (Grand Rapids, 1964) pp 562-575.

Forbes, C "Comparison, Self-Praise and Irony: Paul's Boasting and the Conventions of Hellenistic Rhetoric", *NTS 32,* (1986) pp 1-30.

Freeborn, J C K "The Development of Doctrine at Corinth", *StEv 4,* (1968) pp 404-410.

Friedrich, G "Προφήτης", in *TDNT VI* (Grand Rapids, 1968) pp 781-861.

— "Freiheit und Liebe im 1 Korintherbrief", *TZ 26*, (1970) pp 81-98 ("Freiheit").

Furnish, V P *Theology and Ethics in Paul* (New York, 1968) (*Theology*).

— *The Love Command in the New Testament* (London, 1973) (*Love*).

Gale, H M *The Use of Analogy in the Letters of Paul* (Philadelphia, 1964) (*Analogy*).

Gander, G "1 Cor X:2 'Parle-t-il du baptême?'", *RHPhR 37*, (1957) pp 97-102.

Gangler, E Das Abendmahl im Neuen Testament in Abhandlungen zur Theologie des Alten und Neuen Testaments, 2 (Basel, 1943).

Gärtner, B *The Temple and the Community in Qumran and in the New Testament* (Cambridge, 1965).

Gavin, F *The Jewish Antecedents of the Christian Sacraments* (London, 1928) (*Antecedents*).

Genths, P "Der Begriff Καύχημα bei Paulus", *NKZ 37*, (1927) pp 501-521.

George, A R *Communion with God in the New Testament* (London, 1953) (*Communion*).

Georgi, D *Die Gegner des Paulus im 2 Korintherbrief* (Neukirchen, 1964) (*Gegner*).

Geyser, A S "Paul, the Apostolic Decree and the Liberals in Corinth", in *Studia Paulina Festscrift for J de Zwaan* (Haarlem, 1953 ed Sevenster) pp 124-138 ("Decree").

Gill, D H "TRAPEZOMATA: A Neglected Aspect of Greek Sacrifice", *HTR 67*, (1974) pp 117-137.

Gillet, L *Communion in the Messiah* (London, 1942).

Glasson, T F *Moses in the Fourth Gopel* (London, 1963).

Goguel, M *Introduction au Nouveau Testament* (Paris, 1925, 5 Vols).

Gooch, P W "'Conscience' in 1 Corinthians 8 and 10", *NTS 33*, (1987) pp 244-254.

Goppelt, L "Ποτήριον", in *TDNT VI* (Grand Rapids, 1968) pp 148-158.

— "Τράπεζα", in *TDNT VIII* (Grand Rapids, 1972) pp 209-215.

— "Τύπος", in *TDNT VIII* (Grand Rapids, 1972) pp 246-259.

— *Typos. The Typological Interpretation of the Old Testament in the New* (Grand Rapids, 1982 ET Madvig).

Grant, R M "Hellenistic Elements in 1 Corinthians", in *Early Christian Origins Fests for H R Willoughby* (Chicago, 1961 ed Wikgren) pp 60-66.

Gray, G B *Sacrifice in the Old Testament. Its Theory and Practice* (Oxford, 1925).

Green, W S ed *Approaches to Judaism: Theory and Practice* (Missoula, 1978).

Greenup, A W *Sukka, Mishnah and Tosefta with Introduction* (London, 1925).

Greeves, D Christ in Me: A Study of the Mind of Christ in Paul (London, 1962).

Gressmann, H "Ἡ κοινωνία τῶν δαιμωνίων", *ZNW 20*, (1921) pp 224-230.

Grundmann, W "Ἵστημι", in *TDNT VII* (Grand Rapids, 1971) pp 638-653.

Gundry, R *Soma in Biblical Theology with emphasis on Pauline Anthropology* (Cambridge, 1976).

Hainz, J *Koinonia. "Kirche" als Gemeinschaft bei Paulus* (Regensburg, 1982).

Hammerton-Kelly, R G *Pre-existence, Wisdom and the Son of Man: A Study of the Idea of Pre-existence in the New Testament* (Cambridge, 1973).

Hanson, A T *Jesus Christ in the Old Testament* (London, 1965) (*Jesus*).

— *Studies in Paul's Technique and Theology* (London, 1974) (*Studies*).

— *The New Testament Interpretation of Scripture* (London, 1980) (*Interpretation*).

Hanson, R P C "Moses in the Typology of St Paul", *Theology 48*, (1945) pp 174-177.

— *Allegory and Event* (London, 1959).

— "Review of M Smith, Clement of Alexandria and a Secret Gospel of Mark", *TS 25*, (1974) pp 513-521 (*Clement*).

Harnack, A *The Acts of the Apostles* (London, 1909 ET Wilkinson).

Harris, B F "ΣΥΝΕΙΔΗΣΙΣ (Conscience) in the Pauline Writings", *WTJ 24*, (1962) pp 173-186.

Harris, J R *Eucharistic Origins* (Cambridge, 1927) (*Origins*).

Hauck, F "Ἐκών", in *TDNT II* (Grand Rapids, 1964) pp 469-470.

— "Περισσεύω", in *TDNT VI* (Grand Rapids, 1968) pp 58-63.

Hause, H "Μετέχω", in *TDNT II* (Grand Rapids, 1964) pp 830-832.

Hawthorne, G F *Philippians* in *Word Biblical Commentary* (Waco Texas, 1983).

Heitmüller, W *Taufe und Abendmahl im Urchristentum* (Tübingen, 1911).

Hemphill, K S *The Pauline Concept of Charisma* (Cambridge, 1976 unpublished dissertation).

Hengel, M *Judaism and Hellenism* (London, 1974).

Hill, D *Greek Words and Hebrew Meanings: Studies in the Semantics of Soteriological Terms* (Cambridge, 1967) (*Words*).

Hillers, D R *Covenant: The History of a Biblical Idea* (Baltimore, 1969).

Hillyer, N "'Rock-Stone' Imagery in 1 Peter", *TynB 22*, (1971) pp 58-81.

Hinz, C "Bewährung und Verkehrung der Freiheit in Christo: Versuch einer Transformation von 1 Kor 10:23-11:1", in *Gnosis und Neues Testament* (Berlin, 1973 ed Troger) pp 405-422.

Hock, R F "Paul's Tentmaking and the Problem of his Social Class", *JBL 97*, (1978) pp 555-564.

— *The Social Context of Paul's Ministry. Tentmaking and Apostleship* (Phildelphia, 1980).

Hooke, S H "Christianity and The Mystery Religions", in *Judaism and Christianity, Vol I* (London, 1937 ed Loewe) pp 237-250.

Hooker M D ed *Paul and Paulinism. Essays in Honour of C K Barrett* (London, 1982) (*P and P*).

Hooker, M D "'Beyond the Things which are Written': An Examination of 1 Cor IV:6", *NTS 10*, (1963) pp 127-132.

— "Interchange in Christ", *JTS 22*, (1971) pp 349-361.

— *Pauline Pieces* (London, 1979).

— *Studying the New Testament* (London, 1979).

— "Beyond the Things that are Written? St Paul's Use of Scripture", *NTS 27*, (1981) pp 295-309.

— "Paul and 'Covenantal Nomism'", in *P and P* (London, 1982 eds Hooker and Wilson) pp 47-56 ("Nomism").

Horsley, R A "Pneumatikos vs. Psychikos. Distinctions of Spiritual Status Among the Corinthians", *HTR 69*, (1976) pp 269-288 ("Pneumatikos").

— "Wisdom of Word and Words of Wisdom in Corinth", *CBQ 39*, (1977) pp 224-239 ("Wisdom").

— "Consciousness and Freedom among the Corinthians: 1 Cor 8-10", *CBQ 40*, (1978) pp 574-589 ("Consciousness").

— "The Background of the Confessional Formula in 1 Kor 8:6", *ZNW 69*, (1978) pp 130-135.

— "Gnosis in Corinth: 1 Corinthians 8.1-6", *NTS 27*, (1981) pp 32-51.

Howard, J K "Christ our Passover: A Study of the Passover-Exodus Theme in 1 Corinthians", *EQ 41*, (1969) pp 97-108.

Hübner, H *Law in Paul's Thought* (Edinburgh, 1984).

Hurley, J B *Man and Woman in 1 Corinthians* (Cambridge, 1973 Unpublished PhD dissertation) (*Man*).

Jacobs, H E "Cup", in *ISBE I*, (Grand Rapids, 1979) pp 836-837.

James, M R trans *The Biblical Antiquities of Pseudo-Philo* (London, 1917).

Jaubert, A *La Notion d'alliance* (Paris, 1963) (*Alliance*).

Jeremias, J "Der Ursprung der Johannestaufe", *ZNW 28*, (1929) pp 312-320.

— "Zur Gedankenführung in den paulinischen Briefen: Die Briefzitate in 1 Kor 8, 1-13", in *Studia Paulina in Honorem Johannis de Zwaan*

Septuagenarii (Haarlem, 1953 ed Sevenster and Unnik) ("Briefzitate").
— "Chiasmus in den Paulusbriefen", *ZNW 49*, (1958) pp 145-156.
— "Moses", in *TDNT IV* (Grand Rapids, 1964) pp 848-873.
— *The Eucharistic Words of Jesus* (London, 1966 3rd ed ET Perrin) (*Eucharistic*).
— *New Testament Theology Vol I Study Edition* (London, 1971 ET Bowden).
— "This is My Body", *ExT 83*, (1972) pp 196-203.
— "Paulus als Hillelit", in *NeotestSem* pp 88-94.
Jeske, R L "Christology and Covenant", *Dialog 18*, (1979) pp 271-276.
Jewett, R *Paul's Anthropological Terms: A Study of their Use in Conflict Settings* (Leiden, 1971).
Johnson, S L *The Old Testament in the New* (Grand Rapids, 1980).
Jones, P *The Apostle Paul: A Second Moses According to 2 Corinthians 2:14-4:7* (Princeton Theological Seminary, 1973 unpublished PhD dissertation) (*Apostle*).
Jourdan, G V "Koinonia in 1 Cor 10:16", *JBL 67*, (1948) pp 111-124.
Judge, E A *The Social Pattern of Christian Groups in the First Century* (London, 1960).
— "Paul's Boasting in Relation to Contemporary Professional Practice", *ABR 16*, (1968) pp 37-50 ("Boasting").
— "St Paul and Classical Society", *JAC 15*, (1972) pp 19-36.
— *Rank and Status in the World of the Caesars and St Paul* (New Zealand, University of Canterbury, 1982).
Kadushin, M *The Rabbinic Mind* (New York, 1952).
Kaiser, W C "The Current Crisis in Exegesis on the Apostolic Use of Deuteronomy 25:4 in 1 Corinthians 9:8-10", *JETS 21*, (1978) pp 3-18 ("Crisis").
Kane, J P "The Mithraic cult Meal in its Greek and Roman environment", in *Mithraic Studies, 2* (Manchester, 1975, ed Hinnels) pp 313-351.
Käsemann, E *Essays on New Testament Themes* in *SBT 41* (London, 1964) (*Essays*).
— *New Testament Questions of Today* (London, 1969) (*NTQT*).
— *Perspectives on Paul* (London, 1971) (*PP*).
— "A Pauline Version of the "Amor Fati"", in *NTQT* (London, 1971) pp 217-235 ("Amor").
Keck, L *Paul and His Letters* (Philadelphia, 1979).
Kempthorne, R "Incest and the Body of Christ: A Study of 1 Cor 6:12-20", *NTS 14*, (1968) pp 568-574 ("Incest").
Kennedy, H A *St Paul and the Mystery Religions* (London, 1913).
Kennedy, J H *The Second and Third Epistles of St Paul to the Corinthians* (London, 1900).

Kerst, R "1 Kor 8.6 - ein vorpaulinisches Taufbekenntnis?", *ZNW VI*, (1975) pp 130-139.

Kijne, J J "We, Us and Our in 1 and 2 Corinthians", *NovT 8*, (1966) pp 171-179.

Kilpatrick, G D "Eucharist as Sacrifice and Sacrament in the New Testament", in *Neues Testament und Kirche* (Freiburg, 1974 ed Gnilka).

Kim, S *The Origin Of Paul's Gospel* (Grand Rapids, 1982).

Kittel, G "Ἔρημος", in *TDNT II* (Grand Rapids, 1964) pp 657-659.

Klauck, H-J "Thysiasterion — eine Berichtigung", *ZNW 71*, (1980) pp 274-277.

— *Herrenmahl und Hellenistischer Kult* (Münster, 1982) (*Herrenmahl*).

Knox, J "The Pauline Chronology", *JBL 58*, (1939) pp 15-29 ("Chronology").

Knox, R A *Enthusiasm. A Chapter in the History of Religion* (Oxford, 1950).

Knox, W L *St Paul and the Church of the Gentiles* (Cambridge, 1939) (*Gentiles*).

Koester, H "Paul and Hellenism", in *The Bible in Modern Scholarship* (New York, 1965 ed Hyatt) pp 187-195 ("Hellenism").

Kraft, R A and Nicklesburg, G W E ed *Early Judaism and Its Modern Interpreters* (Philadelphia, 1986).

Kramer, J *Christ, Lord, Son of God* in *SBT 50* (London, 1966).

Kuhn, K G *Konkordanz zu den Qumrantexten* (Göttingen, 1960) (*Konkordanz*).

Kümmel, W G *Introduction to the New Testament* (London, 1966 ET Mattill) (*Introduction*).

Kuss, O *Paulus. Die Rolle des Apostels in der theologischen Entwicklung der Urkirche* (Regensburg, 1971).

Lampe, G W H *The Seal of the Spirit* (London, 1951).

Lampe, G W H and Woollcombe, K J *Essays on Typology* (London, 1957).

Lane, W "Covenant: The Key to Paul's Conflict with Corinth", *TynB 33*, (1982) pp 3-30 ("Covenant").

Le Deaut, R *La Nuit Pascale Essai sur la signification de la Paque juive à partir du Targum d'Exode 12:42* (Rome, 1963) (*La Nuit*).

Lee, G M "1 Cor 9:9", *Theology 71*, (1968) pp 122-123.

Leonard, P E *Luke's Account of the Lord's Supper against the background of Meals in the Ancient Semitic World* (Manchester Unpublished PhD dissertation, 1976).

Lietzmann, H *Messe und Herrenmahl. Eine Studie zur Geschichte der Liturgie* (Bonn, 1926).

Lightfoot, J *Horae Hebraicae et Talmudicae* (Oxford, 1859, 4 Vols).

Lincoln, A *Paradise Now and Not Yet* in *SNTSMS* (Cambridge, 1981) (*Paradise*).

Lindars, B *New Testament Apologetic: The Doctrinal Significance of Old Testament Quotations* (London, 1961).

Lindblom, J "Zum Begriff 'Anstoss' im N T", in *Strena Philologica Upsaliensis Fests für Per Persson* (Upsala, 1922) pp 40-45.

Lock, W "1 Corinthians viii.1-9: A Suggestion", *Expositor 6*, (1897) pp 65-74.

Lohmeyer, E *DIATHEKE: Ein Beitrag zur Erklärung des neutestamentlichen Begriffs* (Leipzig, 1913).

Lohse, E "Zu 1 Cor 10:26. 31", *ZNW 47*, (1956) pp 277-280.

Lohse, E ed *Die Texte Aus Qumran* (Darmstadt, 1964).

Loisy, A "The Christian Mystery", *HibJ 10*, (1911/12) pp 45-64.

— *Les Mystères Païens et Le Mystère Chrétien* (Paris, 1914) (*Mystères*).

Longenecker, R N *Biblical Exegesis in the Apostolic Period* (Grand Rapids, 1975) (*Exegesis*).

Lütgert, D W *Freiheitspredigt und Schwarmgeister in Korinth: Ein Beitrag zur Charakteristik der Christus-partei* (Gütersloh, 1908).

Lyons, G *Pauline Autobiography. Toward a New Understanding* in *SLBDS 73* (Atlanta, 1985).

MacGregor, G H C *Eucharistic Origins. A Survey of the New Testament Evidence* (London, 1928) (*Origins*).

Macho, A D *Neophyti 1. Targum Palestinense. Ms de la Biblioteca Vaticana* (Barcelona, 1968, 6 Vols).

Malan, F S "The Use of the Old Testament in 1 Corinthians", in *The Relationship between the Old and New Testament. Neotestamentica 14* (Bloemfontein, 1981) pp 134-170 ("Use").

Malina, B J *The Palestinian Manna Tradition. The Manna Tradition in the Palestinian Targums and its Relationship to the N T Writings* (Leiden, 1968) (*Manna*).

Manson, T W *Studies in the Gospels and Epistles* (Manchester, 1962 ed Black) (*Studies*).

Manson, W *Jesus the Messiah* (London, 1943).

Marshall, I H *Last Supper and Lord's Supper* (Grand Rapids, 1980) (*Supper*).

Martelet, G "Sacrements, figures et exhortations en 1 Cor 10:1-11", *RSR 44*, (1956) pp 323-359, 515-559 ("Sacrements").

Martin, R P *Philippians* in *The New Century Bible Commentary* (Grand Rapids, 1976).

— *The Spirit and the Congregation. Studies in 1 Corinthians 12-15* (Grand Rapids, 1984) (*Congregation*).

Marxsen, W *Introduction to the New Testament. An Approach to its Problems* (Oxford, 1968 ET Buswell).

— *The Lord's Supper as a Christological Problem* (Philadelphia, 1970 ET Nieting).

Maurer, C "Grund und Grenze Apostolischer Freiheit", in *Antwort. Karl Barth zum siebzigsten Geburtstag* (Zürich, 1956) pp 630-641.

— "Συνείδησις", in *TDNT VII* (Grand Rapids, 1971) pp 898-919.

Mauser, U *Christ in the Wilderness* in *SBT 39* (London, 1963).

McCarthy, D J *Treaty and Covenant* (Rome, 1963).

— "Notes on the Love of God in Deuteronomy and the Father-Son relationship between Yahweh and Israel", *CBQ 27*, (1965) pp 144-147 ("Love of God").

McCasland, S V "Christ Jesus", *JBL 65*, (1946) pp 377-383.

McCree, W T "The Covenant Meal in the Old Testament", *JBL 45*, (1926) pp 120-128.

McDermott, M "The Biblical Doctrine of Koinonia", *BZ 19*, (1975) pp 64-77; 233 ("Koinonia").

McKelvey, R J *The New Temple* (London, 1969).

McNamara, M *The New Testament and Palestinian Targum to the Pentateuch* (Rome, 1966).

— *Targum and Testament* in *AnBib 27* (Shannon, 1972) (*Targum*).

Meeks, W A "'And Rose up to Play': Midrash and Paraenesis in 1 Corinthians 10:1-22", *JSNT 16*, (1982) pp 64-78 ("Midrash").

Mendenhall, G E "Ancient Oriental and Biblical Law", *BA 17*, (1954) pp 26-46.

— "Covenant Forms in Israelite Tradition", *BA 17*, (1954) pp 50-76.

Meslin, M "Convivialité ou communion sacramentelle? Repas mithraïque et Eucharistie chrétienne", in *Paganisme, judaisme, christianisme. Mélanges offerts à M Simon* (Paris, 1978) pp 296-305.

Metzger, B A *Textual Commentary on the Greek New Testament* (UBS, 1971).

Michaelis, W "Πίπτω" in *TDNT VI* (Grand Rapids, 1968) pp 161-166.

Michel, O "Οἰκοδομέω", in *TDNT V* (Grand Rapids, 1967) pp 136-148.

Millard, A R "Covenant and Communion in First Corinthians", in *Apostolic History and the Gospel* (Exeter, 1970 ed Gasque and Martin) pp 242-248 ("Covenant").

Minear, P S "Paul's Teaching on the Eucharist in First Corinthians", *Worship 44*, (1977) pp 83-92 ("Teaching").

Moberley, R W L *At the Mountain of God. Story and Theology in Exodus 32-34* in *JSOT Supplement 22* (Sheffield, 1983).

Montefiore, C and Loewe, H *A Rabbinic Anthology* (London, 1938).

Moore, G F *Judaism in the First Centuries of the Christian Era. The Age of the Tannaim* (Cambridge, 1927, 2 Vols).

Morton, A Q "Dislocations in I and II Corinthians", *ExT 78*, (1967) pp 119.

Moule, C F D *An Idiom Book of New Testament Greek* (Cambridge, 1953).

— "The Judgment Theme in the Sacraments", in *The Background of the N T and its Eschatology: in Honour of C H Dodd* (Cambridge, 1956 ed Davies) pp 464-481 ("Judgment").

— *The Holy Spirit* (London, 1978) (*Spirit*).

Müller, K "I Kor 1,18-25 Die eschatologisch-kritische Funktion der Veründigung des Kreuzes", *BZ 10,* (1966) pp 246-272 ("I Kor 1,18-25").

— *Anstoss und Gericht. Eine Studie zum jüdischen Hintergrund des paulinischen Skandalon-Begriffs* (München, 1969) (*Anstoss*).

Munck, J *Paul and the Salvation of Mankind* (London, 1959) (*Paul*).

Murphy-O'Connor, J "Eucharist and Community in 1 Corinthians", *Worship 51,* (1977) pp 56-69 ("Community").

— "1 Cor 8:6: Cosmology or Soteriology?", *RB 85,* (1978) pp 253-267 ("Cosmology").

— "Freedom of Ghetto", *RB 85,* (1978) pp 541-574 ("Freedom").

— "Food and spiritual gifts in 1 Cor 8:8", *CBQ 41,* (1979) pp 292-298 ("Food").

— *St Paul's Corinth Texts and Archaeology* (Wilmington, 1983) (*Corinth*).

Neuenzeit, P *Das Herrenmahl Studien zur paulinischen Eucharistieauffassung* (Munich, 1960).

Neusner, J "Method and Substance", *SJ,* (1976) pp 89-111.

— "Comparing Judaisms: review of PPJ", *HistRel 18,* (1978) pp 177-191.

— "The Use of the Later Rabbinic Evidence for the Study of First Century Pharisaism", in *Approaches to Ancient Judaism* (Missoula, 1978 ed Green) pp 215-228 ("Use").

— "From Scripture to Mishnah", *JBL 98,* (1979) pp 269-283.

Nickle, K "A Parenthetical Apologia: 1 Cor. 9:1-3", *CTM 1,* (1974) pp 68-70.

Nineham, D E *The Gospel of St Mark* (London, 1968).

Nock, A D *Early Gentile Christianity and its Hellenistic Background* (New York, 1964) (*Background*).

Omanson, R L "Some Comments about Style and Meaning: 1 Corinthians 9:15 and 7:10", *BiTr 34,* (1983) pp 135-139.

Osborn, H "ΣΥΝΕΙΔΗΣΙΣ", *JTS 32,* (1931) pp 167-179.

Osburn, C D "The Text of 1 Corinthians 10:9", in *New Testament Criticism: Its Significance for Exegesis. Essays in Honour of Bruce M Metzger* (Oxford, 1981) pp 201-212 ("Text").

Panikulam, G *Koinonia in the New Testament. A Dynamic Expression of Christian Life* (Rome, 1979) (*KNT*).

Pathrapanal, J "Pauline Understanding of the New Covenant", *Jeevadhara 11*, (1981) pp 113-126.

Patte, D *Early Jewish Hermeneutic in Palestine* in *SBLDS 22* (Missoula, 1975) (*Hermeneutic*).

Pearson, B A *The Pneumatikos-Psychikos Terminology in 1 Corinthians. A Study in the Theology of the Corinthian Opponents of Paul and Its Relation to Gnosticism* in *SBLDS 12* (Missoula, 1973) (*Pneumatikos*).

— "Hellenistic-Jewish Wisdom Speculation and Paul", in *Aspects of Wisdom in Judaism and Early Christianity* (London, 1975 ed Wilcken) pp 43-66 ("Speculation").

Perrot, C "Les Examples du Désert (1 Co. 10.6-11)", *NTS 29* (1983) pp 437-452.

Pfitzner, V C *Paul and the Agon Motif. Traditional Athletic Imagery in the Pauline Literature* (Leiden, 1967).

Pierce, C A *Conscience in the New Testament* in *SBT 15* (London, 1955).

Porteous, N W "Second Thoughts. II. The Present State of Old Testament Theology", *ExT 75*, (1963) pp 70-74 ("Present").

Preisker, H "Μισθός", in *TDNT IV* (Grand Rapids, 1967) pp 695-728.

Proudfoot, C M "Imitation or Realistic Participation", *Interp*, (1963) pp 140-160.

Rauer, M "Die Schwachen in Korinth und Rom", in *BibS 21* (Freiburg, 1923).

Rees, J M "Paul Proclaims the Wisdom of the Cross: Scandal and Foolishness", *BTB 9*, (1979) pp 147-153 ("Paul Proclaims").

Reitzenstein, R *Hellenistic Mystery Religions. Their basic ideas and significance* (Pittsburgh, 1978 ET Steely) (*HMR*).

Richardson, G P *Israel in the Apostolic Church* in *SNTSMS 10* (Cambridge, 1969).

Richardson, P *Paul's Ethic of Freedom* (Philadelphia, 1979).

— "Pauline Inconsistency: 1 Corinthians 9:19-23 and Galatians 2:11-14", *NTS 26*, (1980) pp 347-362.

Richardson, P and Gooch, P W "Accommodation Ethics", in *TynB 29* (1975) pp 89-142.

Ricoeur, P "Science and Technology", in *Hermeneutics and the Human Sciences* (Cambridge, 1981 trans and ed Thompson).

Ridderbos, H *The Epistle of Paul to the Churches of Galatia* (Grand Rapids, 1956).

— *Paul. An Outline of his Theology* (Grand Rapids, 1975 ET deWitt).

Roberts, A and Donaldson, J *The Writings of the Ante-Nicene Fathers Vols1-10* (Grand Rapids, 1956).

Robertson, A T *A Grammar of the Greek New Testament in the Light of Historical Research* (Nashville, 1923 3rd ed reprinted).

Robinson, D W B "Charismata versus Pneumatika", *RThR 31*, (1972) pp 49-55.

Robinson, J A T *The Body: A Study in Pauline Theology* (London, 1952) (*Body*).

— "Review of Gundry's SOMA", *JTS 28*, (1977) pp 163-166.

Roetzel, C J *Judgment in the Community: A Study of the Relationship between Eschatology and Ecclesiology in Paul* (Leiden, 1972).

— *The Letters of St Paul. Conversations in Context* (Atlanta, 1982 2nd ed).

Rogerson, J W "Sacrifice in the Old Testament", in *Sacrifice* (London, 1980 eds Bourdillon and Fortes) pp 45-59.

Rood, L A "Le Christ comme Dunamis Theou", in *Litterature et Theologie Pauliniennes* (Bruges, 1960 ed Descampes) pp 93-108 (*Dunamis*).

Sampley, J P *Pauline Partnership in Christ* (Philadelphia, 1980).

Sandelin, K-G *Wisdom as Nourisher* in *Acta Academiae Aboensis 64 No 3* (Abo, 1986).

Sanders, E P *Paul and Palestinian Judaism. A Comparison of Patterns of Religion* (London, 1977) (*PPJ*).

— "Puzzling out Rabbinic Judaism", in *Approaches to Ancient Judaism II* (Missoula, 1980 ed Green) pp 65ff.

— *Paul, the Law, and the Jewish People* (Philadelphia, 1983).

Sandmel, S "Parallelomania", *JBL 81*, (1962) pp 1-13.

Saussure, F de *Course in General Linguistics* (New York, 1974 orig 1915).

Savage, T B *Power Through Weakness. An Historical and Exegetical Examination of Paul's Understanding of the Ministry in 2 Corinthians* (Cambridge, 1986 unpublished PhD dissertation).

Sawyer, W T *The Problem of Meat Sacrificed to Idols in the Corinthian Church* (Southern Baptist Theological Seminary, 1968 Unpublished ThD dissertation).

Scharlemann, M H *Qumran and Corinth* (New York, 1962).

Schlatter, A *Die korinthische Theologie* (Gütersloh, 1914).

— *The Church in the New Testament Period* (London, 1955 ET Levertoff) (*Church*).

— *Paulus der Bote Jesu. Eine Deutung seiner Briefe an die Korinther* (Stuttgart, pp 1969 4th ed) (*Bote*).

Schlier, H "Ἐλεύθερος", in *TDNT II* (Grand Rapids, 1964) pp 487-502.

Schmauch, W *In Christus. Eine Untersuchung zur Sprache und Theologie des Paulus* (Gütersloh, 1935) (*In Christus*).

Schmithals, W *Gnosticism in Corinth* (New York, 1971 3rd ed, ET Steely).

Schnackenburg, R *Baptism in the Thought of Paul* (New York, 1964).

— *The Gospel According to St John* (London, 1968 ET Smyth).

— *The Church in the New Testament* (London, 1974).

Schneider, J "'Ολεθρεύω", in *TDNT V* (Grand Rapids, 1967) pp 169-170.

Schoeps, H J *Paul. The Theology of the Apostle in the Light of Jewish Religious History* (Philadelphia, 1959) (*Theology*).

Schreiber, R *Der Neue Bund im Spatjudentum und Urchristentum* (Tübingen, 1955 dissertation).

Schrenk, G "Εὐδοκέω", in *TDNT II* (Grand Rapids, 1964) pp 738-742.

— "Πατήρ", in *TDNT V* (Grand Rapids, 1967) pp 945-1014.

Schütz, J H *Paul and the Anatomy of Apostolic Authority* in *SNTMS 26* (Cambridge, 1975).

Schweitzer, A *The Mysticism of Paul the Apostle* (New York, 1931) (*Mysticism*).

Schweizer, E *The Lord's Supper according to the N T* (Philadelphia, 1967).

— "Πνεῦμα", in *TDNT VI* (Grand Rapids, 1968) pp 332-451.

Scott, C A "The Communion of the Body", *Expositor 8th Series 18*, (1919) pp 121-130.

— "The 'Fellowship', or 'Koinonia'", *ExT 35*, (1923/24) pp 567.

Scroggs, R "Paul: Sophos and Pneumatikos", *NTS 14*, (1967-1968) pp 33-55 ("Sophos").

Seesemann, H *Der Begriff KOINΩNIA im Neuen Testament* (Giessen, 1933).

Segal, H J B *The Hebrew Passover from the Earliest Times to A D 70* (London, 1963).

Selwyn, E G *The First Epistle of St Peter* (London, 1946).

Sevenster, J N *Paul and Seneca* in *SNT IV* (Leiden, 1961).

Shurer, E *The History of the Jewish People in the Age of Jesus Christ* (Edinburgh, 1979 revised and edited Vermes, Millar, Black) (*History*).

Sigal, P "Another Note to 1 Corinthians 10:16", *NTS 29*, (1983) pp 134-139.

Silva, M *Biblical Words and Their Meaning. An Introduction to Lexical Semantics* (Grand Rapids, 1983) (*Meaning*).

Sloyan, G S "Primitive and Pauline Concepts of the Eucharist", *CBQ 23*, (1961) pp 1-13.

Smedes, L B *Love Within Limits. A Realist's View of 1 Corinthians 13* (Grand Rapids, 1978).

Smith, M "Pauline Worship as seen by Pagans", *HTR 73*, (1980) pp 241-249 ("Worship").

Smith, P *A short history of Christian Theophagy* (Chicago, 1922).

Smolar, L and Aberbach, M "The Golden Calf in Postbiblical Literature", *HUCA 39*, (1969) pp 91-116.

Soden, H von "Sakrament und Ethik bei Paulus", in *Das Paulusbild in der Neueren Deutschen Forschung* (Darmstadt, 1976 ed Rengstorf) pp 338-379.

Spicq, C "La Conscience dans le Nouveau Testament", *RB 47*, (1938) pp 50-80.

Stacey, W D *The Pauline View of Man* (London, 1956).

Stählin, G "Ἐγκόπτω", in *TDNT III* (Grand Rapids, 1965) pp 855-860.

— "Προσκόπτω", in *TDNT VI* (Grand Rapids, 1968) pp 745-758.

— "Σκάνδαλον", in *TDNT VII* (Grand Rapids, 1971) pp 339-358.

Stauffer, E "Ἀγαπάω", in *TDNT I* (Grand Rapids, 1964) pp 35-55.

Stegner, W R *The Self-Understanding of the Qumran Community, Compared with the Self-Understanding of the Early Church* (Drew University, 1960, Unpublished PhD thesis).

— "Wilderness and Testing in the Scrolls and in Matt 4:1-11", *Bibl Research XII*, (1967) pp 18-27.

Styler, G M "The Basis of Obligation in Paul's Christology and Ethics", in *Christ and Spirit in the New Testament* (Cambridge, 1973 eds Lindars and Smalley) pp 175-187.

Sweet, J *Revelation*, in *Pelican Commentaries* (London, 1977).

Talmon, S "The 'Desert Motif' in the Bible and in Qumran Literature", in *Biblical Motifs: Origins and Transformations* (Harvard, 1966 ed Altmann) pp 31-63 ("Desert Motif").

Taylor, V *Jesus and his Sacrifice* (London, 1937).

— *The Names of Jesus* (London, 1953).

Teeple, H M *The Mosaic Eschatological Prophet* in *JBL Monograph Series* (Philadelphia, 1957).

Thackeray, H St John *The Relation of St Paul to Contemporary Jewish Thought* (London, 1900).

Theissen, G *The Social Setting of Pauline Christianity. Essays on Corinth* (Philadelphia, 1982 ET Schütz).

Thiselton, A C "Realized Eschatology at Corinth", *NTS 24*, (1977-78) pp 510-526.

Thrall, M E "The Pauline Use of ΣΥΝΕΙΔΗΣΙΣ", *NTS 14*, (1967) pp 118-125.

— "The Meaning of οἰκοδομέω in Relation to the Concept of συνείδησις (1 Cor 8:10)", in *StEv 4* (Berlin, 1969 ed F Cross) pp 468-472 ("Meaning").

— "The Origin of Pauline Christology", in *Apostolic History and the Gospel* (Exeter, 1970 ed Gasque) pp 310-312 ("Origin").

Thurian, M *L'Eucharistie* (Neuchatel, 1959).

Tischendorf, C *Novum Testamentum Graece* (Lipsiae, 1872, 3 Vols).

Trumbull, H C *The Blood Covenant. A Primitive Rite and its Bearings on Scripture* (London, 1887).

— *The Threshold Covenant or the Beginning of Religious Rites* (Edinburgh, 1896).

Urbach, E E "The Rabbinical Laws of Idolatry in the 2nd and 3rd centuries in the Light of Archaeological and Historical Facts", *IEJ 9*, (1959) pp 149-165; 229-245.

Van Roon, A "The Relation between Christ and the Wisdom of God according to Paul", *NovT 16*, (1974) pp 207-239 ("Relation").

van Unnik, W C "La Conception Paulinienne de la Nouvelle Alliance", in *Sparsa Collecta: the Collected Essays part 1* (Leiden, 1973) ("Conception").

Vermes, G "La Figure de Moïse au tournant des deux Testaments", in *Moïse, L'Homme de l'Alliance. Cahiers Sioniens* (Paris, 1954) pp 63-92 ("La Figure").

— *Scripture and Tradition in Judaism* (Leiden, 1961) (Scripture).

— *The Dead Sea Scrolls in English* (London, 1975 2nd ed) *(DSSE)*.

Vielhauer, P *Oikodome. Das Bild vom Bau in der christlichen Literatur vom Neuen Testament bis Clemens Alexandrinus* (Karlsruhe-Durlach, 1939).

Volf, M "The 'Foolishness' and 'Weakness' of God: An Exegesis of 1 Corinthians 1:18-25", *StBTh 9*, (1979).

Von Rad, G *Old Testament Theology* (London, 1962).

— *Wisdom in Israel* (Abingdon, 1972).

Wagner, G *Pauline Baptism and The Pagan Mysteries* (Edinburgh, 1967).

Weber, M E *'Eschatologie' und 'Mystik' im neuen Testament Ein Versuch zum Verständnis des Glaubens* (Gütersloh, 1930).

Wedderburn, A J M *Gnosticism and Paul's First Letter to the Corinthians* (Cambridge, 1969 unpublished dissertation for King's College) *(Gnosticism)*.

— "The Body of Christ and Related Concepts in 1 Corinthians", *SJT 24,* (1971) pp 74-96 ("Body").

Weinfeld, M "Covenant", in *Encyclopaedia Judaica Vol 5* pp 1012-1022.

Weiss, J *The History of Primitive Christianity* 2 Vols (London, 1937) *(History)*.

— *Earliest Christianity* (New York, 1959 ET 1937).

Whiteley, D E H *The Theology of St Paul* (Oxford, 1964) *(Theology)*.

Wickert, U "Einheit und Eintracht der Kirche im 1 Korintherbrief", *ZNW 50*, (1959) pp 73-82.

Wikenhauser, A *Pauline Mysticism* (New York, 1960).

Wilcken, R L ed *Aspects of Wisdom in Judaism and Early Christianity* (London, 1975).

Wilckens, U *Weisheit und Torheit: eine exegetischreligionsgeschichtliche Untersuchung zu 1 Kor 1 und 2* (Tübingen, 1959).

— "Σοφία", in *TDNT VII* (Grand Rapids, 1972) pp 465-529.

— " Ὕστερος", in *TDNT VIII* (Grand Rapids, 1972) pp 592-601.

— "Das Kreuz Christi als die Tiefe der Weisheit Gottes zu 1 Kor 2:1-16", in *Paolo a Una Chiesa Divisa* (Roma, 1980 ed de Lorenzi) pp 43-81 ("Kreuz").

Willis, W L *Idol Meat in Corinth (See under Commentaries).*

— "An Apostolic Apologia? The Form and Function of 1 Corinthians 9", in *JSNT 24* (33-48, 1985).

Wilson, R McL "How Gnostic were the Corinthians?", *NTS 19*, (1972) pp 65-73.

Wilson, S G ed *Paul and Paulinism. Essays in Honour of C K Barrett* (London, 1982) (*P and P*).

Windisch, H *Der zweite Korintherbrief* (Göttingen, 1924).

Winter, B W "The Lord's Supper at Corinth", *RThR 37*, (1978) pp 73-82.

— *Philo and Paul among the Sophists. A Hellenistic Jewish and Christian Response* (Macquarrie Australia, 1988 Unpublished PhD dissertation).

Winter, M *Pneumatiker und Psychiker in Korinth. Zum religionsgeschichtlichen Hintergrund von 1.Kor. 2,6-3,4* (Marburg, 1975).

Wiseman, J R *The Land of Ancient Corinthians: Studies in Mediterranean Archaeology* (Götenborg, 1978).

Woollcombe, K J *Essays* (see Lampe, G W and Woolcombe, K J).

Worgul, G S Jr "People of God, Body of Christ: Pauline Eschatological Contrasts", *BTB 12*, (1982) pp 24-28 ("People").

Wright, A G "The Literary Genre Midrash", *CBQ 28*, (1966) pp 105-138, 417-457 ("Genre").

Wright, N T *The Messiah and The People of God. A Study in Pauline Theology with Particular Reference to the Argument of Romans* (Oxford, 1980 unpublished DPhil dissertation) (*MPG*).

Wuellner, W "Haggadic Homily Genre in 1 Corinthians 1-3", *JBL 89*, (1970) pp 199-204 ("Genre").

— "Greek Rhetoric and Pauline Argumentation", in *Early Christian Literature and the Classical Intellectual Tradition in Honorem Robert M Grant* (Paris, 1979 eds Schoedel and Wilcken).

Yamauchi, E *Pre-Christian Gnosticism. A Survey of the Proposed Evidences* (London, 1984 2nd edition).

Ziesler, J A *The Meaning of Righteousness in Paul. A Linguistic and Theolgoical Enquiry* (Cambridge, 1972).

— "Σῶμα in the Septuagint", *NovT 25*, (1983) pp 133-145.

Zuntz, G *The Text of the Epistles* in *The Schweich Lectures of the British Academy* (London, 1953).

Made in the USA
San Bernardino, CA
22 July 2019